ROLE OF PANCHAYATS IN WELFARE ADMINISTRATION

ROLE OF PANCHAYATS IN WELFARE ADMINISTRATION

A Study with Special Reference to Centrally Sponsored Schemes

Abraham Mathew

Publications

KALPAZ PUBLICATIONS

DELHI - 110 052

Role of Panchayats in Welfare Administration: A Study with Special Reference to Centrally Sponsored Schemes

Rs. 750

ISBN : 81-7835-450-0

Published in 2005 in India by
Kalpaz Publications,
C-30, Satyawati Nagar,
Delhi-110 052
Email : kalpaz@hotmail.com

Lasertype Setting by: Tact Computer Graphics, Delhi
Printed at: Ajit Printers, Delhi

Contents

Acknowledgements

This book is a revised version of my Ph.D. thesis submitted to the University of Kerala in April 2003.

It was under the supervision and guidance of Dr. P.J. Alexander (formerly Director of the Institute of Management in Kerala and Director General of Police in Kerala) that the research was completed and the dissertation prepared. I place on record my deep sense of gratitude to him for his constant guidance and intellectual support.

Dr. Varghese M. Mathunny (formerly Principal, St. John's College, Anchal) who deputed me for Ph.D. under the Faculty Improvement Programme of the UGC has been a source of great help during various stages of this work. I express my sincere thanks to him.

Besides, I have received help and encouragement from several individuals and Institutions. They include Mr. Rudra Gangadharan of the Indian Administration Service and Dr. G. Bala Mohan Thampi former Director of the Institute of Management in Government and Mr. S. Girijathmajan, Dr. Alexander Jacob of the Indian Police Service and Mr. A.G. Sasidharan Nair, former secretaries of the Institute. To them I extend my sincere thanks for providing the necessary facilities at the IMG to carry on the research.

I am also grateful to Dr. M. Bhaskaran Nair, Head of the Dept. of Political Sciences, University of Kerala, Kariavattom and Dean of the Faculty of Social Sciences, University of Kerala and Dr. G. Gopakumar, Professor, Department of Political Science, University of Kerala and all teaching staff of the Department for their encouragement and valuable suggestions. I also acknowledge with gratitude the assistance received from Dr. Kalyana Raman, Professor, Department of Statistics, University of Kerala, Kariavattom and Dr. K.K. Mathew, my former colleague, in the form of comments and corrections. I am thankful to Dr. John Pulparambil and Dr. T.I. Menon (Professors, IMG) for their encouragement and support at various stages of this work. I also appreciate with thanks the keen interest and support shown by Dr. T. Varghese (Reader and Head of the Dept of Political Science and Public Administration, St. John's College, Anchal) and colleagues of St. John's College, Anchal, in the progress of this study.

I acknowledge with gratitude the help by the Director, Joint Director, Research Assistant, S. Sasidharan Nair and staff of the Rural Development Commissionerate, Thiruvananthapuram. I thank officials various Grama Panchayats and Block Panchayats, for their valuable help in collecting data and in sparing time for detailed discussions. I am equally grateful to the elected representatives of various Panchayat Raj bodies for enlightening me through their ideas and views.

I also sincerely thank the encouragement given by Rev. Dr. Samuel Kattukallil, Principal, St. John's College, Anchal.

Thanks are also due to the Librarian and the staff of the State Planning Board, Centre for Development Studies, University Library, Legislative Library, the British Council Library, Thiruvananthapuram. The Librarian, Department of Politics, University of Kerala, Kariyavattom, the Campus Library deserve special mention. I wish to express my sincere thanks to Rev. Fr. Mathew Manakarakavu, Lecturer, Department of French and the Bursar, Mar Ivanios College, Thiruvananthapuram, for providing me with hostel facility during the research.

My parents and my lone sister (the late Mrs. Philomina Chrnm) have always been a source of strength and inspiration in my academic pursuit. To them, I dedicate this work. I also appreciate the fortitude and forbearance shown by my wife Suma and children throughout the course of this study.

Abraham Mathew

Thiruvananthapuram

1
Introduction

One of the strong sources of influence to shape human thought and action has been the quest for justice and fairness. They spring from the belief that, all men are equal and entitled to equal opportunities for growth and development and for development of his abilities. A moral evaluation of life with accent on distributive justice is at the core of these concepts. Scholars and thinkers of all ages, from past to the present, have articulated strongly on the compelling need for justice and fairness for the progress and development of human society. Epoch-making cultural and political events like the Renaissance, the Reformation, the Glorious Revolution, the French Revolution, and the Russian Revolution have contributed significantly in strengthening and developing the concepts of justice, liberty and equality in society. The notions of utilitarianism and liberalism also laid stress on social justice and welfare in the management of the state. Along with the development of democratic political institutions, these ideologies influenced the governance of states in all liberal democracies. The emergence of the 'Welfare State' was the next important development.

The term 'Welfare State' is however of post World War II vintage. The concept originated in Britain with the Beveridge Report on Social Insurance in 1942 and it had spread fast. With the advent of the modern nation states, both the concept and its content gained prominence over the 'Laissez Faire' state. Now, most governments, irrespective of their nature and ideology tacitly claim to be Welfare States, though, democratic states alone are generally considered as Welfare State. Welfare States provide a wide range of social services to the citizens and guarantee a minimum standard of subsistence or living to those who fall below the acceptable national minimum.

The State has been initiating several programmes for the general welfare of the people, and of the whole society. It has been recognised as a positive State, and it works for the prosperity of all citizens. The entire administration of the State is being directed to provide assistance to the whole population from 'the cradle to the grave'.

This scenario is undergoing vast changes; limits are being set to the role of the State, and the State is being rolled back in favour of privatisation. However, in developing and underdeveloped countries, the 'Caring State' cannot be dispensed with so hastily as is being advised. For the poor and the deprived, the State has to remain as a source of succour and support.

Welfare States with mixed economies or otherwise, stand for freedom of choice, of both the producer and the consumer. In that sense, they try to establish a society based on the merits of both socialism and capitalism and assures maximum welfare and equal opportunities to all citizens. These objectives of the Welfare State may be attained to a certain extent through progressive taxation on the one hand and socially useful expenditure on the other.

1.1 Concept of Welfare

It is difficult to define the concept of welfare, because it is interpreted and practised differently in different societies. Welfare State is 'a system whereby the State undertakes to protect the health and well being of its citizens by means of grants, pension etc.'[1] The term welfare is closely related to 'equality'. Equality implies that a minimum of welfare is guaranteed to all members of the society. The concept of welfare is necessarily moral and is related to distribution of power and distributive justice which can only be ensured through strong political policy.

Happiness and welfare are often used synonymously. It may be noted that happiness is strictly personal and subjective. It may or may not be related to one's own material conditions. Welfare, on the other hand, focuses on the material circumstances of the individual- adequate food, housing, education etc. There are certain objective criteria to measure the level of welfare in every society.[2]

Welfare is not a matter of charity, but of right; it is a responsibility of the State to its citizens. A civil society in which the instrumentalities and the authority of government are employed to establish, maintain and guarantee certain specific conditions of physical and sociological protection to its citizens can be defined as a Welfare State.[3] It is also responsible to provide beneficial services and institutional opportunities to the general public.

Aristotle viewed the State as a means of securing the highest aggregate welfare to all its citizens. He argued that a considerable degree of individual liberty should be allowed to attain welfare. Since men differ in abilities and needs, the best development of their powers would result from a system that guarantees them a certain freedom in conducting their lives.[4]

Bentham, one of the chief exponents of Utilitarianism, measured welfare in terms of additions to utility with every increase in production. In that sense, it favoured maximisation of utility irrespective of distribution. What prevented economies from being pro-poor was the absence of value judgement in a system, where market and self interest were supposed to ensure rational choice for social production and justified rich growing richer even if poverty existed.[5]

The neo-classical economist Marshall, however, compromised with low utility surplus of the poor consumers, provided production was high and prices low. According to him, both the rich and the poor could maximise their satisfaction by equalising marginal utilities. He however, expected some limitation in such a system and suggested subsidies to overcome under production and taxes to discourage over production.[6] Pigou and other neo-classical economists have conceived welfare as the sum of the utilities of different households.[7] Pareto has argued that consistent social choices in production could add to general welfare if some one was better off without anybody else being worse off.[8] But social choices often made income distribution in favour of the poor quite redundant. It resulted in the rich becoming richer without making the poor, poorer.

Though the concept of Welfare State is not directly discussed, Marx's perception of economic and production relations is a clear indication towards that direction. Marx envisaged a system in which private ownership of means of production is replaced by social ownership. In his view, the social ownership of means of production would ensure equality of opportunity for all. However, there are some basic differences between Marxism and Welfarism.

The welfare theorists postulate the State as a permanent institution and a neutral instrument of power. In their view, every human being is entitled to: (1) a minimum of material well-being such as food, clothing and decent housing; (2) expand living standards with existing physical resources and scientific knowledge; (3) should accept the fact the State has a right and duty to act when private initiative fails. Marx views the institution of State as a historical development to wither away when a communistic society, after a revolution of the proleterate, is established. According to him, the State is 'an organ of class domination, an organ of oppression of one class by another, its aim is the creation of the 'order' which legalises and perpetuates this oppression by moderating the collision of the classes.[9]

The concept of welfare has a significant place in Gandhism. The Gandhian thought is rooted in the welfare of the masses. Gandhiji wanted a decentralised bottom-up State built on a foundation of village 'Swaraj' or 'Village Republic' which would ensure the welfare of all.[10] He believed that 'Swaraj' could not be accomplished unless the lowest and the humblest sections enjoyed all the ordinary amenities of life. He was quite convinced that the establishment of 'Rama Rajya' or 'good government' is possible only through decentralisation of economic and political power and with party-less democracy. The concept of 'Antyodaya', i.e., the upliftment of the poorest among the poor is also based on the same conviction. Welfare, in Gandhian philosophy was Sarvodaya- the welfare of all. Sarvodaya is the title given by Gandhiji to Ruskin's 'Unto This Last'. According to Gandhiji, the central idea of Ruskin's work is that the good of the individual is contained in the good of all. This meant that social welfare and individual welfare are inseparable. Gandhiji was against mass production, but wanted every economy to produce goods and services required for the masses. He regarded the rich as the trustee for the poor and exhorted them to share their resources with the poor.[11]

Nobel laureate Amartya Sen has explained the concept of welfare in terms of capability and entitlement. According to Sen, what creates welfare is not goods as such, but the capacity to acquire them. Poverty arises from the failure to secure goods and services. The entitlement of a person includes employment benefit or social subsidy, that can be obtained through the claims against the State. These entitlements enable the people to consume goods and services which raise their capabilities.[12]

Sen also explains development from the angle of freedom that people enjoy in society. Extension of freedom is viewed as the primary means of development. He points out several distinct but inter-related components instrumental to freedom. They are economic entitlement, political rights, social opportunities, transparency guarantees and political security. According to him, these components of freedom not only directly promote the capabilities of the people, but also supplement and reinforce one another. He views poverty as a severe failure of basic capabilities, which are influenced not merely by personal income but also by social facilities. He also asserts that giving a boost to the income of the poor by itself does not remove poverty unless it reaches the worst off. [13]

1.2 Evolution of the Welfare State

The 'Laissez Faire' State which dominated the scene till about the end of the 19th century performed mostly police functions - the maintenance of law and order, collection of revenue and the protection of the country from external aggression. It was called, perhaps, pejoratively, hence, as 'Police State'. Promotion of social welfare did not fall within the limits of the State. It was left to the free play of market forces. Laski was the first political thinker who turned the attention of the world from 'Police State' to 'Welfare State'.[14]

Though the Welfare State is said to have been born after World War II, its gestation period was spread over four centuries. The major historical forces which influenced the emergence of the Welfare State were the Renaissance and Reformation in the fifteenth and sixteenth centuries, the political revolutions in England, France, USA and Russia during the seventeenth , eighteenth, nineteenth and twentieth centuries. The basic principles which greatly influenced the concept of welfare during these periods were freedom, dignity, prosperity and justice.

The 'Poor law' enacted by Queen Elizabeth I of England in 1601 had laid the foundations of State-sponsored security schemes for the first time. The Poor Law and its subsequent amendments served as a basis for similar legislations in many other countries during the 19th century.[15] In the middle of the ninenteenth century, Napolean III of France intitiated certain social policies. In 1854, Austria pioneered in adopting compulsory old age pension scheme. Later, in 1883, Imperial Germany, under Bismarck, established compulsory health and disability insurance. Subsequently, many Acts were passed such as 'Workmen's Compensation' (1884) and 'Old Age Security Programme' (1889). In Great Britain an unemployment insurance scheme was introduced in 1909 and a society was established in 1911 to protect members against contingencies of sickness, maternity, old age and death. The ideology of liberalism and also the writings of authors like Charles Dickens which popularised the concept of social justice, had a great impact on such decisions.

In the United States also, several security measures were undertaken during the first half of the 19th century. In 1908, Federal Workmen's Compensation Law' was passed and President Theodore Roosevelt urged the state governments to pass similar legislations. But social insurance in the strict sense of the term emerged in the USA only in the 1930s. In order to combat the disastrous consequences of the Great Depression in 1935, President Franklin Delano Roosevelt announced a package of social insurance programmes which came to be known as the 'New Deal'.[16] These measures were intended to promote social justice and social security for all sections of the American people. The year 1938 witnessed another epoch making event in the history of social welfare when New Zealand Security Act for Universal and Compulsory Social Insurance came into existence. The government of New Zealand had introduced social security tax to meet the finances for the same.[17]

The decisive event in the evolution of Welfare State began with the adoption of a comprehensive set of social security programmes, initiated in Britain after World War II. These programmes came into being as a follow-up action of the historic Beveridge Report of 1942. It became a landmark in the history of social security programmes all over the world. It recommended extension and revision of existing social insurance programmes in order to establish a national minimum level of subsistence with protection against contingencies 'from the cradle to the grave'. The plan was essentially an insurance scheme 'giving in return for contributions, benefits up to subsistence level, as of right and without means test'.[18] In effect, the proposals also contained sources of financing the same.

The Beveridge Report had played an important role in bringing the Labour Party to power in England and in establishing the Democratic Socialism of Great Britain in 1948. Its impact was felt not only in England, but also in other parts of the world, especially in the USA. However, there are differences between welfare measures introduced in Great Britain and in the US. The welfare measures in Great Britain were uniform throughout the country while in the USA it was extremely uneven and offered a great variety of measures. Unlike the British, many of the American measures were completely self financing.[19]

1.3 Welfare Administration

The administrative system is the most powerful instrument by which the goals of a Welfare State can be realised. In the achievement of socio-economic goals, administration plays a two-fold role. Firstly, it has to assist the process of policy-making, and secondly, it has to take responsibility for its implementation.

In this context, welfare administration can be defined as the process of transforming social policy into social services; it is the process of translating policies into action programmes. Briefly stated, welfare administration refers to the process of applying professional standards, competence and resources to secure successful implementation of the targeted programmes of social welfare through various social agencies, official and voluntary. A properly trained and motivated bureaucracy is an essential pre requisite for the successful implementation of welfare programmes.[20]

No administrative system can be fool-proof or perfect. Some defects within are due to the system itself and some others subjective. Most of the Third World countries have inherited systems of administration which are strong in the performance of regulatory functions, but with little emphasis on development. The evaluation and monitoring of development plans is quite lacking.[21]

In order to achieve social change through social welfare, an organised effort in social planning is needed. New techniques of planning and administration have to be developed for bringing about an integration between change and welfare. Welfare administration is not only a sector administration, but also the goal of community action. It needs new unorthodox rules and approaches. Since it is very complex, coordination is necessary both vertically and horizontally and across sectors.[22]

A strong and viable local government with sound administrative system is essential for a Welfare State. A democratic polity is based on three broad administrative principles; decentralisation, unification of welfare programmes and revision of inappropriate policies, and adoption of new administrative procedures. These changes are essential to achieve the goals of a Welfare State and to ensure easy flow of services to the people.[23]

1.4 India - A Welfare State

In India, even from the hoary past, the concept of welfare had been identified with good life. Emperor Ashoka and Akbar the Great were well known for their welfare oriented approach in administration. During the colonial days, social welfare mattered little for the foreign rulers.[24]

The formation of Village Panchayats was central to the ideological framework of India's national movement. Gandhiji had defined his vision of village panchayats as a 'complete republic based on perfect democracy and individual freedom'. The assumption and programmes of the modern Welfare State were implicit in the economic and social objectives of the Indian National Congress and it was rightly endorsed by the Karachi Congress session. It was further modified by the All India Congress Committee in its meeting at Bombay in 1931.[25] The idea of Provincial Autonomy and evolution of Panchayats in the country had been greatly related to the experiments of Lord Rippon and the Government of India Act 1935. The Government of India Act, 1935 introduced a scheme of three-fold subjects of legislation, namely, Federal, Provincial and Concurrent. In the Act, the provision for the formation of local government was in the State List. The position with regard to the local self-government institutions remained unchanged till August 1947.[26]

The idea of Welfare came into limelight, again after India attained independence. Free India has incorporated in her constitution the concept of welfare. The leaders who participated in the struggle for independence were very particular in incorporating in the constitution the ideals of justice, liberty, equality and fraternity for all without distinction of class, colour or creed.[27] During the discussions, on Directive Principles of State Policy, in the Constituent Assembly, Dr. B.R. Ambedkar stated in unequivocal terms the equal importance of both economic democracy and political democracy for building a Welfare State.[28] With this end in view, the founding fathers of the Republic decided to constitute India as a sovereign, secular and democratic republic. It embodies in a solemn form the ideals and aspirations for which the country had struggled during the British regime.

The Preamble is considered the key to the constitution. It states that, democracy would be hollow if it fails to generate the spirit of brotherhood. The essence of social justice is nothing but distributive justice and it is mainly concerned with the way in which a society allocates its resources to its members. It is believed that equity, equality and needs are universal norms of justice. In the Indian context, 'need' is a more preferred norm than 'equity' or 'equality', because it gives thrust to providing the basic necessities of life to all citizens. The term 'Economic Justice' in the Preamble denotes the commitment of India to bring about a socio-economic revolution.[29] Further, the word 'socialist' inserted in the Preamble through the 42nd Constitutional Amendment reinforces the responsibility of the State to expand its functions towards establishing a socialistic pattern of society.

Part III and Part IV of the Indian Constitution dealing with Fundamental Rights and Directive Principles of State Policy respectively contain provisions to ensure social justice and fundamental freedom. Hence, this part of the constitution is popularly known as the conscience of the constitution. It contains several provisions to safeguard individual liberty on the one hand and ensuring social and economic justice to the citizens on the other. Many ideologies have influenced the shaping of this crucial part of the constitution. It includes Bill of Rights of the U.S Constitution, Declaration of Rights of Man and Citizen of the French Revolution

(1789), the Political Liberalism of the 19th century, the Socialist Ideologies of the Russian Revolution (1917) and the Charter of the United Nations as well as the Declaration of Universal Human Rights (1948). Besides, it also has the strong influence of Gandhism.[30]

During the discussion in the Constituent Assembly of the Fundamental Rights, the Universal Declaration of Human Rights had great appeal all over the world. It prompted the makers of the constitution to incorporate a number of rights such as equality, basic freedom etc. in Part III of the Constitution. Very few constitutions in the world offer such a large number of provisions to ensure freedom with justice to the people. Since Part IV of the constitution is considered a permanent instrument of instruction to the governance of the country, the government in power is committed to work out policies and programmes accordingly.

Article 14 which provides for equality before law may be considered important for establishing a Welfare State. Article 38 of the Constitution specifically authorises the State to work for establishing a Welfare State. It states that, 'the state shall strive to promote the welfare of the people by securing and protecting effectively as it may, a social order in which justice, social economic and political shall prevail in all the institutions of national life.' [31] Articles 335 to 350 also stresses the need for the upliftment of the backward and minority communities.

India took to planning with a view to achieving the objectives of Welfare State. The major objectives of the successive Five Year Plans have been economic development and eradication of poverty. Poverty alleviation became the main plank of planning in India from the 6th Five Year Plan onwards. According to the Planning Commission, 'the major thrust of the 6th Five Year plan was on socio-economic infrastructure development in rural areas, alleviation of rural poverty and reduction of regional disparities' [32] During the 7th Plan period also, the agenda of eradication of poverty received top priority. Moreover, the Plan stressed the significance of decentralisation and involvement of the people in rural development. During the 8th Five Year Plan period, poverty alleviation got further momentum. Specific poverty alleviation programmes were launched along with the existing ones to ensure productive employment and certain minimum level of income to the poor.

1.5 Welfare Administration in India

India has a long tradition of maintaining and promoting social welfare. Its roots can be traced to the social system and in the religious and philanthropic sentiments of the people. Welfare was considered to be an individual responsibility, obligation and a mechanism to attain salvation. People used to take care of the weak and the needy through a variety of institutional arrangements.[33]

Based on the principles enshrined in the Constitution, several welfare programmes have been initiated by the Government from time to time. Traditionally the area of social welfare was concerned with the protective function of the State. With the emergence of Planning, several concrete steps have been taken for the welfare of the masses. From the Fifth Five Year Plan onwards, the development dimensions of the vulnerable section gained importance. Welfare services are now promoted, taking the family as a unit of development. Many diverse programmes were integrated in order to maximise the capabilities and capacities of the individuals as target groups. The current strategy is therefore aimed at reducing incidence of poverty and to bring improvement in the quality of life of the people providing opportunities for self-employment.

Social services are rightly considered to be additive and supplementary to other services for development such as health, nutrition, education, housing, labour welfare etc. With a view to achieve the objectives of social welfare, the central, the state and local governments are obliged to provide required organisational and administrative mechanisms in their respective jurisdictions. The administrative structures for social welfare are spread over the three tiers of federal polity.

The social welfare administration at the national level was initially allied to other departments. In 1964, with the establishment of a Department of Social Security, subjects related to social insurance have been pooled together. The need for a separate Ministry at the Centre for welfare programmes and its implementation were very seriously articulated by various committees. Accordingly, a new Ministry for Welfare was constituted in 1968 and 32 subjects pertaining to social welfare were brought under its jurisdiction.[34]

The Ministry of Welfare is headed by a Cabinet Minister. The Ministry has a Consultative Committee of the Members of Parliament.

The Ministry has been allocated many subjects including welfare of various sections of society, policy, planning and coordination of programmes, operation of central and centrally sponsored schemes etc. In 1985, the Central Ministries were restructured and the Ministry of Human Resource Development was established and the Department of Women and Child Development was also created and placed under it.

At the State level also there is a Social Welfare Department headed by a Minister. The activities of the Social Welfare Department can be broadly categorised into: child welfare, welfare of women, welfare of the aged, welfare of the handicapped, and general welfare. These departments would advice the Government in formulating policies and plans.

Welfare programmes of the Centre and States can be categorised into four basic types. They are (i) health care (ii) social insurance that requires contribution from the benefeciary (iii) personal services and (iv) benefits that do not require any contribution, such as grants to the needy. The Centre and States have also set up Corporations for development and Welfare Programmes of weaker sections of society and gave financial assistance to help them undertake economic activities. Housing and Urban Development Corporation Ltd., Tribal Cooperative Marketing Development Federation, National Backward Classes Finance and Development Corporation etc, are some such agencies.

1.6 Role of Panchayats in Welfare Administration

The dawn of Independence brought in its wake a new orientation of society in general and village panchayats in particular, permeated by ideas of 'Welfare State', planning and socialistic pattern of social order.[35] Accordingly, a provision for constituting village panchayats has been incorporated in the constitution. Article 40 of the Constitution reads, 'The State should take steps to organise village panchayats and endow them with such power and authority as may be necessary to enable them to function as units of self government'.[36]

Removal of poverty and unemployment are the twin objectives of welfare programmes of the panchayats. With these objectives in view, two programmes were launched in early 50s. They were the Community Development Programme and the National Extension

Service. It was conceived for the socio-economic reconstruction of rural communities in India. It was launched with American aid through the Ford Foundation under the Indo-US Technical Co-operation Agreement signed in January 1952.[37] Development Blocks were established for the effective implementation of these programmes.

Thereafter, several schemes were launched as part of the rural development programme like the Intensive Agriculture Development Programme (IADP) and Intensive Agriculture Area programme (IAAP) introduced in the early 60s and the High Yielding Varieties Programme (HYVP) started in 1966. In 1976, the Integrated Rural development Programme (IRDP)was launched in 20 selected districts. It was further extended on October 2, 1980 to all the development blocks in the country. It is a strategy package which seeks to achieve enhanced rural production and productivity, greater socio-economic equity, a spatial balance in social and economic development and broad based community participation in the process of development.

Training of Rural Youth for Self Employment (TRYSEM) which was an integral part of the IRDP was launched on 15 August 1979. The main thrust of the scheme was on equipping the rural youth, from families below the poverty line, with technical and entrepreneural skills to enable them to take up self-employment in the fields of agriculture, industries, business and allied activities.[38] The programme for Development of Women and Children in Rural areas (DWCRA) was introduced as a pilot project in 50 selected districts in 1982. In 1985-86, it was extended to almost all districts. It was a programme intended to provide income generating opportunities to women belonging to poor families.

Another programme known as National Rural Employment Programme (NREP) was started in October 1980. It was followed by Rural Landless Employment Guarantee Programme (RLEGP) launched in 1983. Both these programmes were intended to generate additional gainful employment for rural unemployed persons and create productive community assets. In April 1989, both NREP and RLEGP were merged into one programme known as Jawahar Rozgar Yojana (JRY). The primary objective of the programme was to generate additional employment for the rural poor. The secondary objectives were to create productive community assets and improve the overall quality of life in rural areas. From 1999, it came to be known as Jawahar Gram Samaridhi Yojana (JGSY) [39]

1.7 The Panchayati Raj System

The Indian villages are known to have been governed by their own institutions of a self governing nature from time immemorial. Even before the emergence of democratic polity, democratic ideals and institutions in some form or other, flourished in ancient and medieval India.[40] There was a multitude of functions entrusted to and performed by the panchayats which included development of rural economy, the management of village schools, sanitation, irrigation, organisation of temples and police. They also exercised civil and criminal jurisdiction over the society that constituted them.

Autonomous villages with self-governing institutions thrived in all parts of South India even during the Sangam period. At the eastern region of south India, popular institutions known as Tharakuttam, Desakuttam, Munnuttavar and Arunuutavar existed in the whole length and breadth of the Chera Country (Kerala) in the past.

After the advent of the English, conditions changed drastically. The British brought with them an urban, mercantile and industrial civilization. They introduced urban government institutions in towns and cities which sprang up in the provinces under their control. Rural organisations like the village panchayats tended to be over looked and neglected. Consequently the gap between the urban and rural India continued to widen. [41]

However, the period of Viceroyality of Lord Rippon was an exception. Through a resolution of 18 May, 1882 he had taken a bold step to revamp local government institutions in the country. This resolution is known as the 'Magna Carta' of local democracy in India. It provided for a large majority of non-official members in the Panchayats and is presided over by a non-official Chairperson. But it did not make any major breakthrough in the Local Government set up in the country. [42]

1.8 Village System after Independence

After Independence, the urge for a system of Local Government suited to Indian conditions had become very strong. Accordingly, some provisions for the same was incorporated in the constitution. Imbibed by the spirit of Article 40 of the constitution, village panchayats were established in almost all States of India. Several welfare and development programmes were entrusted with the village panchayats right from 1952. But the programmes carried out by the panchayats failed to produce the required results due to lack of people's participation. The Government of India appointed a committee in 1957 headed by Balwant Rai Mehta to suggest measures to rectify the defects of the Panchayat administration and recommended a three tier system of panchayats to revamp the same. The committee recommended immediate devolution of power and resources to the panchayat bodies to ensure participation and welfare of the people. [43] The Report also recommended that the functions of the Panchayat should be made development-centered.

The recommendations of the committee were accepted by the government in January, 1959. However, the Panchayati Raj System remained uneven amongst different states because it was included in the State List in Schedule VII of the constitution. [44] Thus the State Government had the freedom to make their own patterns in the system. The post 1959 Panchayati Raj institutions functioned as executive agencies of development policies formulated by the Union and State governments and would not be regarded as units of self government. The spirit of the Report, however, slowly withered. The Ashok Mehta Committee set up in December 12, 1977 identified the factors that were responsible for the sorry state of affairs of the panchayats. The Committee observed that the powers of the Panchayti Raj institutions were limited, their resources weak and the overall attention given to them by state governments, almost disappointing. They had suggested a two tier system of Panchayati Raj for the whole country. The Committee also favoured participation of political parties in panchayat elections with their symbols. But, no concrete steps were taken to implement these recommendations.[45]

1.9 The New Panchayati Raj System in India

The failure of the Panchayati Raj system for more than four decades triggered off an interest in their revival. Consequently, the Rajiv Gandhi Government introduced the 64th Constitutional Amendment Bill on May 15, 1989. It culminated in the 73rd Constitutional Amendment Act of 1993 for revamping the Panchayati Raj system. This Amendment to the Constitution brought about a fundamental change not only in the realm of local self-government but also in India's federal structure. Thus, the journey from the local self government idea of Lord Rippon to the institutions of self-government concept in the 73rd amendment took more than a century. [46] This evolution is epoch making in the federal structure of the country. By this amendment, Panchayati Raj institutions became a part of the Constitutional scheme of the country. In addition to the Central, State and Concurrent Lists of subjects, a fourth list of subjects for Panchayati Raj institutions was made. A separate Election Commission, an Ombudsman, Audit Commission, and State Development Council also came into being for Panchayati Raj institutions.[47]

The 73rd Amendment ensured greater decentralisation in administration and greater autonomy for the Panchayati Raj institutions. One of the most positive outcomes of the Amendment has been women's participation in Panchayati Raj institutions. Several measures were taken to ensure greater participation of the benefeciaries in the development activities. These include the constitution of a District Planning Committee and Grama Sabha. The District Planning Committee is designed to supervise the planning process at the District level. The Grama Sabha offers equal opportunity to all the citizens of a village to discuss, evaluate and approve or reject proposals of the panchayat executive and assess its past performance. It is a watchdog of democracy at the grass root level. In fact, Gram Sabha works as an agency for social audit in the new Panchayati Raj system.[48]

The provision for the participation of Non Government Organisations (NGOs) in Panchayati Raj activities is also crucial. They can play a catalytic role in creating conditions for the success of the panchayats in several ways such as awareness building programmes, training elected members especially women, ensuring their active participation in planning and implementation of development programmes etc. Moreover, their voluntary effort, financial aid and technical assistance can enrich the Panchayat Raj system. The NGOs also can mobilise and ensure the improved participation of vulnerable groups in the development process of the country.

1.10 The Panchayati Raj System in Kerala - Developments After the 73rd Constitution Amendment

In the wake of 73rd Constitution Amendment a new Panchayati Raj legislation was enacted in Kerala in April 1994. The legislation provided for a three tier Panchayati Raj set up for Kerala. The first elections to the three tier Panchayats were held in September 1995 and the new governing bodies came into being in 2nd October 1995.

In September 1995, the State government issued an order transferring several institutions and staff to the Panchayati Raj bodies. In the budget of 1996, a separate document known as Annexure IV containing the details of the grants-in-aid to the local bodies was incorporated. Thus the allocation of funds for the local bodies was made part of the State budget giving it the stamp of legislative approval and protecting it from the vagaries of executive decision making. [49]

1.11 People's Planning

Along with the installation of the Panchayati Raj institutions, a new experiment in development planning known as 'People's Planning' was launched in Kerala. It was formally inaugurated on 17 August 1996. The central idea behind this programme was to ensure people's participation in planning from below. With the implementation of people's planning, every citizen got involved in the planning process by discussions in the Grama Sabha. People's planning can also be considered as a system of multi-level planning where the lowest unit is allowed to plan and implement programmes quite suitable to them. The primary objective of the people's campaign has been to motivate and empower the local self-government to take up the new challenge of development planning at micro level.[50]

1.12 The Sen Committee

When the 9th Five Year Plan was poised to take off with reliance on people- centered approach to planning and development in Kerala, a Committee on Decentralisation of Powers under the chairmanship of Dr. S.B. Sen was set up on 4 July 1996. The Committee consisting of ten members was entrusted with the responsibility to consider and recommend modification for decentralisation of power under the Kerala Panchayati Raj Act, 1994 and other related regulations.

It submitted the Report in 1999 and its recommendations were incorporated in the Kerala Panchayathi Raj Act in February 1999 providing the legal foundation for a healthy and accountable institution of local self-government. The Grama Sabha, Committee System, reduced the role of control of government over the PRIs, Finance Commission, Ombudsman, Audit Commission, State Development Council, Responsible Governance, Anti-defection Act and Legal Entitlements, are the major features of this Report. The Report has contributed immensely towards institutionalisation of the gains of people's planning campaign and other efforts towards decentralisation. It also provided a solid foundation for local self-government.[51]

1.13 Panchayats and Welfare Administration in Kerala

The development of local government system of Kerala had a chequered history. The first attempt to decentralise power to local bodies came in 1957 immediately after the reorganisation of Kerala State. The Kerala Government had prepared two Bills - Kerala Panchayat Bill (1958) and Kerala District Council Bill (1959). Due to the imposition of President's rule, it could not be enacted. In 1960, the first Kerala Panchayat Act was passed. It provided more authority and financial resources for local bodies. In 1964, another Bill, Kerala Panchayat Samithi and Zilla Parishads Bill were made almost on the lines of Balwanth Rai Mehta Commitee's recommendations. However, it could not be enacted due to the dissolution of the Assembly in 1967. Another Bill, the Kerala Panchayati Raj Bill, was introduced with two-tier system- Panchayat at Village level and Zilla Parishad at District level. It also met with the fate of the earlier Bills. In 1979, Kerala District Administration Act was passed. Due to unprecedented political upheavals and differences, it could not be implemented till 1991. Though it was implemented in 1991 and elections held, it could neither function effectively nor last long. [52]

In the wake of the 73rd and 74th Constitution Amendment, the State Government introduced the Kerala Panchayati Raj Bill in March 1994, in conformity with the provisions of Article 243 (G) and 11th Schedule of the Constitution. Substantial changes were made in the proposed Bill. Finally, the Government enacted the Conformity Act in April 1994. The Kerala Act classifies the functions of the

Panchayati Raj Institutions as mandatory functions, general functions and sectorwise functions. The amended Kerala Panchayati Raj Act contains several provisions which drastically reduces the powers of direct governmental control over Panchayati Raj institutions. The first elections to the new three-tier Panchayati Raj setup were held in September 1995.

The Panchayats in Kerala have been associated with developmental activities on a moderate scale for a reasonably long time. The main functions performed by the Panchayats include those related to agriculture, protection of animals, cooperatives, public works, public health and education. There are educational institutions and public health centres run by the Panchayats. Panchayats also construct and maintain village roads. In addition, the responsibility of implementing most of the welfare programmes launched by the Union and State governments are vested with the Panchayats.[53]

Several poverty alleviation and employment generation programmes that were launched earlier, continued during the 8th Plan period also. They are: Integratred Rural Development Programme, Training of Rural Youth for Self Employment, Development of Women and Children in Rural Areas, Jawahar Rozgar Yojana etc. JRY was an important self employment rural infrastructure development programme started by Central Government in 1989. This has been renamed as Jawahar Grama Samuridhi Yojana (JGSY) in April 1999 when a new package of poverty alleviation programmes were declared by the finance minister in his budget speech. This programme was put under the direct control of the Grama Panchayats from its very inception. Afterwards, JGSY and EAS programmes were renamed as Sampoorna Grameen Rozgar Yojana (SGRY) when the Prime Minister announced a new package of poverty alleviation programmes on August 15, 2001.

At the village level, the execution of the programme was the responsibility of the Grama Panchayats and Block Panchayats. At the district level, the implementation of the programme was left to the District Rural Development Agency. Of the funds under this scheme, 70 per cent was available to Grama Panchayats, 15 perc ent to the Block Panchayats and the rest 15 per cent to the District Panchayats.[54]

1.14 Statement of the Problem

Planning has been one of the pillars of our programmes for national development. In the five decades of planning, the efforts at rural development has expanded with the introduction of various projects and programmes. Many welfare programmes have been initiated with a view to augumenting resource mobilisation on the one hand and labour quality and employment on the other, besides increasing productivity and growth rate.

The last fifty years have seen changes in the strategy for rural development as it made distinct shift from Community Development in 1950s to Agriculture Development in 1960s to Area Development in1970s and to Self-employment and Wage Employment in 1980s and 1990s. In 1989, in the last year of the 7th Plan, a special wage employment programme, JRY was taken up with a specific thrust on invloving Panchayati Raj institutions. The JRY was to be implemented as a Centrally sponsored scheme on a cost sharing basis between the centre and the states in the ratio of 75:25. It aims to create additional gainful employment for the unemployed and underemployed persons in rural areas, strenthening of rural economy through the creation of durable community assets and to improve the quality of rural life as a whole.

Only a few studies have been conducted on the performance of JRY at the National and State level. A concurrent evaluative study by the Planning Commission in 1992 was the first one. Another one was the study conducted in Karnataka in 1992-93 by the Ministry of Rural Development. In 1996-97, a National level study of the performance of the programme was done by Gupta.

It has been observed in the evaluative studies that the JRY did not provide employment to the extent expected. The quality of the assets created and its maintenance were not satisfactory. The local initiative and involvement were very poor. Many works did not conform to the JRY stipulations and had large scale leakages of funds. The implementation of the programme was adversely affected due to maladministration and over politicisation.

The study by Gupta, also has revealed similar problems and lacuna. However, he argues that in Kerala, the performance of the programme was a success compared to other States. He has observed that in Kerala, there was greater participation of the beneficiaries and most works were found socially useful. He has further stated that the PRI functionaries have played their role very well and the administrative machinery had adequate forward and backward linkages.

In the official records, the performance of the programme is positive or encouraging. But large scale errors and lapses were reported on its implementation from various quarters. It is argued that the performance has been far below official estimation. Significant variation can be seen across the States with regard to its implementation, generation of employment, the quality of the assets and maintenance of assets. The present study is an attempt to critically evaluate the performance of the programme in Kerala during the 8th Plan period.

1.15 Objectives

The objectives of the study are:

(i) to assess the extent to which the JRY helped in generating employment to the target groups;

(ii) to analyse the type of assets created under the Yojana – their quality and usefulness;

(iii) to examine the problems encountered during the implementation of the Yojana;

(iv) to suggest the mechanisms for the maintenance of the assets created;

(v) and to evaluate the impact of the new Panchayati Raj system on welfare programmes for the rural poor.

1.16 Hypotheses

Based on the above objectives, the following hypotheses have been formulated for empirical testing and scientific validation:

1. There are perceptible changes in asset creation since the inception of the JRY, praticularly during the 8th Plan.
2. There has not been uniform progress all over Kerala.
3. The official machinery has been inadequate in implementing the programmes, especially in ensuring the quality, maintenance of the assets and generation of employment.

4. The achievements have not been commensurate with the resources spent on the programme.
5. The Panchayati Raj system can enhance the efficiency of the welfare programmes.

1.17 Methodology

The methodology adopted for the study is empirical. In order to test scientifically the hypotheses formulated above, both primary and secondary data have been utilised. Secondary data were mainly collected from the statistical records on the performance of JRY, from the State Planing Board and the Rural Commissionerate (Trivandrum). The data obtained from these sources provided the basis for the macro analysis of the JRY performance in the State. However, as this data was found to be inadequate to make an indepth assessment of the implementation of the programme, a micro level analysis has been attempted to identify the problems associated with the implementation of JRY and to identify proper mechanisms to rectify the same.The records maintained at Block Panchayats and Grama Panchayats of the three selected Distircts provided the empirical support for the micro level study.

Primary data was collected by a field survey using a pre-tested interview schedule. The survey was conducted in the 12 Panchayats spread over the Block Panchayats of Anchal, Pattambi and Taliparamba and the method of selection of the units is discussed in Chapter IV. These Blocks were taken at random from the medium, best and lower performed districts with regard to JRY performances during the 8th Plan.

1.18 The Scope and Relevance of the Study

There are provisions in the Constitution that envisage the welfare of the people. Based on this, programmes and projects have been introduced from 1952 beginning with the launching of the Community Development Programme. Since the 6th Plan, it can be seen that there is a substantial increase in the financial outlay for rural development and poverty alleviation programmes. The amount spent on agriculture and rural development was Rs. 2,633.1, Rs. 4,809.9, Rs. 10,272.8 crores in 6th, 7th and 8th Plan respectively. The amount spent for rural development alone in 1991-92 was Rs. 3,021 crores and it increased to Rs. 9,844 crores in 1998-99.[55]

The present study is based on a very important wage employment and rural infrastructure development programme, the Jawahar Rozgar Yojana, launched in 1989 and continued during the 8th and the 9th plans. The official data collected from the Rural Commissionerate, and State Planning Board, Trivandrum, show that programme was a great success and created large scale employment and rural infrastructure facilities in Kerala during the 8th Plan.

To assess the success, an objective and analytical study was essential. Within the scope of the study falls the extent of the success of the programme in employment generation, asset creation and asset maintenance. It is necessary to identify appropriate administrative mechanisms and organisational inputs to make the Yojana more effective and useful.

Research and evaluation provide useful information on different dimensions of social problems to facilitate effective planning, policy formulation and implementation of programmes. Effective social welfare programmes demand a good knowledge regarding the structure and functioning of the scheme. It will help the State and Central Governments which implement such programmes to rectify and remodel the programme in future.

The present study examines the State-wise and district-wise performance of the programme during the 8th Plan using secondary data. This is followed by a micro-level study of 3 Districts of Kerala in which the data collected from the individual beneficiaries and benefeciaries of community projects were the mainstay. The study also attempts to cover the role of the Panchayati Raj system in the implementation of the JRY programme by collecting the opinion of representatives of the people and officials of the Panchayati Raj bodies. A study of this nature is essential to evaluate the achievements of the programme and to identify the lacuna and lapses in its implementation.

1.19 Limitations of the Study

The insufficiency of the secondary data used for the study has been a major limitation experienced by the researcher. The information on the number of persons available for employment and actually employed under the Yojana had not been maintained in Block

Panchayats and Grama Panchayats. Some of the Grama Panchayats had not maintained even the muster rolls. Out of 300 persons identified as individual beneficiaries of JRY, only 143 persons reported that they got employment under JRY. The assessment of employment generated under the Yojana, it may be conceeded, is subject to this limitation.

The conclusions made from secondary data have been unified by collecting primary data from selected areas. But the study is not free from the inherent limitations involved in the selection of sample and collection of data. However, adequate attention has been paid to make the study accurate and scientific.

1.20 Scheme of the Study

Chapter I is an introduction to the study. It deals with the concept of welfarism including the origin and development of the Welfare State and welfare administration with special reference to India, the development of local self government in India, Kerala and the new Panchayati Raj system. The statement of the problem, objectives, hypotheses, methodology, scope and limitations of the study are included in this Chapter.

Chapter II explains the conceptual framework of the study. An overview of the existing literature on the subject is given here.

Chapter III gives a brief account of the planning process in India with special reference to poverty alleviation programmes during the 8th Five Year Plan.

The results of the analysis of the data collected by the researcher is given in Chapters IV and V. It is a scientific assessment of the validity of the evaluation of the secondary data obtained from the Rural Commissionerate, Trivandrum, and the State Planning Board, Trivandrum, regarding JRY performance during the 8th Plan. It makes a critical study of the employment generated and the individual and community assets created during the period. The inferences drawn by the researcher from personal interactions with the officials and peoples' representatives in the local bodies also find a place in this Chapter.

Chapter VI gives the Conclusion and Suggestions. There are suggestions to improve the implementation of poverty alleviation programmes in the days to come in the light of the study and analysis, especially under the Panchayati Raj system.

References

1. Pearsall, Judy (ed.) *The New Oxford Dictionary of English*, (New Delhi: Oxford University Press, 1998) 2095.
2. Happiness is a necessary objective of society and welfare an input towards it. Welfare cannot be the final end. The external material circumstances of a person such as food, housing, health etc., may or may not be related to his happiness. (a) Jhunjunwala, Bharat, *Welfare State and Globalisation: Critique of Amartya Sen.* (New Delhi: Rawat Publications, 2000). Nobel laureate economist Prof. Amartya Sen was concerned for the welfare of the poor. Most of the research of Prof. Sen was on development economies and the welfare of the poorest sections of the people. He constructed an index to judge the improvement in welfare. Human Development Index of the United Nations was also the idea of Professor Sen. He argues that, per capita income is not an adequate mechanism to measure welfare and human development. Education, health, nutrition, infant mortality etc. are some other important criteria to measure human development. (b) Ray, Biswanath, (ed.) *Welfare Choice and Development, Essays in Honour of Prof. Amartya Sen*, (New Delhi: Kanishka Publishers, 2001) 257, 258.
3. Mark, Heald, M., *The Concept of Welfare State*, (ed.) Aiyar S.P. Perspectives on the Welfare State (Bombay: Manaktalas 1966), 133.
4. Wanlass, Lawrence, C., *(ed.) Gettel's History of Political Thought*, (London: George Allen and Unwin Ltd., 1924) 65.
5. Datt, Ruddhar and Sundaram, K.P.M., *Development Issues of the Indian Economy*, (New Delhi: S. Chand & Co. Ltd., 1985).
6. Roll, Eric. *A History of Economic Thought*, (London: Faber and Faber Ltd., 1953) 396-397.
7. Fisher, Irving in his Nature of Capital and Income (1906) explicitly set himself to the task of evolving concepts suitable to economic accounting. In the Marshallian System too, the national dividend and the causes which produce change in it are at the core of the analysis. This is still more obvious in Pigou's Economics of Welfare (1920) in which particular policies are examined almost exclusively in relation to their effects upon, first, the distributive and second, the total size of the national dividend. Roll, Eric, 511.
8. Pareto (1906) in his New Welfare Economics, reasoned self interest and all the time consistent social choices for production could add to general welfare if someone was better off without anybody else being worse off. Roll, Eric, 464-465.
9. Desai, A.R., The Myth of Welfare State in Aiyar S.P. (ed.) *Perspectives on the Welfare State*, (Bombay: Manaktalas, 1966) 164.

10. Singh, Kirth, *Philosophical Importance of Gandhism*, (New Delhi: South Asia Publicaton, 1994) 127.
11. Gandhi, M.K., *Ruskin- 'Unto This Last'*, (Ahmedabad: Navjeevan, 1956) 34-40.
12. Sen, Amartya, 'Development, Which Way Now?' *Economic Journal*, Vol. 193, 1983) 745-762.
13. Sen, Amartya and Dreze, Jean, *India Economic Development and Social Opportunity*, (Oxford: Clarendon Press, 1999) 103-113.
14. Asirvatham, E., *Political Theory*, (New Delhi: Upper India Publishing House Ltd., 1965) 180.
15. Bruce, Maurice, *The Coming of the Welfare State*, (London: B.T. Batsford Ltd., 1967) 18.
16. Srinivasan, R. The Welfare State in Britain and in the USA, in Aiyar S.P. (ed.) *Perspectives on the Welfare State*, (Bombay: Manaktalas, 1966) 110-112.
17. Stack, Maurice, 'Social Insurance in Latin America' *International Labour Review,* July 1941.
18. It was a report prepared by Lord William Beveridge (1942) at the request of the Labour Government in Britain. It envisages social welfare provisions for the entire population of a country from 'cradle to grave'. In pursuance of the Report, Britain developed a comprehensive social security system to fight what Beveridge had called the five giant evils such as want, disease, ignorance, squalor and illness. The social policy prescription of Beveridge and the economic policy plans of Keynes had greatly influenced the Labour Government reforms of 1940s. Its emotional content has influenced the States all over the world to undertake State sponsored income support welfare programmes for the weak and vulnerable. Beveridge Sir William, *Report on Social Insurance and Allied Services*, (London: George Allen & Unwin Ltd., Repr. 1948) 6, 7.
19. Srinivasan, R. The Welfare State in Britain and in the USA, in Aiyar, S.P. (ed.) *Perspectives on the Welfare State*, (Bombay: Manaktalas, 1966) 110-112.
20. Sachdeva, D.R. *Social Welfare Administration in India*, (Allahabad: Kitab Mahal, 1993) 55.
21. Sharma, R.D., *Administrative System of Developing Societies*, (New Delhi: Mittal Publications, 2000) 19-20.
22. Ramachandran, Padma, *Public Administration in India*, (New Delhi: National Book Trust, 1995) 86.
23. Pattanayak, Ryaimann, *Dynamics of Development Administration*, (New Delhi: Anmol Publications (Pvt.) Ltd., 1997) 129.

24. Jagannadham, V., Welfare State in India in Aiyar S.P., (ed.) *Perspectives on the Welfare State*, (Bombay: Manaktalas, 1966) 235.
25. For the full text of the Karachi Congress Resolution, as modified by the AICC meeting (August 6-8, 1931) at Bombay, see Jawaharlal Nehru, The Unity of India, Collected Writings, 1937-40 (London, 1941, 3rd Imp, 1948) Appendix A, 406-408.
26. Basu, Durga Das, *Introduction To the Constitution of India*, (13th edn.) (New Delhi: Prentice-Hall of India 1991), 9- 11.
27. Rau, B.N., *India's Constitution in the Making*, (Bombay: 2nd Rev. ed. 1963) 275, 276.
28. *Constituent Assembly Debates,* Vol VII 494-495.
29. *Constitutuent Assembly Debates*, Vol. XI, 686.
30. Pylee, M.V. *Constitutional Government in India,* (New Delhi: S. Chand and Co.,1984) 236-37.
31. Art 38, *The Constitution of India,* 1950.
32. Government of India, 8th Five Year Plan, (New Delhi: Planning Commission, 1992) 36, 37.
33. Sachdeva, 63.
34. Sachdeva, 131.
35. Pathak, Harbans, Rural Development Administration and Panchayati Raj: Need for Institution Building in Mohinder Singh (ed.) *Rural Development in India*, (New Delhi: Intellectual Publishing House, 1992) 103.
36. Art 40, *The Constitution of India,* 1950.
37. For details refer Pathak, Harban, *Revitalizing Panchayati Raj: A Need For Effective Channel of People's Participation,* ICSSR North West Regional Seminar. *People's Power in India., A Reality or A Myth,* Kaithal, March 8-10, 1991.
38. Government of India, *A Manual on IRDP and Allied Programmes*, (New Delhi: 1988) 20.
39. Government of Kerala, Development Guide, (Thiruvananthapuram: Rural Information Bureau, 2000) 120-123.
40. Visalakshi, N.R., *Administration of Village Panchayat in Kerala*, (Thiruvanantha-puram: Education Supplies Depot, 1967) 212-213.
41. Visalakshi, 215-218.
42. Mathew, George, *Status of the Panchayati Raj in the States and Union Territories of India,* (New Delhi: Institute of Social Science, 2000) 4.
43. Government of India, Report, *Committee on Plan Projects,* (New Delhi: 1957).

44. Basu, Durga Das, 430.
45. Government of India, Report, Committee on Panchayati Raj Institutions, (New Delhi: Ministry of Agriculture and Irrigation, Dept. of Rural Development, August 1978).
46. Ramachandran, V. *Panchayat Raj in Kerala.* (ed.) George Mathew, *Status of the Panchayati Raj in the States and Union Territories on India,* (New Delhi: Institute of Social Science, 2000) 155-163.
47. Mathew, George, 4,5.
48. Grama Sabha is a unique element of the Kerala model of decentralisation. It aims at the empowerment of the common people and ensure civic participation in the governance of the local bodies. There is a Grama Sabha in each ward of a Grama Panchayat in Kerala. The Grama Sabha has to meet atleast 4 times a year. The quorum of the Grama Sabha is 10% of the number of voters in the area. It is the village assembly in which all voters in the area are supposed to participate. It enables the voters to associate in the decision-making process. The decisions are minuted and forwarded to the Panchayats. Necessary action will be taken subsequently. The Panchayat cannot change the order of priorities in the list send by the Grama Sabha for approval. It also helps to strengthen people's initiatives through citizen's groups, neighbourhood organizations, voluntary organizations etc. Grama Sabha has the power to control the whole process of village administration comprising project formulation to implementation. The performance audit and social audit are some other effective mechanisms that strengthen the Grama Sabha. The scale and magnitude of decentralization process in Kerala has been gigantic. Ramachandran, 156-57.
49. Kannan, K.P., *"Janakeeyaasoothranam: Kalayku Mumbil Kettiya Vandi"*,(Malayalam) *Mathrubhoomi Weekly*, Kozhikode: Sept. 2000, 14-16.
50. Ramachandran, 158-159.
51. Government. of Kerala, Sen, S.B., *Report of the Committee on Decentralisation of Powers*, (Thiruvananthapuram: 1999) 59-148.
52. Bhargava, B. S. and Thomas, Jose, C., "Kerala Panchayat System: Some Aspects" *Kerala Journal of Political Studies*, Thiruvananthapuram:University of Kerala, Vol. 1 No. 1, 1986.
53. Visalakshi, 212, 213.
54. Development Guide, 117-136.
55. Estimated from the respective data of Plan Document.

2
The Conceptual Framework of the Study

The study examines the administration of welfare projects, in particular the JRY scheme, in Kerala under the Panchayati Raj system. To this end, an effort has been made to look into the development of the concept of welfare and Welfare State by a review of existing literature on the subject. This review extends to the related areas such as Public Administration, Sustainable Development, Panchayati Raj system, Planning and Poverty Alleviation. The survery of literature presented in the ensuing pages also provide the necesary theoretical base for the study.

2.1 Welfare

There is no unanimity with regard to the nature and extent of the concept of welfare. Its content and practice differ widely among the different states and countries. The term is generally used to indicate government and private programmes aimed at providing food, monetary support and other necessities for people in need.[1] The concept stands for social justice and the distributive principle. The legitimisation of redistribution is the prime motto of the concept of welfare. Social integration is also a major element associated with the concept of welfare. It is a processs through which people are being conditioned to fit into the society inorder to avoid social exclusion. The well-being and material prosperity of the people is the ultimate objective of the concept.[2]

The roots of the idea can be traced to European Hedonism and Utilitarianism. Jeremy Bentham and J.S. Mill as the chief propounders of the concept in the 19th century, defined the goal of government in terms of the 'greatest good of the greatest number of the society'. Later, Harold Laski popularized the concept of Welfare through liberalism. It led to the growth of a new political philosophy based on social and economic equality.[3]

The contribution of Mahatma Gandhi to the concept of Welfare State is quite significant. His vision of 'Sarvodaya' and 'Rama Rajya' are mainly centered on the concept of Welfare State. The idea of 'good government' cherished by Gandhiji was based on decentralisation of economic and political power and he strongly advocated party-less democracy. John Ruskin's, 'Unto This Last' had influenced Gandhiji in shaping his thoughts and principles of life.[4]

Nobel laureate Amartya Sen has explained the concept of welfare in terms of capability and entitlement. According to him, what creates welfare is not goods as such, but the capacity to acquire them. The entitlement of a person includes what can be obtained through the claims against the State, for example, the entitlement to employment benefits or social subsidy. He also explains the concept of welfare in relation to freedom. He states that, extension of freedom is viewed as the primary means of development.[5]

The genesis of Social Welfare or Social Security can be traced to England when the first Poor Relief Act of 1601 was introduced by Queen Elizabeth. Later, in 1854, Austria adopted a Compulsory Pension Scheme for people in their old age. This was followed in 1883 by Imperial Germany, under Bismarck, who introduced Compulsory Health and Disability Insurance. Immediately after that, Workmen Compensation Act (1884) and Old Age Security Programmes (1889) were introduced in Germany. In a major development, Great Britain inaugurated Unemployment Insurance Scheme in 1909, and a society was established in 1911 particularly to protect its members against contingencies like sickness, maternity, old age and death.

Federal Workmen's Compensation Law was passed by the United States in 1908 under the guidance of President Theodore Roosevelt. However, only at the time of the Great Depression of 1935, Social Insurance in the strict sense of the term emerged in USA. The Social Security Act passed in 1935 contained provisions for unemployment, insurance, old age and Survivor's Insurance.

The influence of Keynesian economics was also a factor that contributed in introducing such an Act.[6]

A landmark in the history of Social Security came into being in England with the historic Beveridge Report of 1942. The Report recommended extension and revision of existing social insurance programmes inorder to establish a national minimum of subsistence, with protection against contingencies from 'the womb to the tomb'. Social Insurance was the corner stone of the Beveridge plan of Social Security. The Report visualised a free, democratic, efficient, progressive, public spirited government using material resources for the service of British people.[7] The foundations of modern Welfare State, based on Fabianism, rests on the idea of William Beveridge. His concept of the Welfare State was rooted on principles like redistrubutive taxation, nationalisation, full employment and national minimum to all. From Britain, the idea of Welfare State spread throughout the world. Many countries have included provisions for the welfare of the people in their constitutions, which exemplifies the far reaching influence of the concept.[8]

India has written into her Constitution the philospohy of Welfare State. The Preamble of the Constitution promises to the people of India not only political justice but also economic and social justice. It entrusts the government to work for establishing a State based on social justice and egalitarian principles. It denotes India's commitment to bring about a socio-economic revolution. The term 'Socialsim' inserted in the Preamble of the Constitution through the 42nd Constitutional Amedment specifically mandates the Government to work for the establishment of a socialistic pattern of society, based on mixed economy.

Fundamental Rights and Directive Principles of State policy in Part III and Part IV of the Constitution also reflect the commitment of the country to establish a Welfare State. The Bill of Rights of the US Constitution, Democratic Socialism of the Fabian Type, Universal Declaration of Human Rights etc. have greatly influenced in formulating this vital part of the constitution.[9]

The right to equality embodied in Article 14 of the Constitution is a clear indication of the State to work for social justice. Articles 38, 39, 39A, and 46 of the Constitution reiterate the commitment of the government to introduce policies and programmes for the uplift and welfare of all sections of the people. Artcile 39 of the Constitution states that 'the State shall, in particular, direct its policy towards securing (a) citizens, men and women, equally, have the right to an adequate means of livelihood'. True, the Directive Principles are non-justiciable, but they provide important guidelines for the achievement of welfare objectives.[10] In fact, they have helped to transform the character of the State in India.

Thus, Welfare State now symbolises a wide variety of attributes. It works for such efforts which would diminish the gap between the rich and the poor, the fortunate and the unfortunate, the educated and illiterate, the empowered and the marginalised. Ultimately, it helps inculcate a sense of fellowship and public spirit among the members of the society. Further, it ensures freedom and dignity of the citizens in social life, and prosperity and justice in the national life.

The Report submitted by ***Sir William Henry Beveridge*** (1940) to the Government of Britain is a landmark in the realm of welfare administration. This Report makes an extensive review of the social welfare programmes in England in the post-War period. The welfare programmes initiated by the labour government in the 1940s were largely on the lines suggested by Beveridge. The major features of the policy were development of public social services, nationalisation of major industries and the commitment to full employment.

Social Insurance has been described by Sir William Beveridge as the 'giving in return for the contributions of benefits upto subsistence level, as of right and without means test'. Social Insurance and National Assistance organised by the State are designed to guarantee, on condition of service, a basic income for subsistence. Its aim was to prevent poverty by guaranteeing social security payments to certain categories of people such as the unemployed and the sick.[11]

Agarwala, A.N. (1950) seeks to explain the origin and development of social insurance and the meaning of the concept of welfare in India and abroad. He also makes an assessment of the institutional growth of social insurance all over the world. He makes a distinction between social insurance and social security. He further analyses the relevance of economic planning and social insurance in India and the future of social insurance.[12]

Maurice Bruce (1966) examines how the Welfare State of the present day has grown out of the needs of the English people and out of the struggles for social justice. He narrates briefly the historical concept of the development of social insurance. He gives a comparison of the social security schemes of Britain and the USA and also traces development of the term Welfare State in history by drawing various examples from European history. [13]

William R. Robson (1976) makes a distinction between Welfare State and Welfare Society. He states that Welfare State is what Parliament has decreed and the Government does and Welfare Society is what people do, feel and think about matters which bear on the general welfare. He is of the opinion that a genuine Welfare State cannot be established without a Welfare Society and each is complementary to the other. He also gives an account of the economic, social and political policies suited for a Welfare State and shows how far the hopes and aspirations which were centered in the Welfare State during the post-war years, have been realised.[14]

Rath, S.N. (1977) explains the growth of modern polity in Orissa and the development of the welfare state. He narrates briefly the different facets of Welfare State, its development in the west and its adoption in the Indian constitution. He further analyses the relevance and significance of the Directive Principles of State Policy and its influence on building a welfare state in India. He has also attempted to put briefly the welfare record in Orissa in the larger perspective of welfare government in India.[15]

Maurice Mullard and Paul Spicker (1988) seeks to examine the importance of social policy in a democratic state. According to them, the social policy of a State should be formulated in such a way that it conforms to its social objectives. The social policy of a State determines the broad dimensions of the welfare programmes. They suggest that the prime objective of social policy would be social justice and it must be based on distributive principle. They also assert that the concept of redistriubtion is related to equality or egalitarianism. This is essential for avoiding marginalisation and social exclusion. They advocate elimination of poverty is a pre-requisite to avoid social exclusion and ensure social welfare.[16]

Howard Jones (1990) analyses the kind of policies which the Third World Governments need to adopt. He states that, the problems of the Third World countries are different from those of the industrialised countries. He makes it clear that poverty is the central problem in such countries and their peoples are subject to different forms of deprivation, such as powerlessness, hunger, urban squalor, landlessness, illiteracy, ill-health, financial deprivation, exploitation of women and so on. Most of the poverty in underdeveloped countries is concentrated in rural areas where most of the people live. He states that, the concept of growth and welfare are not necessarily opposed to each other. He further explains that domestic economic policies are more useful for development rather than other factors. He believes that, poverty has to be attacked through the pursuit of growth and more equitable distribution of resources like land, capital and a healthy environment. He argues that the income maintenance services on the style of the developed countries is not at all suited to the Third World. He advocates that a human face is to be given to welfare services through social work and community development.[17]

Paul Chowdhury, D. (1992) traces the origin of the development of the welfare state. He explains that mutual aid has been part of every society and points out the role played by voluntary agencies in India for social welfare. He observes that, Christian missionaries were very sincere and committed in rendering service to the under privileged and suppressed sections of the society. He makes it clear that the British colonial Government spent only very little on social welfare. He also states that the Constitution of India contain many provisions for establishing a Welfare State. Moreover, social welfare services became part of the Five Year Plans in India. Under the Five Year Plans huge amount of money is being spent on the welfare of the weaker sections through different programmes and projects.[18]

Sachdeva, D.R. (1993) explains the concept of welfare in its different perspectives. He states that the concept of a Welfare State is clearly reflected in the Preamble of the Constitution of India, the Fundamental Rights and Directive Principles of State Policy. In these areas of the Constitution, there are numerous provisions aimed at promoting the welfare of the people. These welfare policies and programmes have received emphasis during the post independence years. The increasing financial outlays in the successive Five Year Plans substantiate this contention. He also highlights the role of voluntary organisations in formulating and implementing social welfare programmes. He critically analyses the shortcomings of the existing policies and programmes and those of the procedures and mechanisms for their implementation. It also incorporates suggestions for remedying the deficiencies in our policies and execution of programmes. The quantum and quality of social welfare programmes are not uniform in all the countries due to several reasons. He states that the Scandinavian countries have the best models for providing welfare services from the cradle to grave than any other country in the world.[19]

Jain, M.P. (1993) analyses the concept of Welfare State, the Preamble of the Constitution, the Fundamental Rights and Directive Principles of State Policy with adequate explanation from current derivations. He explains that, the Indian Constitution has been conceived and drafted in the mid- twentieth century when the concept of Social Welfare was popular around the world. The concept of Welfare State embodied in the Preamble has been reinforced by the provisions of Directive Principles of State Policy which set out the economic social and political goals of the Indian constitutional system. He makes it clear that political democracy would be meaningless without economic democracy, especially in a poor country like India.

He explains that since the advent of the Constitution, State action is being directed towards attaining the goals embodied in the Directive Principles of State Policy so as to create a Welfare State in India. Being committed to socialism, eliminating inequality in income, status and standard of life is a major concern of the State.[20]

Kamala Jain (1995) seeks to explain the concept of Welfare from different angles. First of all she examines the Preamble of the Constitution of India. It promises justice to all citizens, social, economic and political. She states that democracy would indeed be hollow if it fails to generate the spirit of brotherhood among all sections of people. The Preamble states that the people of India, belong to a fraternity, and they are people belonging to one country. She also examines the idea of socialism and observes that India's socialism is democratic socialism and not a 'communist socialism'. She has also examined the concept of equality citing different examples.[21]

Peta Alcock (1996) He analyses major issues in social policy in Britain, it particularly with British social policy from the broader.

International and theoretical context. He states that social policy can be treated as a discipline. The changes in the way social policy has been conceived and studied are also discussed. He also deals with the structure of the welfare mix in Britain and examines some of the major contextual influences upon policy development and policy analysis, and seeks to explain how these have been addressed in the study of social policy. He makes it clear that social policy has great force for social change, in spite of some hinderances visible on its way.[22]

Durga Das Basu (1998) the well known authority on the Indian Constitution, makes a detailed account of all the major Constitutional amendments in India related to the Preamble, Fundamental Rights, Directive Principles of State policy, etc. and states that the 42nd Constitutional amendment has inserted three new terms in the Preamble. These are: Secularism, Socialism and Integrity. Socialism is implicit in the Preamble and in the Directive Principles of state policy. The term 'economic justice' in the preamble denotes nothing but India's resolve to bring about a socio-economic revolution. He makes a thorough analysis of the relationship between the Fundamental Rights and Directive Principles of state policy. [23] This is a handy source book for the theoretical basis of the Constitution of India.

Seervai H.M., (1996) gives a exhaustive discussoin of the various provisions of the Indian Constitution, specially those highlighting the theoretical background in his well-known four volume commentary.[24]

Rodney Lowe (1999) examines the development of the concept of welfare state in Britain. He makes it clear that the 1942 Beveridge Report, is conventionally regarded as the principal blueprint of the Welfare State. It was under Prime Minister Atlee that the foundations of Welfare State was land in England in 1950. The British Welfare state reflect popular aspirations, accompanying the growth of industrialisation and political democracy, not only in Britain but also in all western countries. He further states that Welfare State is expected to ensure not only social security of the citizens but also a wide range of other services-including health, education and housing at a standard well above the barest minimum.[25]

Bhart, Jhunjhunvala (2000) explains the concept of 'Welfare State' and touches the principle of Pareto Optimalism while explaining the concept of Welfare. Pareto Optimalism speaks of a situation where no one can be made better off, without making another worse off. He is also of the view that a universally acceptable definition is not possible with regard to the concept of welfare state. He further points out that Welfare State also can be considered as a state which follow the merits of both communism and unbridled individualism.[26]

Ruddar Datta and Hirendra N. Konar (2000) makes a comparison between Amartya Sen's Welfare Ethics and Gandhism. Amartya Sen has argued that men suffer mainly on account of their economic incapability, which arises out of their failure to attain the power of 'exchange entitlement'. Gandhiji had no regard for market rationality. Gandhiji strongly condemned mass production and favoured production for the masses. Sen's welfare concept has no ethical value judgement but at the same time Gandhiji was very emphatic on this respect. Gandhiji asserted that the poorest of the poor should be the main unit of welfare. Giving merely a boost to the income of the poor does not by itself remove poverty unless it reaches the worst off.[27]

Bishwanath Ray (2001) reappraises the economic thinking of Amartya Sen such as social choice, measurement of inequality, and relationship between inequality and welfare. He also discusses the concept of development as visualized by him and his views as a critique on welfare economics from the perspective of post-modern theories.[28]

2.2 Public Administration

Public administration is perhaps the most visible component of a democratic government. To ensure well being and prosperity of the people, through good governance is the hallmark of a Welfare State. In fact, people assess the performance of a government through its administration. The efficiency and economy are among the fundamental principles of good administration. The quality of the life of a society depends to a great extent on the quality of administration. No administrative system is perfect and mistakes are bound to occur. The task ahead in public administration is to codify public bureau pathologies and design practical guidelines for remedial treatment. Excessive bureaucracy and red-tapism are the two giants which destroy the spirit of public administration.[29]

General administration and development administration are integral parts of modern Public Administration. The values of the indigenous society must be incorporated into the modern administrative system. In that respect, a top heavy and bottom loose structure of administration is neither good nor desirable. It will not strengthen the solid base required for a Welfare State. Public participation is an essential part of public administration. It is an inevitable aspect in development administration. The concept of decentralisation offers room for public participation. The views of Pai Panandiker and Fred W. Riggs as the exponents of modern participative administration are of immense value. It has been realised that, the classical Weberian system of administration is rigid, closed and bureaucratic. A development oriented system of administration should be evolved by the State while sustaining the good values of the classical system. Putting the people first should be the essence of modern administration.[30]

In a democratic set up, administration is considered as a vehicle or tool of implementing public policy. Efficiency and effectiveness are the two wings of modern administration. Administrative failures become the starting point of the alienation of the people from administration. There is an increasing recognition of the fact that the needs of the people should be at the centre of the development process.[31] The Panchayati Raj system and the concept of decentralisation can play a major role in strengthening the participation of the people in nation-building process. It may be recalled that, Gandhiji had emphasised the need of participation for the people in administration at grassroot level. His concept of Gram Swaraj itself is based on such participation. He believed that, through the Panchayati Raj system, the participation of the people can be effectively and easily ensured. However, bureaucracy and political elites create road blocks in the way of effective participation of the people.[32]

The participation of the people must be expedited by an effective system of administration. The present system of administration should be made to ensure the participation of the people, instead of alienating the people from taking responsibility. It is to be understood that, the success of public participation lies in the extent to which decisions are being taken with unanimity. This unanimity has a great force in promoting spontaneous and speedy implementation of the programmes. The livelihood and development of the people should be taken into consideration when concept of participation is being piloted. What would be the nature and extent of participation? This is a very important question and an urgent answer has to be found for the same. [33]

Panikkar K.K. (1971) unveils the merits and demerits of the Community Development Programmes initiated in Kerala. He has conducted a study of the Community Development Administration undertaken in Kerala in the 1950s and 60s. His study is based on three major objectives. viz. to assess the extent of physical and financial achievements; to analyse the sociological and political aspects of the projects implemented; and to enquire into the feasibility and efficiency of administrative machinery to achieve economic and social development.

He has undertaken a study in 16 Blocks based on the above objectives. The study has brought to light where the administration went wrong and how ill equipped the channels of communications and the official reporters were. It also brought to the fore the bottlenecks, troubles and delays faced during the time of implementation. He has explicitly stated that when Community Development Programmes are being implemented, greater attention should be given to the means rather than the ends.[34]

Mishrad, S.N. and Kushal Sharma (1983) analyse the necessity of public participation in rural development. They argue that growth and development are not the same. Growth refers only to quantitative and tangible increase in the G.N.P. But development refers to a relatively stable long-range increase in real national income that is accompanied by a change in the attitudes of the people. They are of the opinion that attempts at radical changes in administration cannot be dealt with in isolation. So a multi pronged approach is necessary for the all-round development of the country. They advocate an integral approach to development.[35]

Chaturvedi, T.N. (1988) explains that, a policy which fails to take into account the possible constraints of performance cannot be deemed a good one. He asserts that policy and performance constitute a continuum. He also believes that administrative feasibility and support are as vital as the technical viability, economic validity and even the political acceptability of policy, programmes or projects. He advocates the need for efficiency and effectiveness with regard to administration.[36]

Mishra N.L., (1991) gives an account of responsive adminstration and states that administration is the art of getting things done. The British rulers and their administrative machinery did not give much respect for the feelings of their subjects. The administration was accountable only to the Imperial Master and not to the people of the country. After independence, the scope of administration continued to enlarge as it had to shoulder new responsibilities and undertake tasks covering a wide spectrum of activities, ranging from planning and implementation of development schemes to removal of public grievances and human resource development. Later, the focus of public administration shifted to building up the 'Welfare State'.

He further states that an administrative system, responsive in the true sense, is supposed to be conducive to public needs and sensitive to public grievances. In a country like India, the concept of development encompasses economic growth and distributive justice. The system of administration should have deep commitment for the alleviation of poverty and orientation to the needs of the poor and the under privileged. He makes it clear that in order to achieve these objectives, certain values are indispensable to the administrative structure. It may include flexibility, consistency, stability, competence, prudence, due process, candour, efficiency, accountability, neutrability and integrity etc. As these values are invariably related with human beings, these are not only interlinked but also interdependent.[37]

Aravind, A., (1992) explains the programmes initiated for the welfare of women in India. Article 15(3) of the Constitution provides for special programmes for women and children. He states that the various poverty alleviation programmes have adequate provisions for the welfare of SC/ST and women. Many States have set up special Corporations for promoting the development of women and weaker sections. Thus, development of women and children receives special attention at the hands of the central and state governments in India. He further says that implementation of programmes meant for the society in general is easier than the implementation of such target group oriented special programmes for weaker sections. In such programmes, there is the need to adequately identify the target groups who may be placed below the poverty line such as women, children, illiterate adults etc. He believes that it is very difficult to identify the right beneficiaries and wrong beneficiaries. Besides, the monitoring officials are the least concerned about the achievement of the goals laid down for the targeted groups.[38]

Ram K. Varma. (1995) tries to explain the need for people's participation in anti-poverty programmes. The author says that India is wedded to establish a socialistic pattern of society. But no society can be built from above. He agrues that the manpower resources of our country, if not properly utilised, will become a great liability in future. He reiterates the importance of community development programmes for the uplift of the rural masses. He states that society is an organism which, like vegetation, has to grow organically, from the ground up.[39]

Padma Ramachandran (1995) explains the constitutional provisions to ensure social justice for the traditionally depressed and backward classes and for weaker sections. She argues that, the principle of social justice contained in the Constitution have had a great impact on the administrative process of our country. She makes it clear that the emphasis on planning for people's welfare has greatly increased the responsibility of the government and has strongly influenced Public Administration during the last five decades. The goals of welfare state has changed the strategy of economic growth. It has changed the nature of the administrative system and also governmental activity. The modern Governments are constantly seeking to enhance the quality of the life of the citizen through new administrative mechanisms. Administration is no longer merely Public administration, it has become development administration. Development administration needs new unorthodox roles and approaches. She is of the opinion that it became very complex due to the multiplicity of programmes and unweildy officialdom associated with it. To co-ordinate different functions both vertically and horizontally and across sectors is a difficult affair.[40]

Furquan Ahmed (1995) makes a detailed study of the role of civil service in a modern society. At the very out set he explains the features of the classical system of administration and puts forth the different models of administration. He believes that there are a lot of operational bottlenecks with regard to the functions of bureaucracy. He points out five important factors of administrative deficiency. They are failures attributed to the people, failures attributed to the Government workers, failures due to administrative deficiencies, failures due to defective and unrealistic planning and finally, due to defective implementation. He also makes it clear that the bureaucrats in our country should act as a catalytic agency of development and change. Thus, unless the administration gives up the arbitrary and arrogant style of functioning and enthuse public participation, it may not be possible for them to successfully achieve the desired developmental tasks.[41]

Ferrel Heady (1996) states that public administration is an aspect of governmental activity and has co-existed along with the political system. Public Administration as a field of systematic study, is of recent origin. The author explains that the publication of the book entitled. 'The Study of Administration by Woodrow Wilson' in 1887 is generally considered as the beginning of the study of Public Administration.

He further says that Robert Dhal and Edward Weidner contributed much for the development of Public Administration. Robert Dhal brought public administration to the status of a science. On the other hand Weidner brought to the fore the concept of development administration. He also states that public administration has become a well recognised area of specialised study for social scientist.[42]

Balakrishnan Nair A. (1996) states the need and importance of development of rural areas in Kerala. He States that it is the first requisite to general development. He also advocates that the community development programmes should be implemented with great care and sincerity. He is of the view that local level leadership should be promoted for village development.[43]

Remesh K Arora (1999) seeks to explain the development of public administration in India. He states that since we were under foreign domination for a long term, administrative reforms could be introduced only by trial and error. Hence the strategy of reforms also becomes incremental, gradualist and cautious. He further states that the two pristine premises of administrative reforms are nothing but efficiency and economy. He also makes a critical assessment of the recommendation of Committees and Commissions of the centre and states which were constituted for the purpose of administrative reforms.[44]

Sharma, R.D. (2000) seeks to explain the nature of functioning of the administrative system in third world countries. He points out that the administrative systems of 'Third World' is having both striking "similarities" and "variations". He has used the Riggsian approach to explain the third world administrative phenomenon. Riggs' administrative structure is having three models such as 'fused', 'prismatic' 'and refracted' The author says that the administrative system should be capable enough to stabilise the permanence of social goods. An administrative act is a public act performed on behalf of the public, for the public, by the servants of the public. The Third World Countries' administrative system is still colonial in spirit. It is strong in the performance of regulatory functions but has little know-how of new functions. Lack of popular participation in the planning and implementation of development programmes is a handicap of the administrative system in Third World countries. He has suggested certain measures for enhancing administrative capabilities and has argued that Public Administration must be recreated, renamed, revitalised to produce the changes and achievements for the transformation of societies. He also holds that administrative planning is important for improving administrative capacity. He points out the need and importance of devolution of power. He further states that, devolution of power would lead to laying the foundation of a new society which ensures economic and political development.[45]

2.3 Sustainable Development

Right to development is nothing but a human right. Right to development emphasis a claim for social order based on equity. 'Development as Freedom' by Amartya Sen, can be described as a milestone towards the development of the concept. He strongly articulates the importance of increasing the capabilities of individuals.[46] Another notable aspect of development is making better off, the existing poor of all categories, without penalising the rich.

Sustainable development is a concept which is currently discussed widely. Poverty and over population are the twin problems affecting sustainable development of developing nations. The former is a disease and the latter can be considered a menace. It is widely recognised that mere growth of assets alone may not reduce economic poverty but the distribution of economic growth should take place. There is also a strong argument for strengthening the economy from with in and thereby creating appropriate models of development and modernity. Development and growth are not the same but a thinking of that sort prevails. In fact, development means change plus growth.[47]

Neo-development is a concept recently developed in the world and stands for activating the dead economy of each and every village by suitable mechanisms. The exponents of this concept argue that Neo-development do not require very huge capital investment, but its results would certainly be very far and wide, and a deep impact. F. Perroux's concept of Growth Pole presupposes that growth does not appear every where at the same time, it manifests itself in points or poles of growth, with variable terminal effects for the economy as a whole.[48]

Amal Ray (1976) explains the dimensions of rural development programmes executed in Karnataka in the 1970s. His study was mainly based on rural development programmes carried out in the different Taluks of Karnataka. It sheds light on a series of issues concerned with the administrative problems of rural development, particularly in key activity areas of agriculture and family planning. The study was mainly directed towards an investigation of the organisational process of rural development programmes and attainment of its goals, priorities and targets. His findings were based on information collected from both field investigation and the available literature on the subject. His work is significant not only for its factual base but ever more for its analysis in the light of a conceptual frame work. He apprehends that the present outflow of the rural poor into cities is likely to create more slums and pose more problems for urban development in India.

He found that in India the rural sector, in terms of method of production, social organisation and political mobilisation is extremely weak. At the same time it has tremendous growth potential. Therefore, extensive development efforts have been undertaken in the rural areas, since the advent of planning. It is necessary to mobilise appropriate administrative and organisational inputs.

Since the primary aim of rural development is reduction of inequalities in rural income, it is necessary to mobilise adequate institutional support for the programmes formulated for the welfare of the rural poor. The experience in India and elsewhere is that the rural development institutions both financial and non financial are manipulated to serve the needs of the rural rich.[49]

Hari Mohan Mathur (1986) analyses the problems and issues of administering development. He describes the inadequacies of the existing administrative system and its inability to cope with the newer developmental challenges. He argues that, the inefficiency of the administrative system is proving to be a major constraint on development. He has suggested participatory development in public administration for ensuring efficiency and economy. There is a growing consensus that people everywhere have the basic human right to take part in decisions that affect their lives. The author contends that many development projects would just not get off the ground, due to the non-participation of the people. He highlights the merits of people centered development programmes. He is of the opinion that the Third World Countries should adopt a policy of putting the people first in every development programmes.[50]

Mohinder Singh (1992) examines the role and functions of bureaucracy in the changing development scenario. He is of the view that the bureaucratic structure in India is defective because they are reluctant to share power with local people's organisations. He observes that the concept of development has been synonymous with the development of rural areas. He argues that the rural development programmes have been conceived and implemented in fragmented, area specific, sector specific and beneficiary specific compartments. He also examines the various problems being faced by rural development in India. He states that the present strategy is multi dimensional and extremely complex and requires systematic planned efforts and strict vigil. He further explains about various poverty alleviation programmes going on in India, and states that rural development has emerged as a major strategy of the development process in India with multiple objectives viz. higher rate of production, generation of more employment, reduction of inequalities of incomes and assets, establishment of participatory development etc. Since 1950, a number of programmes for rural development have been in operation, particularly programmes like the IRDP, NREP, JRY etc., as a resut of which rural development has acquired special significance in the developmental process of our country. Therefore, such a study on the impact of poverty alleviation programmes in India had been taken up. He thoroughly examines the problem and gives suggestions or measures for the better execution of the programme in future.[51]

Remesh K Arora, Sangeeth Sharma (1992) examine the various facets or approaches of development administration They explain that development administration is change oriented, goal oriented and people centered. They highlighted the significance of people's participation in the development process. Development does not start with goods, it starts with people and their education, organisation and discipline. Merely imitating the alien system of administration do serious harm to the administration of third world countries. The local conditions must be taken into consideration while making administrative changes and reforms. They draw the attention of the ideas put forward by Pai Panandiker. He emphatically states that the foreign models have created fresh problems because of their under emphasis on the specific structural issues in different nations and settings.[52]

Retnakar Gedam (1995) examines development in its different angles. First of all, he explains about neo-development and suggests the creation of micro industrial activity, instead of giant industries. He believes that it is futile to create industry and affluence of high magnitude in cities when we have poverty in villages. He stresses the need for activating the dead economy of each and every village by suitable development mechanism. He advocates that there are multiple sites or poles of development.[53]

Kuldeep Mathur (1996) seeks to examine objectives of the Plan and role of the State. He argues that an underdeveloped country should mould and re-fashion the existing framework of economic and social institutions in order to realise wider and deeper social values. He states that economic and social policy has to be changed from time to time in the light of new experiences and circumstances. The removal of large disparities in development between regions requires the flow of resources for reaching them. [54]

Ravikumar and Todd Sandler, Kevin M. Morrison (1999) try to examine the relevance of development assistance to the poor on the basis of the changing situations. They are of the opinion that the social welfare programmes intended for the deprived has to be conceived within an area framework and it should be meticulously planned. The delivery system must be made very effective and scientific inorder to organise the unorganised. They also reveal that planning effort must be directed towards the implementation of agrarian reforms such as land reforms and sectoral planning. These are central to all efforts to alleviate poverty. [55]

Pratima Trivedi (2000) explains the relevance of economic growth, social justice and egalitarian development. The author makes it clear that the development of the social soector is most crucial for the all round development of a country. She advocates that the test for any process of social and economic development must be based on both the principles of efficiency and equity. She reveals that very often, programmes chalked out for the poor were abandoned during the implementation and execution stages mainly because of the elite management of planning policy. She also makes an attempt to distinguish between economic growth and development. In her opinion growth is a narrower idea and refers to the expansion of national income or production. On the other hand, the idea of development is much broader in scope and refers to a general improvement in the material and social well being of the society. Finally, she also makes a critical assessment of egalitarian development and its various aspects.[56]

2.4 Decentralisation and Panchayati Raj System

Decentralisation and Panchayati Raj is not a new concept. It was associated with the rural life of India for a long time. It aims at establishing democracy at the grass roots level and gives a sense of involvement to the people at the village level. Decentralisation is a popular political ideology being discussed everywhere in recent times. Democracy and decentralisation have become the most coveted ideals in most developing countries. It is peculiar that even where democracy was not much of a trumpeted ideology, decentralisation was considered essential for the achievement of development goals. [57]

Decentralisation is indispensable to make administration more democratic and to ensure people's participation in development programmes. It is an essential means to generate in the people, the feeling that they have a right to participate in the Government and that the development schemes being implemented in the country are their own. In a highly centralised economy, people at the grass root level never gets justice. So, it is necessary that we should bring about the devolution of power and decentralisation of economy as a basis of participatory democracy and planning. Decentralisation not only involves transfer of resources from Centre to the State and State to the Panchayat but also encourages the State and the Panchayati Raj institutions to ensure decentralised resource mobilisation. Thus, it ensures a measure of autonomy and self reliance at different levels.[58]

Gandhiji was a great champion of the concept of decentralisation. Decentralisation as envisaged by Gandhiji was very significant and had great practical utility. The idea of 'Village Republic' is one of his long and cherished dreams. Thus, he stood for the same and worked for it till the end of his life. The Gandhian model of decentralisation is based on two fundamental values – Swaraj and non-violence. He built up his theory of decentralisation on the foundation of self-contained village. Gandhiji very strongly made it clear that if India is to develop, the power and responsibilities must be shared by all. He also stated that the greater the power of Panchayats, the better for the people. It provides better involvement and participation of the people in development programmes. This is the only way to take democracy or decision making power closer to the masses. [59]

The Balwanth Rai Mehta Committee and the Ashok Mehta Committee, stressed the need to introduce grass root democracy. The latest, 73rd and 74th, Constitution Amendment is a big step towards this direction. Being a subject in the State list, the implementation of the Panchayati Raj system in India did not take place in a unified manner. It is seen that, in most States, the three-tier system of Panchayati Raj is acting as talking shops, without authority or power. It should be made strong and autonomous at all levels for good governance. It should show its might as a third tier of Government by its functions. Now Panchayats have become constitutional institutions like state and central government. De-bureaucratisation of administration is also an important agenda of the Panchayati Raj System. [60]

Jessy V. Mathews (1989) examines the development of local self-government in Kerala. The author says that the first active step towards the development of local self government in rural areas was taken with the promulgation of the Travancore Village Panchayat Act in 1925. The Act of 1925 provided for the creation of village panchayat on adults suffrage.

She states that local institutions were established in rural areas as a counterpart to those in urban areas. Voluntary bodies in villages were organised in British India during the early years of the second half of the 19th century and given powers of taxation. However, rural organisations did not get adequate support and encouragement from them to function as effective bodies. After independence, imbibed by the spirit of Article 40 of the Constitution, Village Panchayats were established in many states although its sturucture and functioning differed from state to state. Though the inititative for establishment of Village Panchayats began from 1958, in Kerala, a Bill could be enacted only by 1960. It provided more authority and financial resources for local bodies. She also points out that, thereafter, several attempts were being made to revaamp the Panchayats in Kerala.[61]

Neil Webser (1992) seeks to examine the development of Panchayati Raj system in West Bengal. At the very outset, he states that the interests of the poor could be better protected and the need of the party could be best served through the 1973 Panchayati Raj Act.

The 1973 Act had been formulated on the basis of the original Panchayat Acts passed in West Bengal in 1957 and 1967. According to this Act, a four-tier system of Panchayats had been created extending downwards from the district level to the village. To democratise the Panchayats and destroy the existing 'Rock Departmentalism', were the twin goals of the Panchayati Raj system introduced in West Bengal. Rock departmentalism was rooted in the deep elitism and conservatism that permeated much of the bureaucracy, reinforced by the hierarchical administrative structure. Based on this, State policies and programmes were channelled down through the district department to the block and ultimately to the village. From 1985 all state development plans have been drawn up on the basis of Annual District Plans, which in turn are based up on the proposals from the Panchayat committees below. The author argues that the new Panchayat Raj system has altered the structure and functioning of the local bodies. [62]

Baisya, K.N., (1992) points out that state finance is the core of public administration, which also fuels the administrative machinery. A policy decision on financial management attracts policy makers, administrators, statesman, executive authority etc. He further examines that the success and progress of an economy would always demand scientific decision-making and target achieving planning process through sound investment and appropriate resource mobilisation. The undue centralisation leads to blood pressure and tension at the centre and anaemia at the periphery. The results are morbidity and in efficiency. The way out is decentralisation and asserts that it depends on mutual trust, confidence and understanding between the two tiers of the polity. [63]

Morley Mohan Lal, G. (1994) makes an attempt to explain the vision of Mahatma Gandhi on Panchayat Raj and the contributions of late Rajiv Gandhi for its development. The author reveals that a large part of scarce resources was absorbed by the state administrative machinery, leaving very little for development. Rajiv Gandhi in his quest for democracy and development at the grassroots level had conducted five workshops for District Magistrates and Collectors on "responsive administration". While discussing the methodology for the 8th Plan, he insisted that the District plan should be made the core of planning and the aspirations of the poor would have to be taken into account, when formulating programmes. An account of the Panchayat Raj bill put forward by Rajiv Gandhi is also discussed by the author. Importantly, he makes an analysis of the JRY programmes initiated during the 8th Plan. [63]

Nagaraj, K., (1994) explains the decentralisation process initiated in Kerala in the mid 90s. He claims that the process of development initiated in the State is well known as the Kerala model development. Even at a relatively low level of per-capita income, the state of Kerala has been able to attain high levels of social sector development in literacy, health care etc. On the other hand, Kerala faces serious problems in other areas such as low productivity, stagnation in agricultural and industrial sector, large scale unemployment etc. He argues that the various problems that are being faced now can be solved through effective process of decentralisation and refers to the Sen committee constituted to suggest amendments to Kerala Panchayati Raj and Municipalities Act.

He also examines the various stages covered during the preparation of the 9th Plan. It was conducted in six phases and each phase had its own distinct functions and responsibilities. He claims that the campaign for People's Plan has obviously generated the much needed enthusiasm and involvement from below.[65]

Malhotra, D.D. (1995) in his article, states that, during the colonial rule and after independence, we virtually pursued centralised, bureaucratic and hierarchical structures for the machinery of Government. He is of the view that it reduces flexibility, adaptability, creativity and speed in field services. Most of the internationally funded development programmes and projects demand the strengthening of institutional framework at local levels and strongly argues for active local government participation for their success.[66]

Valsan, E.H., (1995) makes a comparative study of the decentralised system of administration existing in India, Egypt and Africa. He states that local Government in India, has deep roots in Indian history. The local bodies offered a stable basis of organised life at the local levels. The grassroots system had shown a peculiar identity and stability despite frequent changes of power at the super structural level. The modern local self government institutions in India, was primarily the creation of the British. There are two categories of local government institutions in India, viz., the rural local government or the Panchayati Raj Institutions and the urban local governments or muncipalities and or corporations. As a result of the 73rd and 74th Constitution amendment local governments are made the third tier of the governmental system. These innovations were intended to increase the efficiency of the political system as a whole by reducing the scope for abuse of power and costly mistakes incidental to excessive centralisation and to strengthen democracy at the grassroot level.

He also gives an account of local government that existed in Egypt and Africa. In Egypt, they had a centralised system of administration since the time of the pharaohs. However the beginning of the creation of a modern system of local government could be found in the constitution of 1923. After the 1952 Revolution, the constitution of 1956 came into existence, which recognised the significance of local government and decentralisation. With regard to decentralisation in Africa the author states that African countries also followed a policy of decentralisation. They found development programmes difficult to implement from the centre. However political parties are not in favour of decentralisation. He explains that, there are several factors which adversely affect the process of decentralisation in Africa such as finances, lack of trained personnel, lack of infrastructure, weak administrative capabilities etc.[67]

The Report on Decentralisation (1997) A Committee on decentralisation headed by S.B. Sen, was set up by the government of Kerala in 1996 to recommend the necessary amendments to the Panchayati Raj Act of 1994. The Committee has taken every effort to strike a balance between the ideas of decentralisation and the requirements of day to day governance, and to ensure that decentralised governance does not relapse into a rut as had happened in the past. Various recommendations were made to strengthen Panchayati Raj system and local level planning. These are Grama Sabha, Committee System, greater autonomy to the Panchayats, supremacy to the Elected Body, Anti-Defection Act, legal entitlements etc.

The Committee hoped that with the implementation of these recommendations, Kerala would become a model for decentralised administrative system not only in India but also in the whole of the developing world.[68]

Pal R.M. (1998) traces the origin of the Panchayathi Raj system in India. He states that the names of Rabindranath Tagore, Mahatma Gandhi and M.N. Roy were closely associated with the development of the Panchayati Raj. He argues that M.N. Roy played a significant role in laying the principles of decentralisation and local self-government system in India. Roy prepared two documents in 1944 namely, Draft Constitution of Free India and People's Plan for Economic Development. These documents contained Roy's conception of organised democracy in which the government will be of the people and by the people, but not for the people. Such a government would be based on a network of Peoples' Committees as against formal democracy. The author is of the opinion that these documents have much relevance in the present scenario of decentralisation. He strongly favoured a system in which power must remain vested in the people both in letter and spirit.[69]

Bhatkal G.R., (1999) states that decentralisation not only involves transfer of resources from Centre to State and State to Panchayats but also encourages the State and Panchayati Raj institutions to ensure decentralised resource mobilisation. He further adds that distribution of wealth as the correct index of development. To think of development in terms of Man and to work out the strategies based on Gandhian experiments was the main thrust of our planning right from the beginning.[70]

Bandyopadhyay D. (1999) states in his article that the Dalits in the Indian society were often suppressed by the elite class even after independence. He explains that the system of administration lacks accountability to the people. The bureaucratic system below the state level, was nurtured in such a way that they are almost non accountable to the people. The author hopes that the new Panchayati Raj System will remove the inherent weakness of the administration at the local level. He states that elected representatives of the people should have the right to exercise superintendence and control over government officials. He argues that the democracy of the elites is on the offensive against the democracy of the Dalits.[71]

Jose Raphael (2000) examines the significance of decentralisation in its practical aspects. He discusses the need of structural arrangements for decentralised planning in India in the light of decentralised system of planning in Kerala. He also examines the dimensions of the concept of decentralisation in the wake of the 73rd and 74th amendments to the Constitution. He asserts that for the successful operation of decentralised planning, adequate structural arrangement is necessary which is quite lacking in India. In order to assess the operational aspects of decentralisation, he has made a case study in Trichur District in Kerala. This study is very informative as it sheds light on the practical aspects of the concept of decentralisation.[72]

Srivastava, I.C. (2000) states that the 73rd and 74th amendments to the Constitution, envisaging empowerment of Panchayats with financial and administrative responsibilities, opened a new vista for good governance. He pointed out that the Panchayats still suffer from the dependency syndrome. He states that, the 'little village republic' envisaged for each Village by Gandhiji, still remains a dream. In other words, grassroot democracy envisaged in Panchayats, 'little village republics', in the true sense remains a far cry. He argues that the Panchayati Raj system is acting as a talking shop, without teeth and powers. He also suggest that an umbrella co-ordination team should be instituted at Panchayat level. [73]

Mai Treesh Ghatak and Maitreya Ghatak (2002) examine the future of the Panchayathi Raj system in West Bengal. They state that the experience of West Bengal under the Panchayati Raj system, stands in sharp contrast with that of other states. Despite its pioneering status in terms of reforms of the Panchayati Raj system, West Bengal lags behind several other states today in terms of development of power, finance and functions of the Panchayat. They also reveal that the extent of people's participation in the planning process is significantly less compared to that of Kerala. They try to explain the organisational structure of Panchayats and make an analysis about Panchayati Raj System in Bengal. [74]

2.5 Planning and Poverty Alleviation

The term planning implies deliberate and purposeful social action for achieving pre-fixed targets or objectives. It is also an important means by which the potential resources available in the country is being utilised. It is an operational blueprint and has no moral or value dimension.

Planning has been one of the pillars of our policies since independence, and our present strength is derived from its achievements. Planning is essential for macro economic management, and for taking care of the poor and the downtrodden, who are mostly outside the market system and have little asset endowments.[75]

A plan in India is a socio-economic document which outlines not only a programme of allocation of resources but also policies to be pursued in the wake of socio-economic development of the country. The planning process has mainly three stages, namely (a) plan formulation (b) plan implementation and (c) plan evaluation. Indian Five Year Plans have been based on selective planning models. We have followed different models during the successive Plans.

The provision for constituting a Planning Commi ssion has been listed under the Cuncurrent List in the Indian Constitution. Thus the responsibility of making planning programmes lies with both the centre and the states. These arrangements have certain distinct advanages. If there is a conflict between the State and the Central Government with regard to planning, the interest of the latter will prevail. The Centre has also the added responsibility of co-ordinating and incorporating the State plans into National plans.[76]

The government of India has prioritised activities towards nation-building and socio-economic progress. Thus, planning has been adopted in India after independence for the promotion of peoples' welfare and to reduce mass poverty. Planning was also necessary to strengthen and revitalise the economy, because it was in bad shape during the post-independence period. So far, we have successfully completed 9 Five Year Plans, the first of which was started in 1951.

Five Year Plans consists of plans for the Centre, Union Territories and States and plans for the private sector, especially the corporate sector. The entire matters related to the planning process in India is the responsibility of the Planning Commission. The Prime Minister is the Chairman of the Commission.

There is hardly any other country in the world which has as much and as long an experience as India in dealing with the problem of poverty. There is no doubt that concrete and time-bound programmes need to be formulated to deal directly with the problem of of rural poverty. Otherwise, the flow of the rural poor to cities is likely to grow, creating more slums and posing more problems for urban development. In India the rural sector, in terms of methods of production, social organisation, and political mobilisation is extremely weak.[77]

Though alleviation of poverty has always been a vowed objective of planning, ever since its beginning and more particularly since the seventies, yet the problem persists in the country. Poverty eradication thus remains a challenge today as it was a decade or two earlier. It is believed that poverty is multifaceted and yet often self perpetuating.

Poverty estimated on the basis of National Sample Survey (NSS) consumption data reveals that poverty is not a regular feature of all families all the time. It is estimated that about 35 per cent of the poor belong to the SC/ST. The incidence of poverty is the highest among agricultural labour households. The poor allocate an average of about 80 per cent of their total expenditure on food. Yet they do not get enough nutrition in terms of calories and fat. By and large, the poor have little formal education. Low investment in human capital prevents them from taking up jobs in the formal sector. Illiteracy was higher (75.83%) among labours, followed by self-employed (61.56%) and least among others. Thus human poverty is the denial of opportunities and choices most basic to human development. It is a social problem and it is undesirable and should be eliminated and alleviated through collective action.[78]

Gunar Myrdal (1968) points out that the fundamental weakness of planning which had affected post-war years, was the lack of adequate and reliable data. He states that, in such a situation there is all probability that planners simply indulge in, planning without facts, making guess estimates on more or less arbitrary assumptions. He further examines the post war growth strategy adapted by the less developed countries. He observes that the less developed countries have adopted capital intensive techniques for economic development and creating employment opportunities.[79]

Lakadawal D.T., (1974) makes an assessment of the need for decentralised system of planning which was adopted by Karnataka in the 1970's. He states that from 1970 onwards the orientation and structure of development planning has changed from growth, to redistribution with growth. He holds that the logic of decentralisation is so powerful that it has been almost universally accepted and it has now become a well-recognised doctrine to enable the people to harness local resources to use it for local needs. [80]

Mehta, M.M. (1976) unveils the importance of human resource planning for the overall economic development and growth. He points out that recent years have witnessed a shift in emphases of study in favour of economics of growth. The earlier preoccupation with the development of physical resources has given way to an appreciation of the importance of human resourses as major growth factor. Planning in developing countries has become increasingly aware of the need for developing human resources as an integral part of general economic planning. The author believes that it is an essential prerequisite for sustained and accelerated economic growth. He examines and analyses the problem in an objective and scientific manner. He also gives an account of various tools and techniques of human resources planning followed by developing countries. He throws light on many conceptual, technical and methodological aspects of the human resources development planning. He stresses the importance of better organisation for fuller development and efficient utilisation of human resources. [81]

Chaturuedi, T.N., and Kamta Prasad (1984) explain planning as a social phenomenon involving the marshalling of great diversity of people, enterprises and organisations to the pursuit of certain collective objectives for the welfare of the masses. They make it clear that planning is neither simply a technical exercise nor only a political or economic device alone. It is also centered on men, their motivation and aspiration. In other words planning is one of the most complicated process because virtually all aspects of human life are involved in it. They add that policy measures also should have a degree of precision and sharpness for effective implementation or execution.[82]

Ruddar Datt, Sundaram, K.P.M. (1985) explain the concept of poverty in its different dimensions. They observe that the concept of poverty in the USA would be significantly different from that of Third World countries. The main aspects that have been focused by them are: policies, strategies, programme design, delivery system, local institutions and management of programmes, implementation of poverty alleviation. It covers macro as well as micro studies of the programmes and also reveals the achievements and failures. It also assesses the effectiveness of the poverty alleviation programmes undertaken by the various states of India.

They also reveal the fact that rural development programmes would not yield the desired result by mere distribution of funds unless administered with great vigil and commitment.[83]

Kamta Prasad (1985) states that poverty, unemployment and inequality are related phenomena. He observes that a weak delivery system is a serious problem with regard to the programmes of the weaker sections. Adequate co-ordination among the different agencies is required for attaining best results. He asserts that free enterprise system has only limited potential for removal of poverty. He also suggest that deliberate public policy measures are needed to tackle this problem.[84]

Malcolm S. Adiseshiah (1985) explains the objectives, sectoral composition and financing of the 7th Plan. He states that the planned economic development being under taken in India is a remarkable experiment unequalled in modern history both in terms of its dimensions and its implications. The original document of the 7th Five Year Plan states, "the guiding principles of Indian planning are provided by the basic objective of growth, modernisation, self – reliance and social justice with in this frame work, each Five Year Plan involves one directional change to take into account new constraints and new possibilities." The document also seeks to emphasise policies and programmes which would accelerate the growth in the food grains production, increase employment opportunities and raise productive employment. The 7th Plan also places particular emphasis on obtaining more output out of assets that have been built up over the years. It is observed that efficiency and employment generation are closely linked with measures for human resource development.

The 7th Plan visualises programmes for alleviation of mass poverty through sectoral development in rural areas. The programmes such as IRDP and NREP will have to be widened and their focus sharpened for taking the benefits to the target groups and households. The author makes it clear that poverty eradication, whether in the rural or in the urban areas, would be incomplete without specific programmes for provision of minimum needs and minimum levels of satisfaction in the areas of health, nutrition, education, safe drinking water, housing and shelter. The 7th Plan has also given adequate emphasis to re-distributive land reforms that provide a minimum level of land holdings to the land less. [85]

Mahendra Reddy S., Yadava Reddy M., Upadhyaya K.S. Reghuram, C.H. (1987) explain that growth with social justice and stability has been the corner stones of India's Five Year Plan. They reveal that social justice is a broad term which includes reduction in inequalities of wealth, income, poverty and unemployment. They also stress the importance of growth with stability and social justice. They are of the view that, in all the Five Year Plans, barring the first Plan, removal of poverty and unemployment, together with reduction in inequalities of wealth and income have been the main objective. The 7th Plan document gave emphasis for strengthening the socio-economic infrastructure in rural areas, alleviating rural poverty and reducing regional disparities.[86]

Padma Ramachandran and Oommen, M.A. (1987) explain that the blending of the participation and initiative from below with the general direction from above alone can correct the distortions of the development process. They argue that it may release new productive energies and also provide the much needed moral direction and depth to development planning in India.[87]

Mrityunjoy Banerjee (1988) seeks to examine the twin principal issues of planning such as determination of priorities and the optimisation of resources. He states that a new history was created in India when she launched the system of comprehensive planning for economic development through democratic means. He traces and analyses the course of Five Year Plans that have been implemented with progressive outlook since 1951. It analyses logically and objectively the broad outlines, outlays, resources, methodogies achievements and failures of the past Five Year Plans. It also contains an account of the assessment of planning, the current economic situation and various programmes of poverty alleviation. He also states that planning means "thinking before action".[88]

Planning Commission (1992) The Planning Commission has made a study in 1992 on the performance of Jawahar Rozgar Yojana in selected areas of the country. The study revealed certain important problems in implementing the programme. It is mainly concentrated on assessing the extent to which the persons from the target group got employment, the types of assets created, arrangements made for its maintenance and the problems faced in the implementation.

The study revealed that, the information on the number of persons available for employment and actually employed under the Yojana had not been maintained at any level of administration. Some of the Gram Panchayats, had not maintained even the muster rolls properly. Although the physical targets in terms of man days of employment generation is achieved satisfactorily, it does not match with the financial performance, and does not give any idea about the number of persons actually employed, under the Yojana.

The illustrative list of assets-to-be-created under the Yojana had become exhaustive at the operational level, for monitoring and review purposes. The list of assets created under "other works" suggests that the Yojana needs to be more flexible so that the assets could be created based on the needs of the area and the people. Arrangements for maintenance of assets have to be made properly and the involvement of Gram Panchayats ensured for the same.

The Report also sheds light on the need and importance of better co-ordination and co-operation among different level of administration and Panchayathi Raj bodies for the effective implementation of the programme in future.[89]

The 8th Five Year Plan (1992) In the Plan document, the Planning Commission explains the objectives, strategies and priorities of planning. The Commission makes a detailed list of programmes to be executed for rural development and poverty alleviation. The problem of rural poverty was brought into a sharper focus during the 6th Plan. The 7th Plan too had emphasised growth with social justice. It was realised, that a sustainable strategy for poverty alleviation has to be based on increasing the productive employment opportunities in the process of growth itself. However, to the extent the process of growth bypasses some sections of the population, it is necessary to formulate specific poverty alleviation programmes for the generation of a certain minimum level of income for the rural poor. Planning Commission holds the view that rural development implies both the economic betterment of people as well as greater social transformation. Increased participation of people in the rural development process, decentralisation of planning, better enforcement of land reforms and so on.

Rural poverty is linked with low rural productivity and unemployment, including under employment. Hence, it is imperative to improve productivity and increase employment in rural areas. About 200 million people are still poor in rural India. In 1987-88, the rural poverty line in terms of per-capita monthly expenditure was

Rs. 131.80. However, there are wide regional variations with regard to poverty. The Commission has suggested that a review of the on-going programme is essential for its effective implementation in the days to come. And the Panchayati Raj system should be activated in its full potential with help of voluntary organisations.[90]

Yogendra Singh (1993) analyses the changes that occured in the social structure, cultural values and institutions in India during the last few decades. He also assesses the implications of the contemporary problems related to social change. The author critically analyses the social mobility and social stratification in one society with another society. He points out the impact of investment in education, agriculture, industry etc. Besides, the reservation policy for the weaker sections and employment and welfare programmes for them are also brought under critical examination. He reveals that the implementation of the welfare programmes and measures for social justice have not yielded the desirable results primarily due to illiteracy of the people. He further states that more stringent steps have to be taken to remove the twin problems of illiteracy and poverty.[91]

Quibrin M.G. (1994) examines the concept of poverty in different dimensions and states that the promotion of economic welfare is the prime objective of economic development. According to the NSS data, the poverty norms of a country should be based on average calorie requirement of the population. It varies depending up on the age, sex and occupation of the individual. He makes it clear that, poverty is not a regular feature of all families all the time. He is of the opinion that, the denial of opportunities and choices are the basic factors which adversely affect human development. He quotes Amartya Sen: "the eradication of poverty entails strengthening the capabilities of the poor, and simultaneously create opportunities in society to enable them to make full use of it".[92]

Ram K. Varma (1996) makes some recollections about 8th Plan approach, rural development and poverty alleviation. He states that alleviation of poverty has been one of the primary objectives of planned development in India. Ever since the inception of planning the policies and the programmes have been designed and redesigned with this aim. He also makes a review of the existing poverty alleviation programmes. Finally he has made an attempt to assess the 73rd Constitution Amendment relating to Panchayathi Raj and 8th Plan approach to special employment programmes.[93]

Laxmi Devi (1997) examines the need of rural development and poverty alleviation programmes. She states that rural development implies both the economic betterment of people as well as greater social transformation. She believes that increased participation of people in the rural development process, decentralisation of planning, better enforcement of land reforms and greater access to credits and inputs go a long way in providing the rural people with better prospects for economic development. She also makes a critical assessment of the existing programmes of poverty alleviation.[94]

Ram Ahuja (1997) explains the strategy of eradication of poverty in its different manifestations. He states that there is no appropriate set of policies and programmes for alleviating poverty. About the concept of poverty, it is a situation that gives rise to a feeling of discrepancy between what "one has" and what one "should have". He suggests mainly three strategies for eradication of poverty; (i) maximisation of economic growth by stepping up investment that would trickle down and diffuse among all sectors of the society, (ii) the distribution of assets through land reforms, community development programmes and nationalisation of big industries, as suggested by the structural school and (iii) intitiating of rural development programmes such as IRDP, TRYSEM, NREP, RLEGP, JRY, JGSY, SGSY etc. He has also made a critical evaluation of the antipoverty programmes going on in India. [95]

Griappa S. (1998) makes a thorough analysis of the rural development programmes undertaken in the state of Karnataka in 1990's. The author is bringing to light a critical evaluation of the JRY programme implemented in Karnataka by the Ministry of Rural Development.

The author points out the following problems faced during the implementation of the programme. The study reveals that inappropriate works were also included under the programme. The local involvement was very much lacking and JRY works have been undertaken from JRY funds only and local contribution was not forthcoming in most of the regions.

There was a lack of specialised staff to maintain and supervise JRY works. Most of the Panchayats felt that the funds received were inadequate and untimely. He further observes that, untimely supply of raw materials and poor supply of inputs affected the programme. The JRY work rate normally was lower than the market wage rate. In some cases, the work were given to contractors. The engineering staff from the district administration did not provide proper technical guidance and supervision. The study also reveals that the problem of politicisation resulting in inappropriate choice of works, mishandling by the Panchayati staff and mis-utilization of funds favouring only a few target groups.[96]

Fernando Franco (1999) examines the gravity and magnitude of the problem of poverty. He criticises the lukewarm attitude of political parties in solving this problem. He believes that reduction of poverty is feasible provided certain conditions are met. He states that after 1991 due to the onset of liberalisation the attention paid to this sector eroded, compared to 1970s and 1980 s. He reiterates the responsibility entrusted with the state to solve this fundamental problem. He further adds that State cannot retreat from its constitutional responsibility in any circumstance. Finally he argues that reducing poverty is not an unattainable dream but it can be attained through active intervention of the State. [97]

Srinath Halder (2000) explains the strategies adopted during the 8th Five Year Plan for the elimination of poverty. He pointed out that the elimination of poverty continues to be a major concern of development planning. The expansion of employment opportunities, augmentation of productivity and income levels of both the under employed and unemployed poor would be the main strategy adopted during the 8th Plan. He states that short term employment will have to be provided to the unemployed and under-employed, particularly for the poor and vulnerable sections, through the existing special employment programmes like IRDP and JRY etc. He further states that by integrating the existing special employment programmes with other sectoral development programmes would generate more employment opportunities. He believes that it will create an atmosphere for sutainable development.[98]

Madhu Dandavate (2000) in his article, reveals certain important facets of Indian Planning. He states that the idea of Planning as a corner stone of economic reconstruction of free India, was first outlined by Netaji Subhash Chandra Bose in his presidential address at the Haripura Session of Indian National Congress in

February 1938 and Pandit Nehru was appointed the chairman of the committee by the congress. This committee became the precursor of the Advisory body of Planning Board set up by the interim government of India in 1946. It had played an important role for the formulation of first Planning Commission of free India.

According to a school of thinking, the process of planning is relevant only in a system in which the Public Sector represents the commanding heights of the economy. To establish an egalitarian economy, an efficient and incorruptible cooperative system is essential. He also cites the examples of the Scandinavian countries where they follow the co-operative system, which helped them to maintain an egalitarian system. He asserts that the planning process of India must have a better methodology for poverty elimination.[99]

Mahendra Dev, S. (2000) explains the impact of the new economic policy referring to the NSS Data, 1997. He states that around 37 crores of people live below the poverty line, in India. He also asserts that the concept of poverty is multi dimensional. Poverty situation of India after the introduction of economic reforms may have differential impact on different regions of the country. The real wages of the people were not increased in the post reform period because of increase in relative food prices. The author observes that direct poverty alleviation programmes would raise the income and purchasing power of the poor particularly in the short and medium runs. He argues that through the new Panchayati Raj system and also with the participation of the people in poverty alleviation programmes, the gravity of the problem can be reduced. He also states that the role being played by voluntary organisations in this regard is quite commendable.[100]

Rumki Basu (2000) states that the introduction of new economic policy in India since 1991 was the major factor that led to the withdrawal of the public sector and down-sizing in public expenditure. The reform process also adversely affected the condition of the poor due to the reduction of public expenditure. The author explains that lack of proper methods for beneficiary hunting under poverty alleviation programmes, deprived the poor from getting much benefits. He also tries to critically analyse the impact of various poverty alleviation programmes being launched by the Central Government, especially during the post-reform period.[101]

Mahesh Prasad (2000) states that poverty eradication is not only a developmental goal but also a central challenge for Human Rights in the 21st century. According to the HDR 2000, India ranks 128 amongst 174 countries. It ranks India above Pakistan (135) but below Myanmar (125). The Report further says that the top ten in the order are the higly industrialised Canada, Norway, the US, Australia, Iceland, Sweeden Belgium, the Netherlands, Japan and the U.K. He explains that the Central expenditure (Plan and non Plan) on social sector (education health and family welfare, rural development etc.) is increased from 9.34 % in 1993-94 to 11.4% in 1999-2000. The report emphasises that the eradication of poverty and related deficiencies in services, need a global effort. Finally he states that only with global efforts can poverty be eradicated the world over.[102]

Gupta D. N. (2001) provides an in-depth study on policy, strategy, programme design, planning, delivery system, Panchayathi Raj system and management of programmes with regard to rural development. An endeavour also has been made to examine comprehensively all the issues that are vital for sustainable development. It attempts to diagnose the rural development from the system point of view in order to address the issues in totality. Rightly so, the system approach has been applied to evaluate the rural development system. He states that rural development has been at the centrestage of development efforts ever since the Five Year Plans were launched. He also makes it clear that though the outlay for rural development programmes increases in the successive Plans, the reduction in poverty ratio is not very encouraging. It makes an important contribution to the current debates on policy issues for comprehensive management of programmes. It covers macro as well as micro study. The findings of the field survey reveals that wage employment programmes have not been a success. He criticises the present rural development strategy mainly because it lacks clear policy direction and efficient delivery mechanism.[103]

The above review of available literature explains briefly the conceptual framework of the study. It is mainly centered on the concepts of Welfare, Administration, Panchayati Raj and Decentralisation, Development Planning and Poverty Alleviation. These are closely associated with the process and procedures of village administration and its welfare programmes. A large number of welfare programmes are being undertaken by them during the past few decades. Thus, it necessitates an independent empirical study on the administration of the Panchayati Raj institutions and their welfare functions. It would be necessary to assess the impact of the welfare programmes undertaken by the Panchayats and suggest ways and means to measure and strengthen the same in the days to come.

References

1. *The World Book Encylopedia*, (U S A Field Enterprises Educational Corpoation, 1977) 156 A.
2. Mullard, Maurice and Spicker, Paul, *Social Policy in A Changing Society,* (London : Routledge 1988) 210-211.
3. Chaturvedi, T.N., *Towards Good Governance*, (New Delhi: Indian Institute of Public Administration, 1999) 38.
4. Gandhi, M.K., *An Autobiography or the Story of My Experiments With Truth,* (Ahmedabad: Navajiban Publishing Hour, 1983), 250.
5. Sen, Armartya and Dreze, Jean, India: *Economic Development and Social Opportunity*, (Oxford: Clarendon Press, 1995) Also see, Sen, Amartya, *Alternative Approaches To Development* (Oxford: Clarendon Press, 1995) 103-13.
6. Bruce, Maurice, *The Coming of the Welfare State*, (London: BT Batsford Ltd. 1966) 20-42.
7. Beveredge, William, *Social Insurance and Allied Services*, (London: George Allen and Unwin Ltd, Repr. 1948) 6,7.
8. Bhandari, D.R., *History of European Political Philosophy,* (Bangalore: The Bangalore Printing and Publishing Co Ltd., 1990) 556-558.
9. Pylee, M.V., *Constitutional Government of India* (New Delhi: S. Chand and Company 1984, 236-237.
10. Art 39, *Constitution of India*, 1950.
11. Beveridge, William, *Social Insurance and Allied Service*, (London: George Allen and Unwin Ltd, Reprint 1948).
12. Agarwala, A.N., *Social Insurance Planning in India*, (Allahabad: Kitab Mahal East End Publishers, 1950).
13. Bruce, Maurice, 134-135.
14. Robson, William, *Welfare State and Welfare Society: Illusion and Reality*, (London: George Allen and Unwin Ltd. 1976).
15. Rath, S. N. *Development of the Welfare State in Orissa*, (New Delhi: Chand and Company 1977).

16. Mullard, Maurice, and Spicker, Paul, *Social Policy in a Changing Society,* (London: Routledge, 1988).
17. Jones, Howard, *Social Welfare in Third World Countries,* (London: Macmillan Press Ltd, 1990).
18. Chowdhary D., Paul, *Social Welfare Administration,* (Delhi: Atma Ram and Sons, 1992).
19. Sachdeva, D. R., *Social Welfare Administration in India,* (Allahabad: Kitab Mahal, 1993).
20. Jain, M. P., *Indian Constitutional Law* (4th ed.) (Nagpur: Wadhwa and Company, 1993).
21. Jain, Kamala, "Social Justice and Indian Constitution", Prashasnika, New Delhi: May-December, 1995.
22. Alcock, Peta, *Social Policy in Britain: Themes and Issues*, (England: Macmillan Press Ltd; 1998).
23. Basu, Durga Das, *Introduction To the Constitution of India,*(13th ed.) (New Delhi: Prentice of India, 1998).
24. Seervai, H.M., *Constitution of India: A Critical Commentary,* (New Delhi: N.M. Tripathi (Pvt.) Ltd., 4 volumes, 1996).
25. Lowe, Rodney, *The Welfare State in Britain Since 1945* (England: Macmillan Press Ltd. 1999).
26. Jhunjhunwala, Bharat, *Welfare State and Globalisation: Critique of Amartya Sen* (New Delhi: Rawat Publications, 2000).
27. Datt, Ruddar, and Konar, N. Hirendra, *Social Choice and Development,* (NewDelhi: S. Chand & Compay Ltd, 2000).
28. Ray, Bishwanth, (ed.) *Welfare, Choice and Development: Essays in Honour of Professor Amartya Sen* (New Delhi: Kanishka Publishers, 2001).
29. Mishra, N.L. *Responsive Administration,* (Jaipur: Amar Jyothi Publications, 1991).
30. Panandiker, Pai and Kshirsagar, S.S., *Bureaucratic Adaptation to Development Administration,* (ed) Sharma S. K., Dynamics of Development (New Delhi: Concept Publishing House, 1978) 208.
31. Sharma, S.K., *Dynamics of Development: An International Perspective,* (New Delhi: Concept Publishing Company, Vol. 2, 1997) 601-616.
32. Gandhi, M.K., "My Idea of Village Swaraj" *Harijan,* July 26,1942.
33. Yadav, Ram, P., *People's Participation in Local Level Planning and Rural Development,* (New Delhi: Concept Publishing House, 1980) 86.
34. Panikar, K.K., *Community Development Administration in Kerala* (New Delhi: S. Chand & Co. Publishers, 1974).

35. Mishra, S.N., and Sharma, Kushal, *Problems and Prospects of Rural Development in India,* (New Delhi: Upper India Publishing House 1983).

36. Chaturvedi, T.N., *Administrative Performance and Accountability,* (New Delhi: Indian Institute of Public Administration, 1988).

37. Mishra, N.L., *Responsive Administration,* (Jaipur: Amar Jyothi Publications, 1991).

38. Aravind, A., *Indian Administration,* (Bombay: Himalaya Publishers, 1992).

39. Varma, Ram K., *Rural Development and Anti Poverty Programmers,* (Jaipur: Print Well, Vol 6.1995).

40. Ramachandran, Padma, *Public Administration in India,* (New Delhi: National Book Trust India, 1995).

41. Ahmed, Furquan, *Bureaucracy and Development Administration,* (New Delhi: Manak Publishers, 1995).

42. Heady, Ferrel, *Public Administration: A Comparative Perspective,* (London: Prentice Hall of India, 1966) 16.

43. Nair, Balakrisnan A. *Landmarks in The Administration of Kerala,* (Trivandrum: The Indian Institute of Public Administration, 1996).

44. Arora Ramesh K., *Indian Administration: Perception and Perspectives,* (Jaipur: Aalekh Publishers, 1999).

45. Sharma, R.D., *Administrative Systems of Developing Societies,* (New Delhi: Mittal Publications, 2000).

46. United Nations Publication, *Decentralisation for National and Local Government,* (New York:1962) 8.

47. Lakadewala, D.T., *Panchayati Raj in Karnatak Today: Its National Dimensions,* (New Delhi: Concept Publishing House, 1994).

48. Perroux, F., *Notes On The Concept of Growth Poles,* (London: Economic Appliquee, Vol. 8. 1955).

49. Ray, Amal, *Organizational Aspects of Rural Development,* (Calcutta: World Press (Pvt.) Ltd., 1976).

50. Mathur, Hari Mohan, *Administering Development in Third World Countries and Choices,* (New Delhi: Sage Publications, 1986).

51. Singh, Mohinder, (ed.) *Rural development in India: Current Perspectives,* (New Delhi: Intellectual Publishers, 1992).

52. Aurora, Ramesh K., and Sharma, Sangeeta, (eds.), *Comparative and Development Administration, (*Jaipur: Arihant Publications, 1992).
53. Gedam, Retnakar, *Poverty in India*, (New Delhi: Deep and Deep Publications, 1995).
54. Mathur, Kuldeep, *Development Policy and Administration*, (New Delhi: Sage Publishers, 1996).
55. Ravikumar & Sandler, Todd and Morrison, Kevin M., *Development Outreach,* (World Bank Institute, Vol. 1, No. 2, 1999).
56. Trivedi, Pratima, *Economic Progress and Social Justice Towards Social Sector Development,* (New Delhi: Deep and Deep Publishers, 2000).
57. Rondinelli, "Government Decentralization in Comparative Perspective: Theory and Practice in Developing Countries", *International Review of Administrative Sciences,* 1981,133-45.
58. Malhotra, D.D., "Local Government Institutions in India: Recent Developments and Dimensions of Reforms", *Administrative Change*, Jaipur: July 1995 – June 1996.
59. Bore, P.M., *The Gandhian Approach to Rural Development*, (ed). Marine R Pinto and Srinivaram (Bombay: Himalaya Publishing House, 1990), 73.
60. Mathew, George, (ed.) *Panchayati Raj in India: An Overview*, (New Delhi : Institute of Social Sciences, 2000) 6 – 10.
61. Mathews, V. Jessy, "Origin of Local Self Government in Travancore" *Journal of Kerala Studies, University of Kerala,* Trivandrum: May – December, 1989.
62. Webser, Neil, *Panchayati Raj in West Bengal: Popular Participation for The People or The Party*, (ed.) Mathur, Kuldeep, (New Delhi: Sage Publications, 1992).
63. Baisya, K.N., *Financial Administration*, (New Delhi: Osmos Publishers, 1992).
64. Mohanlal G., Morley, *Rajiv Gandhi and Panchayati Raj,* (Delhi: Konark Publishers, 1994).
65. Nagaraj, K. *Decentralization in Kerala*, (Thiruvananthapuram: Centre for Development Studies, 1994).
66. Malhotra, D.D., "Local Government Institutions in India: Recent Developments and Dimension of Reforms" *Administrative Change*, Jaipur: July 1995-June 1996.
67. Valsan, E.G., "Democratic Decentralization: Selected Experiments in India, Egypt and Africa", *Administrative Change,* Jaipur: Vol. 1, Nos 1-2, July 1995 -June 1996.

68. Government of Kerala, "Report of The Committee On Decentralization of Powers", Thiruvananthapuram: 1999.

69. Pal, R.M., "Radical Humanism and Panchayat Raj", *Mainstream*, New Delhi : March 21, 1998

70. Ramdas, Bhatkal, (ed.), *Alternative Strategies and India's Development*. (Mumbai: Popular Prakasham, 1999).

71. Bandyopadhyay, "Panchayat and Democracy: Elites Vs Dalits" *Man and Development*, Chandigrah: December 1994, 69-84.

72. Raphael, Jose, *Decentralized Planning in India*, (New Delhi: Anmol Publications, 2000).

73. Srivastva, I.C., "Empowering Panchayats for Good Governance" *Yojana*, New Delhi: October 2000, 29-31.

74. Ghatak, Mai Treesh and Ghatak, Maitreya; "Recent Reforms in The Panchayati Raj System in West Bengal: Towards Greater Participatory Governance" *Economic and Political Weekly*, Bombay: January 5, 2002, 45-58.

75. Joshi P.C., Institutional Aspects of Development Planning (ed.) Ramachandran, Padma & Oommen M.A., *Some Issues in Development Administration*, (Thiruvananthapuram: Institute of Management in Government 1987).

76. Chaturvedi, T.N, and Prasad, Kamta, *Planning and Implementation*, (New Delhi: Indian Institute of Public Administration, 1984).

77. Banerjee, Mrityunjoy, *Planning in India*, (New Delhi: Oxford and IBH Publishing Co (Pvt) Ltd; 1988) 1-2.

78. Fan, Shenggen, Hazel, Peter, Thrat, S.K, "Impact of Public Expenditure on Poverty in Rural India", *Economic and Political Weekly*, Bombay: September 30, 2000, 3581-87.

79. Myrdal, Gunar, *Asian Drama*, (England: Penguin, 1968).

80. Lakadewala, D.T., *Pachayati Raj in Karnatak Today: Its National Dimensions*, (New Delhi: Institute of Social Sciences, Concept Publishing House, 1994).

81. Mehta M. M.; *Human Resources Development Planning*, (New Delhi: The Macmillan Company of India Ltd. 1996).

82. Chaturvedi T. N. and Kamta Prasad, *Planning and Implementation*, (New Delhi: Indian Institute of Public Administration, 1984).

83. Dutt, Ruddar and Sundharam K.P.M., *Development Issues of The Indian Economy*, (New Delhi: S. Chand and Company Ltd, 1985).

84. Prasad, Kamta, *Planning for Poverty Alleviation*, (New Delhi: Agricole Publishing Academy, 1985).

85. Adiseshiah, S. Malcom, *Some Thoughts On The Seventh Five Year Plan*, (New Delhi: Dialogue Publications, 1985).

86. Reddy S. Mahendra, Reddy, Yadava, Upadhyay, K.S. and Ramachandran C.H.(eds.) *7th Five Year Plan: Performance and Perspectives*, (New Delhi: Sterling Publishers, 1987).
87. Ramachandran, Padma and Oommen M. A., (eds.) *Some Issues in Development Administration*, (New Delhi: Oxford and IBH Publishing Company 1987).
88. Banerjee, Mirtynjoy, *Planning in India*, (New Delhi: Oxford and IBH Publishing Co (Pvt) Ltd; 1988).
89. Government of India, *A Concurrent Evaluation,* New Delhi: Planning Commission, 1992.
90. Government of India, The 8th Five Year Plan, New Delhi: Planning Commission, 1992).
91. Singh, Yogendra, *Social Change in India : Crises and Resilience*, (New Delhi: Har- Anand Publications, 1996).
92. Quibrin M. G.(ed.) *Rural Poverty in Developing Asia: Bangladesh, India and Srilanka,* (New Delhi: Asian Development Bank, Vol. 1, 1994).
93. Varma, K. Ram, *Policy Approach to Rural Development* (Jaipur: Print Well 1996).
94. Devi, Laximi, *Planning for Employment and Rural Development*, (Lucknow: Anmol Publications, 1997).
95. Ahuja, Ram, *Social Problems in India*, (Jaipur: Rawat Publications, 1997).
96. Griappa, S., *Evaluation of Rural Development Programmes*, (New Delhi: Mohit Publications, 1998).
97. Franco, Fernado, "Poverty Reduction: Challenges and Opportunities" *Social Action*, New Delhi: October/December 1999.
98. Halder, Srinath, *Indian Economy: Challenges Beyond 9th Plan,* Jaipur: Book Enclave Publishers, 2000.
99. Dantavate, Madhu, "Fifty Years of Planning in India", *IASSI Quarterly,* New Delhi: Vol. 18, No. 4, 2000.
100. Dev, S. Mahendra, "Economic Reforms, Poverty Income Distribution and Employment", Economic and Political Weekly, Mumbai: March 4, 2000, 823-835.
101. Basu, Rumki, *Economic Liberalisation and Poverty Alleviation: Social Sector Expenditure and Centre-State Relations,* (New Delhi: Deep and Deep Publications Pvt. Ltd., 2000).
102. Prasad, Mahesh, "Human Development Report 2000: New Index of Poverty", *Yojana,* New Delh: Vol 44, No 9, September 2000.
103. Gupta, D. N., *Rural Development System : Policy Issues, Institutional Development and Management of Rural Development*, (New Delhi: Book India International, 2001).

3

Poverty Alleviation Programmes Under the 8th Five Year Plan

Economic planning is considered the most viable technique to achieve the objectives of a Welfare State. It aims at some definite and pre-determined objectives to be realised within a stipulated time frame. Planning was initiated in India to achieve faster rate of growth and socio-economic change in a systematic manner. It was essentially intended to give economic content to the policies of Indian polity. In essence, it sought to convert political democracy into socio-economic democracy, and to resolve the contradictions of an unequal society. With the turn of the 20th century, welfare economies succeeded in popularising economic planning by adapting the concept of 'action state' in place of laissez faire.

When India became independent in 1947, it was in the midst of numerous socio-economic problems, like poverty, unemployment and stagnation in agricultural and industrial production. Besides, there were large scale inequality of wealth and income. These basic maladies compelled the introduction of planning in India. The beginning of planning in India can be traced to the many pre-independent initiatives. The renowned socialists and the pioneers of India, Dadabhai Naoroji and Mahadev Govind Ranade prepared schemes for the planned development of the country during the beginning of the 20th century. Both of them sharply opposed the theory of laissez faire and did not tolerate the exploitation of the country by the colonial powers. M. Vishweshwaraiah, had in the 1930s, prepared a blueprint for the development of India. His monumental work, 'Planning for India' contained several proposals for the systematic development of industries, agriculture and other activities.[1]

The National Planning Committe, constituted by the Indian National Congress in 1938 with Jawaharlal Nehru as Chairman was the first collective effort for the planned development of India. Nehru had stated "ending poverty and ignorance and disease and inequality of opportunity", should be viewed as the core agenda of planning. [2] Later, in 1944, the 'Bombay Plan' was drafted. It was a plan prepared by eight leading businessmen of the country for the economic development of India. It was intended to double the per-capita income by having an outlay of Rs. 10,000 crores spread over 15 years. ther major efforts for the planned development of India pertain to the 'Gandhian Plan' and M.N. Roy's 'People's Plan'.[3]

Gandhijis' plan was based on rural development, which was environmentally sustainable, while, Prof. M.N. Roy's plan was based on the principle of decentralisation and autonomy at the grassroots.

The Constitution of India embodies the ideals and aspirations of the people for building a prosperous nation. It was drafted by persons who had dreamt of and struggled for a free India. They were aware of the fact that equity and social justice were as necessary as freedom and a democratic form of government.

There are several provisions in the Constitution to promote social justice for the traditionally suppressed and backward classes and for weaker sections. Economic and social justice for the people envisaged in the Preamble and Directive Principles of State Policy in the Constitution, have had a great influence on the introduction of planning. Pandit Nehru and his socialistic ideology played a vital role in shaping the planning process in India. He was much impressed by the success of planning intitiated in the Soviet Union. When he announced the programe of planning, he stated that "there are so many things we want to do in India, and we want to do them quickly and passionately. The question of finding proper way to reach a certain goal becomes important."[4] Since he was the brain and architect of planning in India, it was popularly known as 'Nehru Model' of Planning.

Planning follows policy making because the two activities though distinct are interrelated. Policies lay down the fundamental principles of governmental action. They provide the framework within which planning has to take place. The formulation of policy is followed by the creation of the machinery and procedure for implementation of policy. This has been to rationalise arrangement of work to produce the desired output.[5] In a democratic setup, administration is a vehicle or a tool for implementing public policy. For the success of planning there must be an administrative machinery capable not only of determining the right proportion needed for all-round growth, but also be effective enough to implement the set goals in the targeted time sequence. The clarity and consistency of objectives are important considerations. Planning policy must enhance administrative capability for its own effectiveness. The emphasis on planning greatly increased the governments' responsibility and has strongly influenced the development of the system. A good policy is not only rooted in the experiences of the past, but also motivated by the compulsions of the present. A policy must be anticipatory or future oriented. The crucial test of efficiency and effectiveness of administration is in the accomplishment of the objectives stipulated in policy decisions. Very often we say that the policy is good but its implementation is poor or bad. There is a wrong notion that a policy once outlined will automatically fructify into performance. But actually this is not so. Policy and performance constitute a continuum.[6]

It is quite well known that development plans and programmes designed to assist the rural poor have in practice not always provided the intended benefits to them. Evaluation studies have brought to light instances where the benefits have gone to people who are already better off rather than the poor and the vulnerable. The question of an adequate machinery for planning, implementation and evaluation is still being debated, so also are the problems of multilevel planning, administrative decentralisation and planning from above or from below. The issues relating to vertical or horizontal co-ordination continue to plague the planning and implementation process. The machinery for project formulation and appraisal is extremely weak or almost non existent for projects in the case of agriculture, rural development and social services.[7]

It is therefore essential that necessary steps are taken to strengthen the administrative structure and adapt suitable administrative process for the success of Planning. Thus, administration will have to be re-oriented completely in its attitude towards people living in rural areas; a task which requires a very human, sympathetic approach towards all people and not one which is fault-finding. The attitude of the administrator, at whatever level he is, should be that of service and of rendering help.[8]

3.1 Planning Commission

The Planning Commission was set up by a Resolution of the Government of India in March 1950 and was charged with the responsibilities of formulating the Plans for the development of the country and for proposing allocation of resources for their implemention. It favoured Five Year Plans which are designed to give concrete shape to the developmental efforts.[9] The composition of the Planning Commission has been changing during the last five decades. At present, it consists of a Chairman (Prime Minister), a Deputy Chairman, 10 full-time Members and 4 Cabinet Ministers. For administrative purposes, the Commission has a Secretary assisted by a Joint Secretary. Besides, they are assisted by administrative staff of different cadres. The three major divisions of the Planning Commission are: the Programme Advisors, the General Secretariat and the Technical Division.

In addition to the Planning Commission, there is a National Development Council to help the Planning Commission to fix the priorities and targets. The members of the Council include the Prime Minister, Chief Ministers of all the States, Cabinet Ministers and Members of the Central Planning Commission. Besides, there is a Planning Board entrusted with the task of formulating and implementing programmes in each State. At District level, in addition to the District Planning Committees, there is a District Rural Development Agency to undertake rural development programmes. The Rural Development Commissionerate is an important institution formed for coordinating the different programmes of rural development.

3.2 Five Year Plans

India was the first country in the non-communist world to begin its post-independence development programme employing comprehensive planning. The development framework of India was deeply influenced by a complex set of political, administrative and complementary factors. Since the ultimate goal of planned development is to improve the welfare of the individuals and the society, political factors do excercise significant influence. It is widely acknowledged that, planned development becomes the most important single unifying force in society. It reflects the wishes and aspirations of the members of the society and pursue democratic planning for social change. The term 'social' indicates dignity and equality of human beings and also growth with social justice. It may be recalled that, it was in order to step up the rate of development and living standard of the people, that the government of India launched its Five Year Plans. It has been a very bold experiment for a vast country with the world's second largest population. It is a scientific process based on information and reasoning. It determines priorities for national development and optimum utilisation of resources. The announcement of the 1st Five Year Plan by Prime Minister Nehru in Parliament in August 1, 1950 was historic, because it has been the beginning of the era of planning in India.

3.2.1 First Five Year Plan (1951-56)

To correct the economic distortions created by the British imperialistic rule was the immediate agenda of the new government of the country. Programmes were, therefore, initiated in such a way as to ensure growth and balanced development. For the first plan, Rs. 2,378 crores was set apart. Since food problem was so serious, top most priority was given for it. Adequate encouragement was also given to the private sector to develop industries. Moreover, community development programmes were initiated in rural areas particularly for the development of marginal and landless labourers. It is observed that the 1st Five Year Plan was a great success. A remarkable progress was visible in national and per capita income, food grain production and in industrial sector.[10] It was thus a good beginning.

3.2.2 Second Five Year Plan (1956-61)

The 2nd Five Year Plan marked the systematisation of the planning process. It came into force on April 1, 1956. The major objectives of the Plan included rapid industrialisation, increase in national income, expansion of employment opportunities and reduction of inequalities. It proposed an outlay of Rs. 6,200 crores. Though the Plan did not fully succeed in fulfilling its objectives, substantial progress was achieved in key areas. The increase in tax revenue, investment and expansion of social services were notable achievements.[11]

3.2.3 Third Five Year Plan (1961-66)

The 3rd Five Year Plan was commenced on April 1, 1961. The watch words of the Plan were, growth, self-reliance, generation of employment and social equality. The Plan proposed a total investment of Rs. 10,400 crores. However, the Chinese invasion in 1962 adversely affected the performance of the Plan. Compared to the 1st and 2nd Plans, it was not a success. Most of the targets could not be realised.[12]

3.2.4 4th Five Year Plan (1969-74)

The 4th Five Year Plan could begin only in 1969. It was not specific about its objectives and achievement of targets. However, the obvious goal was development with justice and equality. The 4th Plan proposed a total outlay of Rs. 24,882 crores. The Plan emphasised the implementation of the projects in such a way that the benefits of development are made to flow in the underdeveloped regions and among the backward sections of the community. It also laid down a new industrial policy which had provisions for encouraging of the private sector.[13]

3.2.5 Fifth Five Year Plan (1975-80)

It has been pointed out that, the earlier Plans did not succeed in alleviating poverty. The 'trickle down' concept did not work out in practice. Thus, planning resulted in making the rich, richer and the poor, poorer. Since poverty was too big and complex a problem, removal of poverty and attainment of self-reliance were made the major objectives of the Plan. For removal of poverty, about Rs. 53,411 crores were set apart under the 5th Plan. It was aimed to raise the average per capita consumption of the poorest 30 percent to Rs. 37.10 in 1978 from the existing level of Rs. 23.24. As a result, the 20 Point Programme was launched in July, 1975. It was a package programme to achieve greater infrastructure facilities, land reforms, housing and employment opportunities in rural areas. Barring certain obvious results in agriculture, irrigation and capital formation, the objectives of the Plan could be achieved only partially. The performance was poor in many important sectors, especially in industry. The decline in the rate of creation of employment opportunities and the price situation showed deterioration at the end of the Plan.[14]

3.2.6 Sixth Five Year Plan (1980-85)

The 6th Plan was different in comparison with the earlier Plans. It laid down certain meaningful objectives for the removal of unemployment, raising the standard of living of the poorer sections and minimum needs programme for the weaker sections. The total Plan outlay was Rs. 156,000 Crores. The Plan was not only the biggest in terms of size, but also in terms of investment. Integrated approach to rural development was one of the outstanding features of the Plan. It included the creation of productive skills and assets to rural poor, special area development programmes and special employment programmes. However, the Plan failed to meet the target under many heads.[15]

3.2.7 Seventh Five Year Plan (1985-90)

Unlike the earlier Plans, the 7th Plan was formulated within the broad framework of a 15 year Perspective Plan. Food, jobs and productivity were the main focus of the Plan. The mechanism chalked out for employment generation included increase in cropping pattern, new agricultural technology, labour-intensive construction works such as houses, roads and rural infrastructure expansion. Besides, primary education, health services and changes in the pattern of industrial growth etc. received adequate emphasis. The total outlay for the Plan was Rs. 3,22,366 crores. The target for growth of gross domestic product was placed at 5 per cent per annum. Broadly, the strategies for the Plan were split into four groups - strategies for poverty alleviation, strategies for employment generation, strategies for agricultural development and strategies for industrial growth.

Poverty alleviation strategies were placed under top priority under the Plan. The various projects like Integrated Rural Development Programme (IRDP), National Rural Employment Programme (NREP) and Rural Landless Employment Guarantee Programme (RLEGP), education, health services and other facilities were the major thrust areas of the Plan. A special feature of the

Plan was to ensure involvement and participation of people in community development programmes. Activating Panchayati Raj bodies to undertake community development programmes was also a major focus of the Plan. The formation of District Planning Boards for efficient execution of planning had a high priority. It is, however, observed that, unrealistic targets, weak balance of payments, lack of clear-cut policy for the private sector and administrative inadequacy etc. created hurdles on the smooth execution of the programmes.[16]

3.2.8 Eighth Five Year Plan (1992-97)

The 8th Five Year Plan could not commence in 1990-91 and was actually begun only in April 1, 1992. A change in the setup of the Planning Commission had to be incorporated, due to the influence of the changed scenario at the national and international levels. To quote the 8th Plan, "from a highly centralised planning system, we are gradually moving towards indicative planning". The 8th Plan had some distinct features which distinguished it from earlier Plans, like : (1) The Plan was indicative in nature (2) it recognised human development as the core of all development efforts (3) the Plan attempted to correct the fiscal imbalances from which the 6th and the 7th Plan suffered (4) it was an integrative Plan (5) it recognised the essential need to involve people in the process of development.

The major objectives of the Plan were (1) to attain an average growth rate of 5.6 percent per annum (2) contain population growth and achieve near full employment (3) universalisation of elementary education (4) provision for safe drinking water and primary health care to all villages (5) growth and diversification of agriculture to achieve self-sufficiency (6) strengthening of infrastructure. The 8th Plan's total outlay was Rs. 7,98,000 crores at 1990-91 price level. The Plan was oriented towards employment generation. The Plan aimed at achieving an overall GDP growth rate of 5.5 per cent to 6.5 per cent, industrial growth rate of 7.5 per cent, service sector growth rate of 8 per cent to 10 per cent and export growth rate of 10 per cent. The Plan size was nearly the double of the previous Plans.

The sources of financing 8th Plan differed significantly from the 7th Plan in many respects, like: (1) 8th Plan financing placed greater reliance on buoyancy in tax and non tax revenues (2) the Plan financing stressed reduced dependence on borrowings, domestic as well as foreign capital and (3) it visualised reduced reliance on deficit financing.

The objective of removal of poverty and unemployment was fundamental in the agenda of the 8th Plan. Several programmes were intitiated in rural areas to modernise agriculture and labour productivity. Special emphasis was placed for strengthening self-employment and rural infrastructure development. These programmes were primarily focussed on the realm of Panchayati Raj system. This was due to the realisation of the fact that a massive and concerted effort at national level is required to tackle the giant problems of poverty and unemployment.[17]

3.3 Manpower Planning and Poverty Alleviation

Planners in developing countries have become increasingly aware of the need for developing human resources. They are of the view that, it is an integral part of economic planning and a prerequisite for sustained and accelerated economic growth. However, in most countries, economic solutions of social reform and development have not generated more opportunities for the poor, nor have they distributed the benefits of growth more effectively. Nearly 399 crore people live in conditions of extreme human suffering. Seventy three percent of humanity does not benefit fully from minimum conditions of human welfare in terms of life expectancy, food, clean water, infant care, basic education, literacy, participatory and democratic governance.[17] Nearly half of the world's population lives with less than $2 a day and 120 crores on even less than $1a day. According to a recent report by the World Bank on World Development entitled "Attacking Poverty", nine out of every 100 boys and 14 out of every 100 girls who reach school age do not live to see their fifth birthday. In India itself there are no less than 10 million children who do not go to school.[19]

The structural imbalance that permeates modern society resulted in unequal distribution of benefits of progress and have accentuated the gap between rich and poor citizen – a phenomenon which the UN Secretary General describes as " Social Darwinism" in which only the fittest survive. The United Nations Report (1997) says that the world has witnessed rampant unemployment in the last decade both in the industrial and developing countries. Little wonder, the Development Committee of the International Monetary Fund (IMF), recently stressed that poverty reduction be made the main objective of globalisation. The World Development Report, says actions are needed in three complementary areas: promoting economic opportunities for poor people through equitable growth, better access to markets and expanding assets. [20]

Many scholarly works have been published on poverty in India. Several have shown that social sector expenditure declined considerably during the first few years of the reforms and this could have adversely affected human development indicators. In any case, India's performance in human development is far from satisfactory, even among Asian countries. ut of 174 countries listed in the UNDP Human Development Report 1999, India ranks among the 'Medium' level standing 132 on the Human Development Scale. Whether poverty has increased or decreased there are still 300 million poor in India and therefore poverty eradication should remain a major thrust of public policy in India.[21]

It is recognised that the development of rural areas is the first requisite to general development since a large majority of Indians live in villages and suffer from poverty and unemployment. In India there are unpardonable waste of highly powerful human resources. n the pretext of competitiveness in foreign markets, to effect low cost and higher efficiency or higher productivity, our leaders and planners repeatedly stressed the need for modernisation and hence the use of sophisticated technology. They are unmindful of the damage being done to the most powerful but cheap and plentiful supply of both skilled and unskilled labour resources.[21]

Rural development is mutli-dimensional in character. It involves a wide range of issues pertaining to social, economic and political aspects. The persistent state of high poverty since Independence has kept the rural development at the center-stage. Thus, Central and State Governments are making increased commitment of resources in successive plans for poverty alleviation. Ever since the inception of Planning, policies and programmes have been designed and redesigned with this aim. Presently the poverty alleviation programmes focus on wage and self-employment of the rural masses. About 50 per cent of the Plan outlay of rural development is spent on these programmes. Besides, other programmes such as rural housing, drinking water, rural sanitation, irrigation development for small and marginal farmers, development of women and children, drought and desert development programmes are also in progress. All these programmes are intended to reduce poverty, whereas the people below poverty line remain almost same over the last two and a half decades.

Government strategy of direct attack on the target groups have achieved only limited success. These programmes may be compared with vitamin therapies of allopathy to soften the "side effects" of the drugs administered. Various employment generating schemes to provide self-employment opportunities to specific target groups have not been very satisfactory. The inadequacy of man hours generated and the failure to achieve the targets etc. are pointed out to be the reasons. For example, though Punjab has made good progress on the agricultural sector, it has not been able to utilise its surplus manpower productivity because of the high level of mechanisation and modernisation in this sector.

Numerous programmes have been launched in the rural sector since the 6th Five Year Plan. But these programmes could not percolate down to the grassroots level to solve the unemployment problem. Actually the IRD programmes have merely touched the periphery of the problem.[23] Modern centralised Governments operate at several disadvantages when they try to move public goods and services down to the local level to benefit the weakest sections of the community. The notable disadvantages is that their system of administration often does not reach effectively much below the district level.

In the mid 70s, when the new large scale sample surveys had shown that over half of India's population continued to live below the poverty line not withstanding continued economic growth. Policy makers and Planners realised that agricultural growth did not trickle down automatically to bring prosperity to all section of society eventhough a number of programmes are being in operation for poverty alleviation.

Thus special emphasis has to be given to manpower planning and human capital development. Vast improvements in the quality and efficiency of human resources and reorientation of educational policy have been identified as important. Special programmes are similarly necessary to help the poor and the weak since the benefit of general growth programmes are mostly bagged by the richer sections of society. The Government very often contemplated numerous programmes, even before the blueprint of it gets ready. This is mainly because of the fact that the Ministry in power is eager to convince the electorate that they are enthusiastic in implementing programmes. To be successful, a multipronged approach to rural poverty is necessary. The strategy for attacking rural poverty must be realistic in terms of costs, and it must have a way of resolving implementation problems that have prevented other approaches from having a developmental impact on the poorest of the poor. In designing projects as part of a strategy for sustained and effective development, we should seek to mobilise local people for their own advancement and progress.[24]

Prominent among the plan agenda were specific programmes for backward areas, food for work programmes, subsidised food supplies through a public distribution system and concessional loan schemes for on and off farm development for both small farmer and marginal farmers and agricultural labourers. Many new programmes were started by merging the old programmes like National Rural Employment Programme (NREP) and Rural Landless Employment Generation Programme (RLEGP) into Jawahar Rozgar Yojana (JRY) in 1989 and later in 1999 it was converted as Jawahar Grama Samardhi Yojana (JGSY) Now JGSY and Employment Assurance Scheme (EAS) scheme were combined and introduced Sampoorna Gramin Rozgar Yojana (SGRY). Another scheme was the Integrated Rural Development Programme (IRDP), Development of Women and Children in Rural Areas (DWCRA) and Training Rural Youths for Self Employment (TRYSEM) merged together and introduced Sampoora Gramin Samrudhi Yojana (SGSY)[25]

3.3.1 Outlay

For the rural development sector as a whole, there has been an increase in allocations at current as well as constant prices over the last five years of the 8th Plan. In fact, the budgetary support in the Central Plan to development heads increased from 38.6 percent in 1992-93 to 42.3 percent in 93-94 and 46.4 percent in 94-95. At the central level, outlays for most social sectors went up significantly in 1993-94. In addition to enhanced outlays for rural development and poverty alleviation, new initiatives have taken to improve the scope of existing supplementary employment generation schemes. There is however, limited scope for growth of agriculture in backward and poverty concentration areas of our country. The major constraints are inadequacy of irrigation for drought prone and hilly areas and drainage congestion for flood prone areas. Inadequate availability of power and other sources of energy is another physical constraint.

The 8th Five Year Plan started with a much greater back log of unemployment, of the order 27 millin compared to only 9.2 million at beginning of the 9th plan. According to the Planning Commission, this meant that roughly 11.5 million new jobs must be created annually during the 8th Five Year Plan to provide jobs to the new entrants into the labour market and to liquidate the existing unemployment. With a view to increasing the employment opportunities an allocation of Rs 35,997 crores was made for rural development during the 8th plan, See Table 3.1.

Realising the importance of rural development, the 8th Plan outlay has been increased steadily in the successive budgets. It may be seen that, for Integrated Rural Development, the amount increased from Rs. 376 crore (92-93) to Rs. 390 crore in 1996-97. When Employment Assurance Scheme (EAS) was started in 93-94 the amount was only Rs. 600 core and it increased to Rs. 1840 crore in 1996-97. Likewise for Million Wells Scheme (MWS) the amount was Rs. 388 crores. During the 8th Plan period both Indira Awas Yojana (IAY) and Million Wells Schemes (MWS) were implemented as part of JRY till 1995-96. The outlay for Jawahar Rozgar Yojana (JRY) also was increased considerably, though the MWS and IAY were separated from it. The amount allocated for JRY during 1996-97 was Rs. 1655 crores. It is observed that the plan outlay for social employment and poverty alleviation programmes has gone up form 1.77 % GDP to 2.23%. Here, there are some important questions and issues about development programmes, viz.,(1) the impact of programmes in the previous years and need for bringing changes, if required, (2) whether the outlay in a particular sector is sufficient to provide the support to all required components and if not, how the resources should be created for total development in that sector, and (3) whether the implementing agency has sufficient capacity to implement the programmes. development efforts that do not answer these issues would lead to

Table 3.1

Outlay for Different Programmes under rural Development (Central Outlay)

(Rs. In Corers)

S.No.	*Name of the Programme*	*98-99*	*97-98*	*96-97*	*95-96*	*94-95*	*93-94*	*92-93*	*91-92*
	Rural Development (Total)	9844	8319	7797	8268	7337	5620	3613	3021
1.	Rural employment	4085	3858	3495	4771	4675	3906	2546	1825
	Jawahar Rozgar Yojana	2095	1953	1655	2955	3535	3306	2546	1825
	EAS	1990	1905	1840	1816	1140	600	-	-
2	Rural Housing*	1660	1144	1194	492	23	10	5	-
	Indira Awas Yojana*	1600	1144	1194	492	-	-	-	-
3.	Million Wells Scheme*	450	373	388	211	-	-	-	-
4.	Integrated Rural Development	740	516	590	640	625	617	376	356
5.	Training of rural youth for self employment	60	46	14	14	9	8	8	4
6	Development of rural women and children	100	62	65	65	31	21	13	12
7	Drought prone areas programme	95	101	110	125	85	77	51	51
8.	Water supply	1628	1303	1096	111	811	739	461	639
9.	Rural sanitation	100	100	60	60	60	32	20	4

Source: EPW, July 18 1998.

* The schemes were earlier included in JRY.

uneven allocations that would make the implementation of programmes unviable. Economic Development with justice has been one of the main objectives of Indian planning since its inception in 1951. Social sector development and anti-poverty programmes have been integral elements of India's development strategy. Several programmes have been in operation over the years focusing the poor as the target groups. These include programmes for the welfare of the backward classes, weaker sections, women and children and a number of special employment programmes for self and wage employment in both rural and urban areas.

3.4 Human Development in Kerala

The position of Kerala is unique with regard to human development and life expectancy. A male in Kerala can expect to live to be 69 years, or 10 years longer than the average Indian and a woman in Kerala can expect to live 74 years, or 15 years longer than the average Indian woman. Kerala's low birth rate is associated with comparatively high rate of literacy of the people and the success of family planning measures, particularly among women. Kerala's development experience has often been referred to as a unique example of achieving high quality of life despite poor growth performance. The performance of Kerala economy over the last few decades, in terms of human resources development and quality of life has been highly remarkable.[27]

While explaining the pace of human development in India, Amartaya Sen and Jean Dreze have praised the achievements of Kerala in expanding social opportunities to the poorer sections. During 1973-74, Kerala's poverty level was nearly 10% of the national level. But with in two decades Kerala not only reduced its incidence of poverty by 58 per cent, but it is now lower than all India by 30 per cent. It shows a faster decline in poverty compared to all India level.This is mainly due to education, both general and technical, imparted to the younger generation in Kerala at a faster pace. Education created a scientific temper in the minds of a large section of the people. It also helped in raising the social and political consciousness of the people in general and that of the poorer sections in particular. It is observed that at least one newspaper or periodical is available for every five person or every three adults in Kerala.[28]

Another significant lesson from Kerala concerns the role of women. The women caught up with men in literacy, school enrolment etc. With regard to people-oriented targeted programmes, the achievement of Kerala is quite encouraging. Kerala is often cited as an example of best performed states in executing people centered programmes. The social development of Kerala with low economic growth is a baffling feature when compared to other states of India.

The success of Kerala has been attributed to a broad nexus of factors including social movement, citizen participation, land reforms, literacy, especially among women and free primary education for all. "Any society that is insensitive and indifferent to the primary needs of the people does not deserve to be called socially developed, much less a 'model' for the rest of the world."[29] It can be inferred that socio-economic dimensions of development are highly interactive, complementary and interdependent and that only a balanced socio-economic development will lead to true development.[30]

Economic development without social development is meaningless and social development without economic development is not sustainable. Kerala has achieved high physical quality of life in terms of literacy, life expectancy and infant mortality, at low per-capita income. Scholars have ascribed several reasons for the high social development of Kerala. A combination of historical, cultural and geographical factors, coupled with the aspirations of the people and social welfare, re-distribution and public policies of State government have contributed to the high social development of Kerala.[31] Poverty alleviation programmes have been playing a dominant role in the administration of the State. Broadly speaking, it has mainly two sides such as 'entitlement' aspect of poverty and 'capability' aspect. The former included providing adequate consumption of food or other necessities of life. The latter include matters regarding education and health. The achievements of Kerala in the area of poverty alleviation are considerable, and has proved that poverty alleviation can be achieved along with a reduction in spatial and gender gaps. The former refers to the gap between rural and urban areas; the latter refers to the gap between men and women. The rural- urban gap is quite narrow in Kerala. In other words there is no such rural urban divide in Kerala and it can be clearly termed rural-urban continuum.

But, it is recognised that per capita income of a country is not an index of the welfare of its people. Welfare depends not only on wealth but also an equity, justice and wisdom. Compared to the developed countries Kerala is a poor State, even poorer than the average of Indian States. According to official statistics, the per-capita income of Kerala is lower than that of the country. This phenomenon is quite unbelievable and contradictory. It is peculiar that the achievement of Kerala is far higher in terms of human capabilities.[32] Inspite of high quality of life and welfare indicators, Kerala lags behind in industrialisation and faces acute massive unemployment.

It is observed that large scale wastage of resources are taking place in state administration. The government is always in fiscal crises and it leads to Treasury ban and such other crises measures. For about a decade the fiscal situation of the state faces the same crises. The Government is struggling hard to equalise income and expenditure. Poor economic growth is the basic factor responsible for this sort of crises. The present fiscal trend of the state indicates that there is not much opening to get rid of the crises. The changing scenario of Kerala's economic performance are to be seen in a sharp contrast to that of the nation's economy. In the period, 1950-51 to 1991, the per-capita income of Kerala at constant prices has risen from Rs. 378 to Rs. 1756 as against the national level increase from Rs. 466 to Rs. 2199. Thus it clearly indicates that in the per capita income growth Kerala's performance is poor.[33]

Kerala's rural population, which accounts for nearly 74 per cent (1991 census) of the total population, have much lower levels of income and consumption per-capita and have relatively poor access to education, health, water supply and such other facilities compared to the people living in urban areas. Improvement in the quality of life of the poorer sections of the population is the basic objective of development planning. In order to achieve this objective, a number of poverty alleviation programmes have been under implementation in the State.[34] Several direct poverty alleviation programmes were started in 1960's and 1970's. The starting of Public Distribution System was also a significant development in the 1960's. The provision of free mid-day meals to primary school children, introduction of supplementary nutrition programmes for pregnant mothers and pre school children from poor households, the granting of old age pension to rural workers and implementation of national poverty alleviation such as the IRDP, DWCRA, TRYSEM etc. were other major programmes. The combined benefit of all these programmes worked out at around 21% of the annual expenditure of rural labour households in 1980's.

3.5 Schemes for Poverty Alleviation: An Analysis

Important poverty alleviation programmes undertaken during the 8th Five Year Plan in Kerala mainly include Integrated Rural Development Programme (IRDP), Training Rural Youth For Self Employment (TRYSEM), Development of Women and Children in Rural Areas (DWCRA), Employment Assurance Scheme (EAS) and Jawahar Rozgar Yojana (JRY). These programmes ensure minimum wages to rural workers and enable them to acquire assets and income through self- employment ventures. Special programmes were also formulated and implemented to improve the quality of life of women and children. A brief account of these programmes, is given in the following pages. A detailed analysis of the JRY attempts to examine how far the programme was successful in fulfilling the objectives.

3.5.1 Integrated Rural Development Programme (IRDP)

The objective of this programme was to enable selected families to cross the poverty line by taking up self-employment ventures in a variety of activities like agriculture, horticulture and animal husbandry in the primary sector; weaving and handicrafts in the secondary sector; and service and business activities in the tertiary sector.

It was introduced in 1976 in a few selected districts on a pilot basis. Later in 1982, it was extended to all districts. It was a strategy package to see that a minimum stipulated number of families are enabled to cross the poverty line with a given investment and within a given time frame. It also seeks to achieve enhanced rural production, greater socio-economic equity, a spatial balance in social and economic development and broad based community participation in the process of development. The functional aspect of this programme can be gauged from the fact that about 97 lakh households are said to have been assisted in four years between 1993-94 and 1996-97.

Since its inception, the programme has been implemented by the Block Panchayats in Kerala. Under the scheme, loans were sanctioned by the Government and subsidy by banks and co-operative institutions. During the 8th Plan, 24,2556 families benefited from this scheme. The beneficiaries also enjoyed Insurance protection.[35]

3.5.2 Training Rural Youth for Self Employment (TRYSEM)

It was a supplementary project of the IRDP. The scheme of Training Rural Youth for Self Employment was started in August 15, 1979 and continued during the 8th Plan. The objective of the scheme was to provide technical skill to the rural youth to enable them to seek employment in the fields of agriculture, industry, services and business activities. Only youth in the age group of 18-35 and belonging to the families living below the poverty line were eligible for training. Priority for selection was given to Scheduled Castes and Scheduled Tribes. One-third seats were reserved for women. The District Rural Development Agency prepares a resource inventory of training facilities which had to be made available to all Block Headquarters. There was also a provision of stipend for the trainees., During the 8th Plan about 29,218 youth were trained and 23,504 youth were settled under this scheme. Now this scheme has been clubbed with SGSY.[36]

3.5.3 Development of Women and Children in Rural Areas (DWCRA)

It was started in 1982 and continued during the 8th Plan. This was also a sub scheme of IRDP and was implemented through Block Panchayats. The main objective of the programme was to organise women in groups. It enabl women to participate in rural development programmes whereby they can improve their earnings and acquire new skills. Under this scheme, a group comprising 10 to 15 can undertake any programme or scheme. They were entitled for subsidy and loan for the successful operation of the scheme. Under this scheme, during the 8th Plan, 3,382 groups were formed in Kerala.[37]

3.5.4 Employment Assurance Scheme (EAS)

The Employment Assurance Scheme was launched in October 2, 1993 in 1,778 identified Blocks on a pilot basis. Later, the scheme was extended to cover all the blocks by April 1997. The primary objective of the scheme was to provide gainful employment or manual work during lean agricultural seasons to all the able bodied adults in rural areas who were in need of work but could not find it. The secondary objective was the creation of economic infrastructure and community assets for sustained employment and development. The scheme was designed to provide up to 100 days of assured manual employment at statutory minimum wages to each employment seeker in rural areas, subject to a maximum of two beneficiaries from each family.

The village Panchayats are required to maintain a record of persons seeking employment. They are also required to coordinate and monitor the works. The applicants who register themselves for employment under the EAS are to be issued family cards in which the number of days of employment are entered, as and when such employment is given to them. It is a Centrally sponsored scheme with a share of 20 per cent by the State. An amount of Rs. 63.78 crores was spent from 1993-94 to 1996-97 in Kerala.[38]

3.6 Jawahar Rozgar Yojana (JRY)

JRY, an intensive rural wage employment programme was introduced in April 1989-90 by merging NREP and RLEGP. There is substantial increase in the flow of funds under this scheme averaging Rs. 6 crores per district. These funds are placed at the disposal of District authorities who are to identify the pockets of unemployment in the District and start public works. Projects can be taken up from among a 'basket of schemes' including the construction of all weather roads, minor irrigation works, soil and water conservation, water harvesting, waste land development and farm forestry. In addition, primary school buildings, anganwadis, public health centres, market sheds and other infrastructure facilities can also be built for generating more employment and for social development. It aims to create additional gainful employment for the unemployed and underemployed persons in rural areas. Strengthening of rural economic infrastructure and the creation of durable community assets to improve the quality of life in rural area are also the objective of the scheme.

JRY had been implemented by 14 District Rural Development Agencies (DRDA), 152 Blocks and all Panchayats in the State. The expenditure is shared between Centre and State on a 75:25 basis. Since JRY is essentially an employment generating scheme, major share of the resources was utilised as wages. Construction of houses, roads, sanitary latrines, drinking water wells, irrigation canals, buildings etc. are the major works/infrastructure created mainly under JRY. The details of the various projects and the amount spent under JRY in Kerala are given in Table 3.2. (See Fig 3.1 for a pictonial representative of the data in Appendix).

Table 3.2

The percentage of amount spent for each item out of the total amount utilised for SC/ST and others under JRY during the 8th Plan in Kerala (1992-93 to 1996-97)

Projects	SC/ST		Other		Total	
	AMT	%	AMT	%	AMT	%
Irrigation	55.03	0.37	799.66	4.39	854.69	2.57
Roads	135.7	0.90	10066.70	55.32	10202.40	30.69
Wells	138.68	0.92	166.14	0.91	304.82	0.92
Latrine	406.95	2.70	291.00	1.60	697.95	2.10
Land Devpt	33.76	0.22	1050.19	5.77	1083.95	3.26
Building	3342.2	22.21	1260.55	6.93	4602.76	13.85
Other works	115.03	0.76	2234.83	12.28	2349.86	7.07
IAY	6305.6	41.91	2038.75	11.20	8344.32	25.10
MWS	4512.8	29.99	290.04	1.59	4802.83	14.45
Total	15046	100.00	18197.86	100.00	33243.58	100.00

* *Amount in lakhs*

** *Source: Estimated from the respective data of JRY from the Rural Commissionerate*

The data from the Rural Commissionerate, Thiruvananthapuram shows that about Rs 332.44 crores were spent for the JRY in Kerala during the 8th Five Year Plan. The Rural Commisionerate is the apex body that co-ordinates the functions of rural development and keep the records of physical and financial achievements of various poverty alleviation schemes. This body also gives Reports to the Centre and the States regarding rural development. It is found that an amount of Rs 150.46 crores (45.26 per cent) was spent on schemes for SC/ST and Rs 181.98 crores (54.74 percent) spent for other categories. (See Tables 3.2 & 3.3)

Mainly 9 important projects were being executed under JRY during the 8th Plan. Minor schemes have been excluded in order to make the present study more scientific and empirical. About 1,16,204 (72.23 per cent) works were taken up under SC/ST category and 44,677 (27.77 per cent) in general category. A total of 1,60,881 works were done under JRY during the plan. The main schemes executed for both SC/STs and general category include irrigation projects, roads, drinking water wells, latrines, land development programmes, buildings; primary schools, panchayat ghars, markets, dispensaries, work sheds, community centres, creshes, anganwadis etc., besides, Indira Awaz Yogana, Million Wells Scheme was also included in the JRY. A District-wise detailed analysis sheds light on the position of each District regarding the performance of JRY. The amount spent for each project between SC/ST and others is given in Table 3.3.

Table 3.3

The percentage of amount spent for each Project between SC/ST and others under JRY during the 8th Plan in Kerala (1992-93 to 1996-97)

Projects	*SC/ST*		*Others*		*Total*	
	Amount	*%*	*Amount*	*%*	*Amount*	*%*
Irrigation	55.03	6.44	799.66	93.56	854.69	100
Roads	135.7	1.33	10,066.7	98.67	10202.4	100
Wells	138.68	45.5	166.14	54.5	304.82	100
Latrine	406.95	58.31	291	41.69	697.95	100
Land Devpt.	33.76	3.11	1050.2	96.89	1083.95	100
Building	3342.2	72.61	1260.6	27.39	4602.76	100
Other works	115.03	4.9	2234.8	95.1	2349.86	100
IAY	6305.6	75.57	2038.8	24.43	8344.32	100
MWS	4512.8	93.96	290.4	6.04	4802.83	100
Total	15046	45.26	18198	54.74	33243.6	100

* *Amount in lakhs.*

** *Source: Estimated from the respective data of JRY from the Rural Commissionerate.*

Table 3.4

Growth of JRY expenditure for each item between SC/ST and others during the 8th Five Year Plan in Kerala (1992-93 to 1996-97)

	92-93		*93-94*		*94-95*		*95-96*		*96-97*	
	SC/ST	*Others*	*SC/ST*	*Others*	*SC/ST*	*Others*	*SC/ST*	*Others*	*SC/ST*	*Others*
Irrigation	0	93.6	0	0	17	375.55	21.63	256.4	16.67	125.44
Roads	0	111.6	9.44	1810.52	9.44	2911.69	15.2	3484.49	4.58	1884.1
Wells	22.28	56.68	22.38	52.92	29.27	52.92	33.96	68.34	28.08	73.98
Latrine	60.69	64.61	103.41	135.31	56.24	124.51	54.24	286.37	135.12	87.15
Land Devpt.	1.22	22.36	0.09	126.23	0	190.96	2.16	382.2	1.51	362.2
Building	601.04	750.66	39.33	1045.87	948.7	977.27	907.98	915.04	845.86	919.04
Other works	14.99	696.94	0	0	5.45	569.6	20.62	549.81	8.27	533.51
IAY	583.79	3143.56	1231.25	3240.35	29.27	1812.47	33.96	73.98	28.08	73.98
MWS	527.98	0	0	0	1889.53	1932.96	1281.09	1442.53	865.87	1427.34

* Amount in lakhs.

** *Source:* Estimated from the respective data of JRY from the Rural Commissionerate.

3.6.1 Growth

An assessment of the growth of expenditure on various JRY projects between SC/ST and others given in the following pages would help to provide a better insight into the implementation of various projects. It would also shed light on the extend to which the objectives of the programme have been accomplished during this period. The details regarding growth of expenditure for each project between SC/ST and others are given in Table 3.4. The graphical representation of the same is given in figures in the appendix (Fig. 3.3, 3.5, 3.7, 3.9, 3.11, 3.13, 3.15, 3.17 and 3.19).

3.6.2 Irrigation

Irrigation facilities are essential for the agricultural development of the State. Though Kerala gets rainfall from both the monsoons and during other periods, due to lack of scientific management of water resources, the State very often faces acute shortage of water for both drinking and irrigation. Agricultural production-both commercial and food crops-could be increased many times, if we had proper irrigational facilities. Small farmers including the SC/ST are facing acute shortage of water for agricultural development. Due to poverty and other problems, they are not in a position to make their own facility for irrigation.

Under JRY lakhs of rupees were spent for irrigation. About Rs. 8.55 (2.57 per cent) crores was spent for irrigation in Kerala. But it was only 2.57 per cent of the total amount spent on JRY during the 8th Plan period. The amount spent for SC/ST and general category differ widely. The amount spent for SC/ST is very low (6.44 per cent) when compared to that spent for the general category (93.45 per cent.) (See Tables 3.4 & 3.5) Table 3.5 shows the district-wise expenditure on irrigation, under JRY see appendix 11 (1). The graphical representation of the same is given in Fig. 3.2 and 3.3 in the appendix variation.

There has been wide Variation is the amount spent in different districts in the state. The Thiruvananthapuram District spent the highest (10.60 per cent) and other Districts except Wyanad and Kannur spent only below 3 per cent. In Wyanad the percentage is 5.56 and in Kannur 4.03 per cent. In the Districts of Pathanamthitta, Alapuzha and Kottayam the amount spent under this scheme was below one per cent. It is observed that the District of Kozhikkode did not spent any amount at all. (See Table 3.4)

Among the fourteen Districts of Kerala, eleven Districts did not spent any amount for this scheme and even the money spent by the three remaining Districts such as Alapuzha, Wyanad and Kasargod are negligible. Of the total amount spent on irrigation, the amount spent for the SC/ST was only 0.37 per cent. The amount spent for general category (93.56 per cent) and SC/ST (6.44 per cent) has a wide difference. (See Table 3.3)

It is observed that there was no amount spent for irrigation under SC/ST category during 1993 and 1994. The amount spent for irrigation under SC/ST was very low compared to the amount spent for general category. For them, only 17 lakhs, 21.63 lakhs and 16.67 lakhs were spent respectively for irrigation from 1995 to 1997.

On the other hand, th4e amount spent for irrigation under general category shows a wide difference. Though no amount was spent for irrigation during 1993-94, the amount spent for it during the preceding and succeeding years were much higher than the amount spent for SC/ST. In 1993, Rs. 93.6 lakhs was spent and during 1994, Rs. 375.55 and in 1995, Rs. 256.4 lakhs was spent for irrigation. But in 1997, only Rs. 125.44 lakhs was spent for irrigation. Thus it shows a decreasing trend. (See Table 3.4)

3.6.3 Roads

Even after 5 decades of Independence, the clamour for roads persist among the people. The difficulties caused by the absence of sufficient roads need no explanation. Since it is the basic infrastructure for development, the availability of sufficient roads is a precondition for sustainable development. The efforts of the Public Works Department of the State is inadequate to provide roads and bridges througout the State.

Under the poverty alleviation programmes, huge amounts of money have been spent for making good roads in rural and urban areas. Under the 'food for work' programme, many rural roads were constructed. At the initial stages, people had shown much interest in such works and schemes. During the 6th Plan, under National Rural Employment Programme (NREP) and Rural Landless Employment Guarantee Programme (RLEGP), crores of rupees were spent for the construction of roads in rural areas. With the inception of the JRY programme, large amounts of money were spent on rural roads in Kerala. The details regarding this are furnished in the following Table. See Fog 3.4 and 3.5 for a graphical representation of the same in the appendix.

Due to the pressure from the people, huge amounts of money have been spent for roads even under People's Planning programmes in Kerala. It indicates the fact that people are direly in need of good roads. To undertake the work of the entire roads by the Government is a big task. For it, the enthusiasm and co-operation of the people, especially the beneficiaries, is highly indispensable. Due to the peculiar geographical conditions of Kerala, it is very difficult to construct all weather roads in all places of the State and to maintain them in good condition.

Under the JRY scheme, Rs. 102 crores were spent for roads during the 8th Five Year Plan. It was 31 per cent of the total amount spent for the JRY. The amount spent for roads under the general category was 55.32 per cent and for SC/St, it was only 0.90 per cent. The District-wise distribution of amount spent for roads show a peculiar growth. In most Districts, the amount spent for roads was the highest. The Districts of Ernakulam, Thirssur, Palakkad and Wyanad spent between 32 to 34.5 per cent of the total expenditure. Out of the total expenditure on JRY, the Districts of Malappuram, Kannur and Kasaragod spent between 39-40 per cent. The amount vary from 2 per cent to 3 per cent in other Districts. It is observed that most of the Districts did not spent any amount for roads with regard to SC/ST. Even Districts which spent money for SC/ST have been very little or negligible except Thrissur and Wayand. Here, only one or two per cent was spent for roads for SC/ST. A wide difference between the percentage of money spent for roads with regard to SC/ST and general category, is observed. It is seen that about 98.67 per cent of the amount was spent for the roads in general category and only 1.33 per cent for SC/ST. The graphical representation of the same is given in Fig. 3.3 in the appendix.

The amount spent for roads under SC/ST is significant. No amount was spent for SC/ST during 1992-93. At the same time, in other category, the amount spent for roads were Rs. 111.6 lakhs during that period. During 1993-94, and 1994-95 the amount spent for SC/ST was Rs. 9.44 lakhs each. On the other hand, the amount spent for roads under other categories show a rapid increase. During this period, Rs. 1810.52 lakhs were spent for roads. The amount spent for roads during 1995-96 was increased to Rs. 2911.69 lakhs. The amount increased to the all time high during 1996-97, i.e., Rs. 3484. 49 lakhs. There was a rise of Rs. 15.2 lakhs during 1995-96 with regard to roads under SC/ST category. But the amount spent for roads under SC/ST had decreased considerably during 1996-97. Only an amount of Rs. 4.58 lakhs were spent for roads under SC/ST during this period. (See Table 3.4).

The above growth of expenditure on roads clearly prove that the amount spent on roads is much higher than the amount spent on any other project under JRY. It also indicates a fact that more roads are still needed in the state because the State is on the path of fast development.

3.6.4 Drinking Water Wells

Water is emerging a scarce commodity, and public is concerned about conservation and economic utilisation of water as never before. The availability of safe drinking water is becoming dearer even in Kerala. In the State, about 70 to 80 per cent of the people depend on open wells for drinking water. It is observed that in most of the harijan colonies there is acute shortage of water in all seasons. There is a general complaint that Kerala does not have a proper water resource management. Moreover, no sincere efforts are taken by the authorities to complete the ongoing water supply schemes in a time-bound manner. Due to the peculiar geographical condition of Kerala, almost all places face water shortage. Open wells are the main sources of water in Kerala. Though the State is getting good rain in all seasons and also having many rivers and water sources through the State, we face acute shortage of water. The details of the amount spent for drinking water wells are given in Table 3.7 see appendix VI (1). The graphical representation of the same is given in Fig 3.6 and 3.7 in thea appendix.

Under JRY, there were schemes for constructing wells for drinking water and agriculture. The total amount spent for this purpose under JRY was comparatively less. Out of the total expenditure, only 0.92 per cent had been spent for wells. (The amount spent for MWS is not included.) The total amount spent for wells was only Rs. 3.05 crores. When looked into from the point of view of the needs of the people, the amount spent for wells is insufficient. The amount spent for SC/ST and general category was only 0.92 per cent and 0.91 per cent respectively. It shows that the allocation of money for the purpose of wells were not on the basis of the actual needs of the people. Thus, a more practical approach to this problem is necessary and special attention must be given to this scheme.

When we examine the District-wise expenditure on wells, it can be seen that majority of the Districts except few like Palakkad, Kozhikode, Wyanad and Kannur had spent only less than 1 per cent of the total amount during the period. Among the Districts, only Wyanad spent 4.54 per cent for wells. The Districts of Palakkad, Kozhikode and Kannur spent 1 to 2 per cent of the total amount spent for the JRY and the remaining Districts spent only less than 1 per cent. This is graphically represented in Fig. 3.6 in the appendix.

An amount of Rs. 22 lakhs and Rs. 22.38 lakhs was spent for SC/ST in1992-93 and 1993-94 respectively. The amount spent for wells was Rs. 56.68 lakhs under other category during 1992-93. However, Rs. 52.92 lakhs was spent for wells during 1993-94 and 1994-95, but the amount for wells under SC/ST category during 1993-94 to 1995-96 shows an increase. The amount spent for wells during this period was Rs. 22.38 lakhs, Rs. 29.27 lakhs and Rs. 33.96 lakhs respectively. However, the amount spent for SC/ST decreased to Rs. 28.08 lakhs in 1997. At the same time, the amount spent for others had increased to Rs. 73.98 lakhs in 1996-97. (See Table 3.4)

3.6.5 Million Wells Scheme (MWS)

It was implemented as a sub-scheme of JRY till 1995-96 and from 1996-97, it was executed as a separate programme. It was a scheme mainly meant for SC/STs which comes in the category of small and nominal farmers. According to the JRY stipulation, out of the total amount for JRY, at least 30 percent was set apart for MWS. Under this scheme, there had been provisions for the construction of open wells, tube wells, bore wells and also for the construction of water tanks for agricultural and water supply schemes. Funds were also spent for land development purposes of the poor. If a well which was constructed did not serve the pupose, the expenditure incurred to the person should be released from the fund. The amount given for each well under the scheme was Rs 14,500 in 1994-96 periods and it was raised to Rs 15,800. The details, with the amount spent on MWS are given in the following Table 3.8 see Appendix VIII (1). The graphical representation of the same is given in Fig 3.8 and 3.9. in the appendix.

Of the total JRY expenditure, about 14.45 per cent was spent for Million Wells Scheme during the 8th plan period. The percentage of amount spent for SC/ST was 30 per cent of the total spent for that group. Under general category the percentage was only 1.59 of the total amount spent for them. When the amount spent for SC/ST and the general category is compared, it is seen that a lion's share was spent for the former (93.96 per cent) and that spent for the latter (6.04 per cent) was very less.

With regard to the performance of Districts, Idukki (18.86 per cent) and Wyanad (18.23 per cent) came first and second respectively. It was also observed that the District of Ernakulam spent 17.66 per cent of money for MWS. Among the remaining Districts, except Kasargod, spent between 14 to 16 per cent for MWS. It was realised that the District of Kasargod spent only 6.87 per cent for MWS. This is graphically represented in Fig. 3.8, given in the appendix.

With regard to the amount spent for MWS, the District of Malappuram spent 41 per cent for SC/STs under MWS scheme. The amount spent by Malappuram for SC/ST except buildings and IAY was very less. Out of the total amount spent for SC/STs the Districts of Trivandrum, Idukki, Ernakulam, Thrissur, Kozhikode, Wyanad and Kannur spent 30 to 35 percent on MWS. The other Districts except Kasaragod spent between 25 to 30 per cent on MWS. The amount spent by Kasargod was only 12.37 per cent for MWS. It is observed that this is far below the State average. It reveals a fact that the distribution of fund for MWS among the district was not done scientifically.

It has been observed that the amount spent on MWS was very high for both SC/ST and other category. No amount was spent during 1992-93 and 1993-94 under other category. During 1992-93, Rs. 527.98 lakhs was spent for SC/ST. However, no amount spent for MWS in 1993-94 under general category. The amount spent for MWS increased to Rs. 1889.53 lakhs during 1994-95. It was the highest amount spent for MWS under SC/ST category. During the period 1995 to 1997, an amount of Rs. 1281.09 and Rs. 865.87 were spent respectively for MWS under SC/ST. During the period,1995-97, an amount of Rs. 1932.96 lakhs, Rs. 1442.53 lakhs and Rs. 1547.34 lakhs were spent for MWS under other category. (See Table 3.4)

3.6.6 Latrine

Availability of proper sanitary facilities is an essential factor to maintain hygiene and health of the people. The Government has undertaken several schemes for maintaining better hygiene among the people. The details regarding this are given in Table 3.9 see Appendix X(1). The graphical representation of the sameis given in Fig 3.10 and 3.11 in the appendix.

Under the JRY scheme, there was provision for construction of latrines for the poor households. Out of the total expenditure on JRY, 2.10 per cent had been spent for the construction of latrines. Altogether, 24,837 latrines were constructed for SC/ST and 9,126 for others. The total number of latrines constructed under JRY in the State during the 8th Plan was 33,963. The amount intially given for this purpose was only Rs. 500 and later it was raised to Rs. 2,000.

When the District-wise performance was examined, it could be seen that Trivandrum stood far ahead of other Districts because Rs. 136 lakhs was spent for it. Of the total expenditure on JRY, 5.27 per cent was spent for latrines. Kottayam came second with 4.37 per cent. Alappuzha and Kannur had spent only 0.65 per cent followed by Idukki (0.72 per cent), Palakkad (0.87 per cent) and Wyanad (0.96 per cent). The other Districts spent between 1 per cent to 3.3 per cent. For SC/ST, the amount spent was 94.4 per cent while 5.6 per cent was spent for the general category.

There are wide variations with regard to the amount spent for latrines for the SC/ST and others. An amount of Rs. 60.69 lakhs was spent for latrines under SC/ST category during 1992-93. It was increased to Rs. 103.41 lakhs in 1993-94. The amount spent for latrine under others also show the same growth. The amount spent under others during 1992-93 was Rs. 64.61 lakhs and it increased to Rs. 135.31 lakhs during 1993-94. During 1996-97, Rs. 87.15 lakhs was spent on latrines under other category. The amount spent during 1994-95 and 1995-96 were more or less the same. During this period, the amount spent for latrine was about Rs. 56.24 lakhs and Rs. 54.24 lakhs respectively. During 1996-97, an amount of Rs. 135.12 lakhs was spent for latrine under SC/ST and it was the highest for the same during the 8th plan period. (See Table 3.4)

3.6.7 Land Development

Land development and agricultural development are closely related. A scientific approach towards land development is essential for agricultural development. Of the total expenditure on JRY, 3.26 per cent (Rs 10.84 crore) was spent for land development. Likewise, out of the total expenditure on SC/ST, only 0.22 per cent could be spent for land development. Of the total amount spent for land development, only 3.11 per cent were spent for SC/ST and 96.89 per cent for others. The details of the same is given in the following Table see Apendix XII (1). The graphical representation of the same is given in Fig 3.12 and 3.13 in the appendix.

With regard to the amount spent for land development, Alapuzha came first because the amount spent for this project is highest there. About 10.16 per cent of money was spent for land development in the District. However, no amount could be spent for land development under SC/ST category in the District.

Out of the total amount spent for JRY, no amount was spent for land development. About 5.91 per cent of amount was spent in the district of Kozhikode. It is the second highest amount spent for land development in the State. In the remaining Districts, the amount spent for land development was only less than 5 per cent. For SC/ST, Ernakulam and Kozhikode spent 15.87 per cent and 13.63 per cent respectively for land development. In the remaining Districts, no amount was spent for land development under SC/ST.

It is observed that the amount spent for land development under SC/ST was very meagre when compared to the amounts spent under the general category. Only Rs. 1.22 lakhs was spent during 1992-93. The amount spent for the same during 1993-94 was also very less (Rs. 0.94 lakhs). During the year 1994-95, no amount was spent for it and during 1995-96, and 1996-97, the amount spent for land development were only Rs. 2.16 lakhs and Rs. 1.51 lakhs respectively.

However, the amount spent for other category show a steady increase from 1992-93 to 1996-97. During 1992-93, the amount spent for land development was only Rs. 22.3 lakhs. It increased to Rs. 126.23 lakhs in 1993-94. It further increased to Rs. 190.96 lakhs in

1994-95. The amount spent in 1995-96 was Rs. 382.2 lakhs. During the last year of the 8th Plan, there was an amount of Rs. 362.2 lakhs spent for land development under general category (See Table 3.4)

3.6.8 Buildings

Construction of buildings appears to be of different types, under the JRY programme. The buildings constructed include, School buildings, Panchayat ghars, Nursery schools, Anganwadis. Since the construction of buildings is an important part of community and social development, government is taking keen interest on the construction of buildings. The details are furnished in Table 3.11. See Appendix XIV (1) The graphical representation of the same is given in Fig 3.14 and 3.15 in the appendix.

During the 8th Plan period, about 13.85 per cent (Rs. 46.3 Crore) was spent for the construction of building under JRY. Out of the total amount spent for SC/ST, about 22.21 percent was spent for buildings. Out of the total amount spent for the general category about 6.93 per cent was spent for buildings. When we take the district-wise performance, Kasargod spent Rs 8.2 crores (27.62 per cent) for buildings. This is the highest amount spent among the Districts of Kerala followed by Pathanmathitta (15.39 per cent). The percentage of amount spent for buildings by other Districts was between 10 to 15 per cent.

Of the total amount spent for JRY, Kasargod spent Rs 6 crores (39.69 percent) and of the amount spent for SC/ST, about 14.50 per cent was spent for buildings. Alapuzha spent only Rs. 0.55 per cent for buildings in the general category. However, of the total amount spent for SC/ST Rs. 21.08 per cent was spent for buildings. Pathanamthitta comes second (9.9 percent) with regard to the amount spent on buildings. Of the total amount spent for SC/ST, 22.15 per cent was spent on buildings. In other Districts, the amount spent on buildings in general category was between 2.77 to 7.73 percent. Out of the total amount spent for SC/ST, 29.55 per cent was spent for buildings alone. The amount spent by other Districts on SC/ST category was between 14.24 to 26.37 percent of the total amount spent on them.

It is observed that, the amount spent for buildings under both SC/ST and general category did not have much variation except in 1993-94. During this period, the amount spent for SC/ST was only Rs. 39.33 lakhs. On the other hand, the amount spent under other category was Rs. 1045.87 lakhs. The amount spent for buildings was Rs. 601.04 lakhs during 1992-93. In 1994-95, the amount increased to Rs. 948.7 lakhs. During 1995-96 and 1996-97, Rs. 907.98 lakhs and Rs. 845.86 lakhs was spent respectively for buildings under SC/ST. Under other category, the amounts spent were Rs. 750.66 lakhs in 1992-93 and during 1994-95, 1995-96 and 1996-97 Rs. 977.2 lakhs, Rs. 915.04 lakhs and Rs. 919.04 lakhs respectively. (See Table 3.4)

3.6.9 Indira Awas Yojana (IAY)

Like food and clothing, shelter is also a basic human necessity. To build a house of one's own choice is an ambition of each person. In India, hundreds and thousands do not have a shelter of their own. Most of the people belonging to SC/ST are not having a house of their own. In Kerala, the percentage of houses for the deprived sections is the highest because many programmes have been undertaken by the Central and State Governments. Due to the introduction of Centrally sponsored schemes like NREP, RLEGP, the construction of houses for the poor has increased. The details of the amount spent for IAY are given in the Table 3.12. See Appendix XVI (1) The graphical representation of the same is given in Fig. 3.16 and 3.17 in the appendix.

Indira Awas Yojana was introduced by the Central Government in 1989-90 with the intention to provide low cost houses to the poor and the deprived. During the 8th plan period under this scheme about 49,765 houses were constructed for SC/ST and other deprived classes in Kerala. Out of the total JRY fund, 25.10 per cent of amount was spent for IAY during this period. An amount of Rs. 8,344 lsks was spent for the same. Out of the total expenditure on SC/ST and general category, 42 and 11.20 per cent was spent for IAY respectively.

When the district wise performance is considered, Kasargod is far ahead of other Districts because, out of the total expenditure on JRY, 34.76 per cent was spent for IAY alone in the District. Out of the total expenditure incurred on SC/ST 68.29 per cent was spent on IAY. However, the amount spent under general category was only 3.89 per cent. In other Districts too, the amount spent on IAY was quite encouraging because the local Panchayati Raj institutions has taken sincere efforts to construct houses under this scheme. In Alapuzha and Kottayam the amount spent on IAY was about 29.21 and 29.03 percent respectively. In other Districts, the amount was between 21 to 28 percent. The District of Kozhikode and Kannur spent only 16.21 per cent and 16.77 percent respectively. Under SC/ST, the amount spent on IAY is much higher than the amount spent on general category. Though the amount spent on housing under JRY was much higher, the problem of housing still persiss among the under privileged and poor.

With regard to the amount spent on IAY, a different growth pattern has been observed. For SC/ST and general category, the amount spent for IAY was very high during 1992-1994. During this period, an amount of Rs. 583.7 lakhs and Rs. 1231.25 lakhs was spent for SC/ST. At the same time, under general category, Rs. 3143.56 lakhs and Rs. 3240.35 lakhs was spent. The amount spent for SC/ST and general category during the remaining period of the 8th Plan shows a decrease. The amount spent under SC/ST category during this period was Rs. 29.27 lakhs, Rs. 33.96 lakhs and Rs. 28.08 lakhs respectively. In the case of others, the amounts spent for the same period were Rs. 1812.47 lakhs, Rs. 73.98 lakhs and Rs. 73.98 lakhs respectively. (See Table 3.4)

3.6.10 Other Works

Besides the above projects, a number of other works were also undertaken under JRY on the basis of regional variations. The details of the amount spent on other works are given in the following Table 3.13. See Appendix XVIII (1) The graphical representation of the same is given in Fig 3.18 and 3.19 in the appendix.

However, there were large scale regional variations with regard to the amount spent on other works. An amount of Rs 24 crores was spent for other works during this period. Out of the total amount, 12.28 per cent was spent on other works under general category.

However, under SC/ST the percentage of amount spent on other works was very low (0.76 per cent). Out of the total expenditure on JRY, Kollam spent 15.53 per cent of money for other works. In other Districts, the percentage varies from 3.25 to 10.57 per cent.

It is seen that, with regard to other works, the amount spent for SC/ST was low when compared to others. The amount spent for other works under SC/ST was only Rs. 14.99 lakhs in 1992-93. However, there was no amount spent for SC/ST and others during 1993-94. It has been observed that the amount spent for other works under other category was high when compared to the succeeding years. An amount of Rs. 696.94 lakhs was spent for other works during this period. In the case of other works, under SC/ST during 1994-95, 1995-96, 1996-97 an amount of Rs. 5.45, Rs. 20.62 and Rs. 8.27 lakhs was spent respectively. But during the period, the amount spent for other works under general category was very high compared to the amount spent for SC/ST. During 1994-95, 95-96, 96-97, an amount of Rs. 549.81 lakhs Rs. 533.51 lakhs, and Rs. 549.81 lakhs were spent respectively for other works under general category. (See Table 3.4)

3.7 JRY and Employment Generation

The performance of the JRY was not uniform among the Districts of Kerala. It could be deduced that certain Districts in Kerala did not implement the programme effectively while others performed well. The details of employment generated in each District of Kerala under JRY during the 8th Plan is given in the following Table (See Table 3.14). The graphical representation of the total and average employment generated and total and average employment generated for women are also given below in Fig 20 and 21 in Appendix.

We may now briefly evaluate the extent of employment generation in different districts.

3.7.1 Palakkad

It is seen that Palakkad performed comparatively better among the districts of Kerala. About Rs 38.79 crores was utilised for JRY for general and SC/ST categories. This is the highest among the Districts of Kerala. About Rs. 20.83 (54 percent) crore was utilised in general category and Rs. 17.96 crores (46 percent) spent for SC/ST. With regard to employment generation, about 27.89 lakh man-days were created for landless, and 2.34 lakhs man-days were created for SC/ST. In the general category, about 44.51 lakh man-days were created for women, and for SC/ST, 23.44 lakh man-days were created. All these show that Palakkad performed well far ahead of others. For details, See Table 3.14

However, the generation of employment was not in proportion to the actual number of persons who were eligible to get employed. Likewise, though the District created the highest number of man days for SC/ST, when compared with the actual population of that category, the employment generated is very low.

3.7.2 Kannur

The performance of Kannur district was for below the state average both in the general and SC/ST category of the total amount of Rs 14.72 spent in the district general and SC/ST category got a share of Rs. 8.54 crores (5.8 per cent) and Rs. 618 crores (4.2 per cent) respectively.

The employment generated for the SC/ST was only 10.19 lakh man-days while the employment generated for the general category was 19.80 lakh. Only 7.80 lakh man-days have been created for to women and only 0.07 lakh man days for the landless. (See Table 3.14)

3.7.3 Thiruvananthapuram

In Thiruvananthapuram, a total of Rs. 25.83 crores were spent for JRY. But the amount spent for SC/ST category is higher than the amount spent for general category. Here, about Rs. 13.17 crores (57 per cent) was spent for SC/ST and Rs. 12.66 crores (49 per cent) for general category.

In the District, for SC/ST and general category, 49.29 lakh man-days were created. While 18.18 lakh man-days were created for general category, the achievement of employment generation was 31.10 lakh man-days. The employment generated among women was 13.55 lakh man-days and only 6.57 lakh man-days for the landless. But comparing the total population in each category, the generation of employment is not encouraging. (See Table 3.14)

3.7.4 Kollam

In Kollam, Rs. 26.47 crores were spent for JRY during 8th plan. The amount spent for general category is higher than the amount spent for SC/ST. Rs. 10.75 crores (41 per cent) was spent for SC/ST and Rs. 15.72 (59 per cent) for others.

With regard to employment generation for both SC/ST and general category about 45.15 lakh man days were created. For SC/ST and general category, about 18.73 lakh man-days and 26.38 lakh man-days were created respectivel. While the employment generated among women and landless was about 11.05 lakh and 6.73 lakh mandays respectively. But when we compared with the total population in each category, the creation of employment is much lower. (See Table 3.14)

3.7.5 Pathanamthitta

An amount of Rs. 15.85 crores was spent for JRY during the 8th Plan period in the District. For SC/ST Rs. 7.04 crores (44 percent) and for general category Rs. 8.81 crores (56 percent) spent in the District.

As regards the generation of employment, for SC/ST and general category, 31.67 lakh man-days were created and for landless 4.96 man-days were created while for women, 11.52 lakh man-days were created. When compared, the employment generated for SC/ST is higher. But for others the employment generated is far below when compared to the actual population of the District. (See Table 3.14)

3.7.6 Alappuzha

In Alappuzha, Rs. 16.48 crores were spent for JRY during the 8th plan period. The amount spent for SC/ST and general category is not having much variation. About 8.19 crores (50 per cent) was spent for SC/ST and 8.29 crores (50 per cent) spent for general category.

Regarding generation of employment for SC/ST and general category, about 31 lakh man-days were created. For SC/ST, about 10.15 lakh man-days were created and for general category, 20.85 lakh man-days were created and 11.49 lakh mandays were created for landless, which is the highest in the State. In the case of women, 10.86 lakh man-days were created. It is observed that there is not much difference between the quantity of employment generated and actual population in that category. But in the case of general category, when compared to the actual population the employment created was very less. (See Table 3.14)

3.7.7 Kottayam

It is one of the least performed Districts after Kannur. Here the total amount spent for JRY was only Rs. 15.73 crores. The amount spent for SC/ST was only Rs. 6.45 (41 per cent) crores and the amount spent for general category was Rs. 9.28 crores (59 per cent).

As regards the generation of employment, only 28.56 lakh man-days were created in the District, out of which 10.77 lakh man-days were created for general category. About 8.48 lakh man-days were created to women and 4.77 lakh mandays for landless.

When we compare the generation of employment with actual population of the District, the employment generated to SC/ST was only 14 lakh man-days. This is higher in proportion to the total population in that category. In other category, the employment generated is low when compared to the actual population of that category. (See Table 3.14)

3.7.8 Idukki

A total of Rs 25.48 crores were spent for JRY during the 8th Plan in the District. Of this, Rs 12.86 crores (50 per cent) was spent for SC/ST and Rs 12.61 crore (50 per cent) spent for general category. The amount spent for SC/ST and general category do not have much difference.

With regard to the generation of employment, 48.55 lakh man days were created for SC/ST and the general category. The employment generated for SC/ST and general category did not have much difference. About 14.34 lakh man-days were created to women and 1.98 lakh man days for landless in the District. More employment was created in this District under JRY after Wyanad. (See Table 3.14)

3.7.9 Ernakulam

In Ernakulam an amount of Rs. 20.59 crores were spent for JRY during the 8th plan period. Out of which, Rs 9.02 crores (44 per cent) was spent for SC/ST and Rs. 11.57 crores (56 per cent) spent for general category.

With regard to employment for SC/ST and general category, 35.67 lakh man days were created in the District. Of this, 14.14 lakh man-days were created for SC/ST and 21.5 lakh man-days were created for the general category. About 10.17 lakh man-days were created for women in the District and 7.75 lakh mandays for landless. But when compared, the generation of employment with the actual population of each category is very low. (See Table 3.14)

3.7.10 Thrissur

It is comparatively a better performed District in Kerala. An amount of Rs. 29.73 crores was spent for JRY during the 8th Plan. Out of which, Rs 14.05 crores (47 per cent) was spent for SC/ST and Rs. 15.67 crores (53 per cent) spent for general category.

With regard to the generation of employment about 51.50 lakh man days were created in the district under JRY. Out of which, 18.74 lakh man-days were created for SC/ST and about 32.76 lakh man-days for general category. About 18.01 lakh mandays and 4.18 lakh man-days were created for women and landless respectively. But when we compare the generation of employment with the total population of the district we can see that the employment generated is very low. (See Table 3.14)

3.7.11 Malappuram

This is one of the best performed district after Palakkad. A sum of Rs 31.13 crores was spent for JRY during 8th Plan It is estimalid that 12.87 crores (41 per cent) spent for SC/ST and Rs. 18.26 (59 per cent) spent for general category.

With regard to employment generation, 53.20 lakh man-days were created for SC/ST and general categories. Of this, 20.34 lakh man days were created for SC/ST and 32.86 lakh man days were created for others. For women, 15.47 lakh man days were created and 9.37 lakh man-days for landless. It is the second highest in the State. When compared with the whole population in each category, the generation of employment is very low in the District. (See Table 3.14)

3.7.12 Kozhikode

An amount of Rs 24.85 crores was spent for JRY during the 8th plan period out of which a sum of Rs 9.28 crores (37 per cent) was spent for SC/ST and a sum of Rs. 15.57 crores (63 per cent) spent for general category.

With regard to employment, 9.18 lakh man days were created in the SC/ST category and 27.44 lakh man days in the general category. For both, 36.60 lakh man days were created in the District. For women, 7.47 lakh man days were created while no mandays were created for landless. When compared with the actual population of the district, the generation of employment is very less. (See Table 3.14)

3.7.13 Kasargod

In the District, a sum of Rs 29.05 crores was spent for JRY during the 8th Plan period. A sum of Rs 13.93 crores (48 per cent) was spent for SC/ST and Rs. 15.13 crores (52 per cent) spent for other categories. In the matter of generation of employment, we can see certain specific features in the District when compared to Wyanad. In fact, only about 10.70 lakh man-days were created in the District for SC/ST. When compared with the total population of that category, the generation of employment increased to 19.24 lakh man days. But for others, the opposite was the case. For SC/ST and general category, about 25.71 lakh man-days were created. The case of women was also the same as that of the other categories. For the landless, 6.24 lakh man-days were created. (See Table 3.14)

3.7.14 Wyanad

A sum of Rs. 17.75 crores was spent for JRY during the 8th Plan period. An amount of Rs 8.71 crores (49 per cent) was spent for SC/ST and sum of Rs 9.04 crores (51 per cent) for others

With regard to the generation of employment, the District shows a different picture when compared to other Districts. Actually, only 14.61 lakh man days were created for SC/ST in the District, but when compared with the population of that category, it came to 20.46 lakh man-days. But the employment generated to others is actually decreased when compared to the total population of the category. For both, 30.99 lakh man days were created under JRY which is the highest among the Districts of Kerala. For women, 12.28 lakh man-days were created while it was 4.6 lakh man-days for the landless. Comparing with the actual population of women in the District, it decreases to 7.44 lakh though it is the highest in the State. (See Table 3.14).

Democratic planning is a powerful mechanism to solve the socio-economic problems of the country. However, even after five decades of planning, the problems of unemployment, poverty, illiteracy and ill-health persist in society. This shows that the 'trickle down' theory and Capital Intensive Technique, that were the hallmarks of planning, did not create the desired impact. Various schemes for poverty alleviation have been implemented during the 8th Five Year Plan in Kerala and JRY was one of the most popular. It is seen that an amount of Rs. 340 crores was spent for JRY alone during this period. However, it is estimated that the benefits accrued with regard to reduction of poverty, generation of employment and infrastructure development, was low. It is seen that the amount spent for projects under JRY had wide variations throughout the State. This indicates that there was wrong prioritisation and unscientific utilisation of JRY funds. It also points to the failure of human resources management at the grass root level. The concept of decentralisation and Panchayati Raj system did not create the expected impact on poverty alleviation. It has been inferred that, Panchayati Raj institutions should initiate public participation on the one hand and restructuring of the administrative system , on the other. This sort of rearrangement in the administrative structure with regard to the implementation of welfare programmes is essential to solve the existing distortions. Needless to say that, to ensure growth with social justice, a restructuring of rural administration is essential.

References

1. Nambudirippad E.M.S., 'Socio Political Dimensions of the New Economic Policy', *Kerala Journal of Social Sciences*, Vol. 1, Trivandrum, Jan-June 1996, 1-7.
2. Nehru, Jawaharlal, *Discovery of India*, (New Delhi: Jawaharlal Nehru Memorial Fund, 1981) 396.
3. Ramachandran, Padma, *Public Administration in India*, (New Delhi: National Book Trust, 1995) 70-87.
4. Dutt, Ruddar and Sundaram, K.P.M., *Indian Economy,* (New Delhi: S. Chand and Co. Ltd., 1998) 133.

5. Bhattacharya, Mohit, *Public Administration and Planning,* (Calcutta: The World Press (Pvt.) Ltd., 1996) 124, 129.
6. Chaturvedi, T.N., 'Administrative Performance and Accountability', *International Training Programme on Audit of Rural Development Programme, Selected Readings* Vol. 1, New Delhi, Sept. 1 to December 3, 1988, 7-19.
7. Korton, C. David, *People Centered Development Contribution Towards Theory and Planning Frameworks,* (New Jersey: Kevmasian Press, 1984).
8. United Nations Organisations, 'Towards improved Multinational Planning for Agriculture and Rural Development in Asia and Pacific, Economic and Social Development', FAO, 1984, 52. Also see, Upoff, T. Norman, *Rural Development and Local Organisation in Asia,* (New Delhi: MacMillan & Company, Vol. 3, 1983) 185.
9. Sachdev D.R., *Social Welfare Administration in India,* (Allahabad: Kitab Mahal, 1993) 74.
10. Government of India, 'The First Five Year Plan', *Planning Commission,* New Delhi: 1951, 70.
11. Government of India, The 2nd Five Year Plan, *Planning Commission,*1956, 51-52.
12. Government of India,The 3rd Five Year Plan, *Planning Commission,*1961, 63-64.
13. Government of India,The 4th Five Year Plan, *Planning Commission,*1969, 76-77.
14. Government of India,The 5th Five Year Plan, *Planning Commission,*1974, 1-52.
15. Government of India,The 6th Five Year Plan, *Planning Commission,*1980, 212-230.
16. Government of India,The 7th Five Year Plan, *Planning Commission,*1985, Vol. 1, 24-50.
17. Government of India,The 8th Five Year Plan, *Planning Commission,*1992, 7-38.
18. Dwaraki, S., *Participation* (ed.) Narayanaswamy, Dwaraki, S., Palanithurai G., (New Delhi: Kanishka Publishers, 1997) 4.
19. 'Poverty and Plenty: Hand in Hand', *Mirror,* Vol. 14, New Delhi: January, 2001, 82-83.
20. Kumar Panda, Pradeep, *Need for Social Policy Reforms,* (ed.) Gosh, Participation in West Bengal Panchayats: Scope and Reality (New Delhi: 1999, 149.
21. Basu, Rumki, *Economic Liberalisation and Poverty Alleviation* (New Delhi: Deep and Deep Publications, 2000) 58-84.

22. Nair, Balakrishnan, *Landmarks in the Administration of Kerala,* (Thiruvananthapuram: The Indian Institute of Public Administration, 1996) 8.
23. Ahuja, Ram, *Social Problems in India*, (Jaipur: Rawat Publications, 1997) 43-265.
24. Kothari, Rajini, 'Development without Deprivation: Can Voluntary Action Help In Rural Development?' *Focus on the Weakest Proceedings of the National Seminar*, New Delhi: Vol 1, 1978, 35.
25. Government of Kerala, 'Guidelines for Centrally Sponsored Schemes', *Panchayati Raj* (Malayalam monthly) Thiruvananthapuram: Vol. 6, September 2001, 32-37.
26. 'Outlay for different Programmes Under Rural Development', *Economic and Political Weekly*, Mumbai: July 18, 1998.
27. Chandran, Rama, V.K., *On Kerala's Development Achievements* (ed.)Drez, Jean Jean & Sen, Amartya, India Development (Delhi: Oxford University Press, 1998) 300-325.
28. Rama, Sundra, Iyer, MacPherson, Steward, *Social Development in Kerala: Illusion or Reality,* (USA: Ashgate, 2000).
29. Govindan Parayil, Quotodin Bissio, (ed.)1999, 76 .
30. Banerjee, Mrityunjoy, *Planning in India* (2nd edn.) (New Delhi: Oxford & IBH Publishing co. Pvt. Ltd., 1988) 246-47.
31. Oommen, M.A.,(ed.), *Rethinking Development: Kerala's Development Experience-I*, (New Delhi: Concept Publishing Compnay, Institute of Social Sciences, Vol. I, 2000) 170-174.
32. Kannan, K.P., *Poverty Alleviation as Advancing Human Capabilities: Kerala Achievement Compared* (ed.) Govindan Parayil, Kerala: The Development Experience (London: ZED Books, 2000) 40-65.
33. Raghavan, U.P., 'Kerala Development Experience: An Overview in Historical Perspective', *International Congress on Kerala Studies*, Vol. 2, Thiruvananthapuram, AKG Centre for Research and Studies, 1994, 14.
34. Raghavan U.P., *Kerala Development Experience*, 1999, 14-25.
35. Government of Kerala, Economic Review, Thiruvananthapuram, State Planning Board, 1997, 115-116. Also see, *'Gramagalil Maatathinte Sankholi'* (Malayalam) 12-14.
36. Government of Kerala, Economic Review, 116. Also see, 'Gramagalil Maatathinte Sankholi' (Malayalam) 20-25.
37. Government of Kerala, Economic Review, 116-117. Also see, 'Gramagalil Maatathinte Sankholi' (Malayalam), 17-20.
38. Government of Kerala, Economic Review, 118. Also see, 'Gramagalil Maatathinte Sankholi' (Malayalam), Rural Information Bureau, Thiruvananthapuram, 1999, 34-36.

4

JRY in Action—the Kerala Experience

Nearly three-fourth of the people of India live in villages. Villages in India have hardly experienced change or benefitted from rural development. The people of our villages face serious unemployment and underemployment due to a number of reasons, leading to inequality and high incidence of poverty in rural areas. To alleviate rural poverty and to increase income generation capacity of the poor, bold and imaginative steps are required. The Government of India has intitiated a number of programmes to bring about rapid and sustainable development in rural areas.

Since rural poverty and unemployment require sustained attention, for a solution, several programmes have been intitiated through the Five Year Plans. Rural development programmes have figured prominently in the policy agenda of the Central and State Governments. In 1952, Community Development and Intensive Agriculture Development Programmes were introduced. They were intended to increase labour productivity on the one hand and economic growth on the other.

During the 6th Plan, large scale specific employment oriented rural development programmes were initiated. National Rural Development Programme and Rural Landless Employment Guarantee Programmes were introduced in 1981and 1983 respectively to expand rural employment opportunities and to create rural infrastructure. These programmes were intended to provide guaranteed employment to one member from every landless labour household atleast for hundred days in an year. In 1989, Jawahar Rozgar Yojana was launched by converting the then NREP and RLEGP. Later, in 1999 the name JRY was changed to Jawahar Gram Samrthi Yojana (JGSY).[1]

The Ministry of Rural Development is co-ordinating the implementation of all programmes that pertain to rural development in India. Under its auspices, high priority is being accorded to provide clean drinking water, rural housing and infrastructure developments. Besides, the ministry is to empower the Panchayati Raj institutions in terms of functions, powers and finance. In the new set up of the Panchayati Raj, the Grama Sabha has become the most significant institution in the process of rural development. Non government organisations and self-help groups have been accorded adequate role to make participatory democracy meanigful and active at the grass root level. The outlay for rural development has been increasing year after year. During the 8th Plan about Rs. 30,000 crores was set apart for the purpose.[2]

4.1 Purpose and Features

1. *The basic objective of Jawahar Rozgar Yojana is generation of additional gainful employment for the unemployed and under employed men and women in rural areas and creation of sustainable employment by strengthening rural economic infrastructure and assets in favour of rural poor for their direct and continuing benefits.*
2. The target groups are people below the poverty line with due preference to SC/STs and 30% of the employment opportunities reserved for women.
3. The programme should benefit the unemployed poor, development of village infrastructure and improvement in the life styles of villagers. The durable community assets like roads, houses, wells, social forestry and buildings result in development and actual participation of the target groups in these programmes.
4. The types of works to be taken up under the programme include social and farm forestry, soil and water conservation works, minor irrigation works, drainage, flood protection works, construction of houses for SC/STs and free bonded labourers, construction of rural roads, construction of schools and community buildings and many others. The basic idea is to provide a durable community infrastructure for other poverty alleviation programmes like IRDP, DWCRA.etc. While utilising

funds for providing infrastructure support, the ratio between wage and material component has to be 60:40. If there is need for supplementary requirement of funds for material components, it may be provided by diverting resources from other programmes and community contribution.

5. The District Rural Development Agency/Zilla Parishad has to prepare the annual action plan equivalent to the value of 125% of its share of funds in the preceeding year and no work can be taken up unless it forms part of the annual action plan. The plans for development of villages have to be discussed in the meetings of the village panchayat and the interests of the weaker sections have to be safeguarded. The Village Assembly has to be appraised of the pace or rate of progress of the implementation at least twice a year. The works have to be selected based on the felt needs of the people and the priorities indicated through the Village Assembly. There is no ceiling on the cost of works to be taken up under the programme; only works whose size and cost structure are such that they may be implemented at the local level and do not involve high levels of technical inputs have to be taken up. Priority should be given for completion of the spill over works over the new ones. No works are to be taken up by the Panchayat which cannot be completed within two years.
6. The Village Panchayat with the implementing agency at village level should appoint a committee to oversee, supervise and monitor the implementation of works under the programme. Contractors or middle-men are not permitted to be engaged for execution of works. The assets created under the programme should be taken over by the concerned departments of state government and should also be maintained by those departments. If maintenance funds are not available, it has to be made available under the programme. Monitoring and supervising of the programme in the District and the maintenance of accounts and taking such steps as are necessary for speeding up the implementation of the programme, are the responsibility of DRDA.
7. Of all the expenditure incurred by the Panchayats in a particular year atleast 60% should be spent on wages of unskilled workers

Fig. 4.1

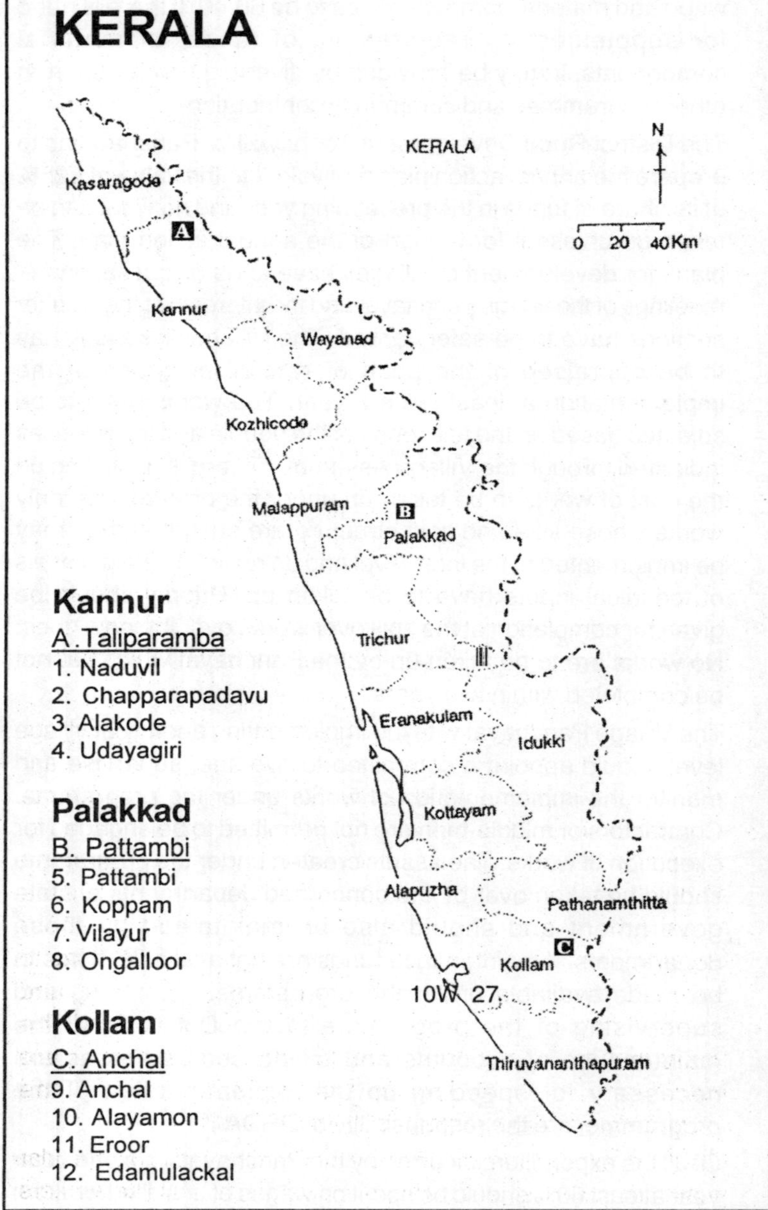
KERALA
KERALA
N
0 20 40 Km
Kasaragode
A
Kannur
Wayanad
Kozhicode
Malappuram
B
Palakkad
Trichur
Eranakulam
Idukki
Kottayam
Alapuzha
Pathanamthitta
C
Kollam
10W 27
Thiruvananthapuram
Kannur
A. Taliparamba
1. Naduvil
2. Chapparapadavu
3. Alakode
4. Udayagiri
Palakkad
B. Pattambi
5. Pattambi
6. Koppam
7. Vilayur
8. Ongalloor
Kollam
C. Anchal
9. Anchal
10. Alayamon
11. Eroor
12. Edamulackal

which shall not be counted towards the wage component. Instead, they will be counted as non-wage (material component). Wages have to be paid as prescribed under the Minimum Wages Act for a particular category of employment. It may be paid partly in cash and partly in food grains.

8. Allocation of resources to village Panchayats is to be made according to the proportion of SC/ST population. Villages are classified as having a population of 1000 onwards. After setting apart funds for the earmarked sectors, 80 percent becomes the share of the Panchayat. Of this, 40 percent will be distributed on the basis of total deemed population and the rest on the basis of total SC/ST population. The resources are released in instalments and the first instalment is released after April. The subsequent instalments are released if atleast 50 per cent of the assistance is utilised by the Panchayat. [3]

4.2 Evaluation Studies of JRY in Kerala

The statistical report of Rural Commissionerate, Planning Board and various Panchayats show that the scheme was a great success although there were large scale leakages in the functioning of the system. Some evaluative studies conducted by the State Planning Board and a study by Gupta, reveal that the execution of the programme was a success. The study conduted by Gupta in 1996 points out that the State of Kerala is far ahead of other States in performance of JRY. He states that most of the works in Kerala were being implemented by the Beneficiary Committees. Moreover, the quality of the work is also higher than that of other States. He argues that this achievement of Kerala was mainly due to high responsiveness on the part of field officers and Panchayati Raj officials.[4]

4.3 Need for an Investigative Study

The official data on the performance of JRY is inadequate to bring out the real facts and the real picture. The various reports, other than by Government agencies, always point out large scale leakages of funds and faulty implementation of the programme. The general public have strong apprehensions about its positive impact because the programme has not succeeded in mitigating the problem of rural unemployment and poverty at the expected rate. Large scale administrative and organisational lacuna has been reported in the implementation of JRY.

The observations of Gupta are also insufficient to bring out the real facts because his study was primarily micro in nature. The sample he had taken was also small and covered only two Panchayats in the State. Moreover, there are a lot of complaints about implementation of JRY as projected by the print and other media. Hence, an independent detailed study about the JRY programme at macro and micro level is necessary to discuss the real performance of the scheme. This is an attempt towards that direction.

4.4 Methodology

The methodology adopted for the study is empirical and both primary and secondary data have been utilised. The secondary data was collected mainly from the Statistical Reports of the Rural Commisionerate and State Planning Board on the performance of JRY. These data provided the basis for the macro analysis of the JRY performance in the State during the 8th Plan.

However, this data alone was not sufficient to assess the implementation of the programme. Hence, a micro level analysis has been attempted to identify the problems associated with JRY implementation and to suggest proper mechanism to rectify the same. The records maintained by Block Panchayats and Grama Panchayats provided the data for micro level study. Primary data were collected by a field survey using a pre-tested interview schedule.

The primary survey was conducted in 12 Grama Panchayats spread over the Block Panchayats of Anchal (Alayamon, Idamulakkal, yeroor, Anchal), Pattambi (Pattambi, Koppam, Vilayur and Ongalloor) and Taliparamba (Naduvil, Chapparapadavu, Udayagiri and Alakode). These Blocks were selected at random in order to represent the medium, best and lower performed Districts of Kerala under the JRY programme. Care was also taken to cover the three regions of the State, namely, the Southern, Central and Northern. From each Panchayat, sample was selected on the basis of population proportion, using random sampling method so as to get 100 beneficiaries from each district. A total of 600 beneficiaries were interviewed during the primary survey. Of these 600 beneficiaries, 300 are benefeciaries of community projects and the other 300 are individual beneficiaries.

Table 4.1 gives details regarding the sample taken for the study.

Table 4.1
Sample Taken for Micro Study

Districts	*Beneficiaries of Individual Projects*	*Beneficiaries of Community Projects*	*Total*
Kollam	100	100	200
Palakkad	100	100	200
Kannur	100	100	200
Total	300	300	600

* *Source:* Personal survey.

4.5 Profile of the Sample Districts

A brief profile of the sample Districts and Block Panchayats is given below:

4.5.1 Kollam

The District came into existence in 1949 and has an area of 2,579 sqkms. According to the 1991 census,the population of the District is 24,07,566. There are more than 4,89,774 families and the literacy level is about 80 per cent. The District extends from the Arabian Sea in the west to the Sahyadri in the east touching the border of Tamilnadu and is in fact a slice of the State extending from the shore of the Arabian sea to the foothills of the Ghats. There are 5 Taluks and 13 Block Panchayats in the district.

Anchal Block Panchayat and 4 Grama Panchayats (Anchal, Alayamon, Edamulakkal, yeroor) were taken as sample for intensive study. The total area of the Block is 950.76 sqkms and it has a population of 2,10,648. Agriculture is the main occupation and it exerts considerable influence on its economy. It is the second biggest classify Block in Kerala in respect of area. There are 3,221 families from the SC group, 73 from the ST group and the rest were 17,943. It is estimated that, about 21,237 people live below the poverty line. There are 9 Panchayats in the Block, and it is estimated that 66.27 per cent of the people are umeployed.[6]

4.5.2 Palakkad

This district which was part of Madras presidency was included in the newly formed Kerala state in November 1957. The area of the district is 4,480 sqkms. with a total population of 23,82,235. The Western Ghats and the Palaghat Gap influence the climate of the district. Far away from the sea, the District at the foothills of the State with extensive hilly region and paddy fields, is well served by a number of rivers which includes the Bharatapuzha. There is a concentration of irrigation dams in the District. There are five Taluks and 12 Blocks in the district.

The Block Panchayat of Pattambi and four Panchayats (Koppam, Pattambi, Vilayur and Ongallur) were taken as sample for intensive study. The Block is located in the north-western part of the District, and lies in between the river Bharatapuzha and Toottapuzha. This comes midway between the 13 agricultural zones identified by the Department of Agriculture in the State of Kerala. There are 8 Panchayats in the Block and agriculture play a key role in the economy. The population of scheduled castes comes to about 33,111. It has been observed that, all Centrally sponsored schemes were being executed in the Block, since its inception.[7]

4.5.3 Kannur

The District also came into existence in 1957 on the recommendation of the State Reorganisation Commission. It has an area of 2,997 sq kms and a population of 22,51,727. About 75 percent of the population is literate. The District has 87 kms of coastline. In the east lies Sahyadri, which borders the State of Karnataka. There are three Taluks and 9 Blocks in the District. Taliparamba Block Panchayat and 4 Grama Panchayats (Naduvil, Chapparapadavu, Udayagiri and Alakode) were taken as sample for intensive study. It is the biggest Block Panchayat in the State of Kerala, in terms of area. The Block is about 580.05 sq kms. The literacy rate is 90.57 per cent. There are 14 Grama Panchayats in the Block.

The economy of the Block is mainly dependent on agriculture and industry. There are 155 scheduled caste colonies in the Block and their population comes to about 25,077. The basic amenities in these colonies are limited; a large number of the people do not have houses and most of the colonies have no latrines, safe drinking water or electricity. There are 101 persons from the Scheduled Tribe group. Geographically, the Block is a typical model of Kerala, with hilly areas and midlands. Almost all centrally sponsored schemes were implemented first in this Block on a pilot basis.[8]

Table Table 4.2 below gives the details of the Panchayats and Grama Panchayats selected for micro level study.

Table 4.2
Block Panchayats and Grama Panchayats Selected for Micro Level Study in Sample Districts

District	*Block Panchayats*	*Grama Panchayats*			
Kollam	Anchal	Anchal	Alayamon	Edamulackal	Yeroor
Palakkad	Pattambi	Pattambi	Koppam	Vilayur	Ongallur
Kannur	Taliparamba	Naduvil	Chappara-padavu	Alamcode	Udayagiri

* *Source:* Personal survey

4.6 Empirical Data: Profile of the Individual Benefeciaries

During the course of the primary survey details pertaining to gender, community, SC/ST status, educational level' income, occupation and marital status have been collected from the 300 individual beneficiencies selected for the semple study. (see Tables 4.3 to 4.9)

Table 4.3
Gender Distribution

	District				
Sex	*Kollam*	*Kannur*	*Palakkad*	*Total*	*Percent*
Male	80	81	72	233	77.6%
Female	20	19	28	67	22.4%
Total	100	100	100	300	100%

* *Source:* Personal survey.

Table 4.4
Community Distrbution

	District				
	Kollam	*Kannur*	*Palakkad*	*Total*	*Percent*
Hindu	91	98	94	283	94.3%
Christian	2	Nil	Nil	2	0.7%
Muslim	7	2	6	15	5.0%
Total	100	100	100	300	10

* *Source:* Personal survey.

Table 4.5
SC/ST Status of Beneficiaries

	District				
	Kollam	*Kannur*	*Palakkad*	*Total*	*Percent*
SC/ST	63	70	65	198	66%
Living below the Poverty line (Others)	37	30	35	102	34%
Total	100	100	100	300	100%

* *Source:* Personal survey.

Table 4.6
Educational Status

	Number	*Percentage*
Level of Education		
Illiterate	140	46.7%
Studied upto Class I to VII	115	38.3%
Studied upto Class Class VIII to X	45	15%
Total	300	100

* *Source:* Personal survey.

Table 4.7
Annual Income

Income	*Number*	*Percentage*
Without Regular Income	30	10%
Between Rs. 3000-3,500/annum	210	70%
Above Rs. 3,500/annum	60	20%
Total	300	100

* *Source:* Personal survey.

Table 4.8
Occupation

	Number	*Percentage*
Not employed	25	8.33%
Casual work	160	53.33%
Regular work	115	38.34%
Total	300	100

* *Source:* Personal survey.

Table 4.9
Marital Status

	Number	Percentage
Married	294	98%
Unmarried	Nil	
Widow/Widower	6	2%
Total	300	100

* *Source:* Personal survey.

Of the 300 individual beneficiaries interviewed, 233 (76.6 per cent) are males and 67 (22.4 per cent) females. 283 (94.3%) are Hindus, 15 (5%) are Muslims and 2 (0.7%) Christians. Most of the 283 Hindus belong to SC/ST.

As regards educational level of the beneficiaries, it is seen that 46.7 per cent are illiterates with no formal education. The number of illiterates is very large, and they belong to the older generation who did not have the benefit of adult literacy programmes introduced in the State. It is also seen that none has education above 10th standard. 38.3% of the respondents is found to have studied up to

VIIth class and 15 upto Xth class. The fact that a large number of people are illiterates, and others have only the bare minimum of education from this deprived section of society is appalling. It is startling to the that most of them belong to either the scheduled caste or the scheduled tribes,

Of the 100 benefeciaries in Kollam, 63 per cent belonged to SC/ST, others constituted 37 per cent. In Palakkad, 70 percent were SC/ST and 30 per cent others. In Kannur, 65 per cent were SC/ST, others constituted 35 per cent. Of the total of 300 individual benefeciaries, 198 (66 per cent) were SC/ST and 102 (34 per cent) belonged to others.

Of the 300 beneficiaries, 294 were married and 6 were widows/ widowers.

Of the 300 respondents, about 25 persons did not have any particular occupation and they were accepting work that occasionally came their way. Among the respondents, 160 were engaged in casual work and only 115 had regular work.

Of the beneficiaries, 10 per cent did not have any annual income at all. and 70 per cent had income between Rs. 3000 and Rs. 3500 per annum. Only 20 per cent had income above Rs. 3500 per annum. An important aspect to be noted was that, for the large majority, the annual income was between Rs. 3,000 Rs. 3,500 which meant that their daily earnings was about Rs. 8.

4.7 Awareness of the Programme

A proper awareness of the various welfare schemes is necessary for the people, especially the deprived classes to take full advantage of the programme. Since most of them are illiterate, they are unable to gather information about such programmes. During the survey, it was found that, most of the beneficiaries came to know about JRY scheme from their Panchayat Ward Members and not directly from other sources. A point that needs to be noted is that, the members of the Panchayats appear to have educated these people from the weaker sections and in this respect, they have been committed and devoted to their constituents. This is an encouraging aspect. Table 4.10 carries these details

Table 4.10
Awareness of the Programme

		District			
	Kollam	*Kannur*	*Palakkad*	*Total*	*Percent*
1. From the people	3	Nil	Nil	3	1.0%
2. Through voluntary Organisation	Nil	3	Nil	3	1.0%
3. Panchayat officer	13	13	28	54	18%
4. Ward members	82	86	72	240	80.0%
Total	100	100	100	300	00.0%

* *Source:* Personal survey.

Of the 300 beneficiaries, 240 (80 per cent) came to know about JRY from the peoples' representatives or Ward members. It shows clearly that the Ward members were keen in informing the persons who are eligible for the assistance. Only 54 (18 per cent) beneficiaries came to know about the scheme from the Panchayat officers. This shows that there was a lack of contact of government functionaries with local people. On the other hand peoples' representatives, though not much educated, are seen showing much attention in providing maximum possible assistance to the people.

4.8 Employment Generated

The generation of employment was one of the major objectives of the JRY scheme. Assessinng the extent to which it had helped in providing employment to persons from the target group, deserves attention. The target group mainly consisted of people below poverty line, who were willing to work. Due preference was given to SC/STs and freed bonded labourers. An attempt was made to give 30 per cent of the employment to women.

The study has revealed that information on the number of persons available for employment and actually employed under the Yojana, were not maintained at Block or Grama Panchayat level. Even muster rolls were not properly maintained by the Panchayats. However, physical performance of man-days of employment generation is recorded at different levels. But, it does not give any clear idea about the number of persons actually employed under the Yojana. Serious efforts were made by the researcher to assess the extent to which JRY had helped in providing employment to the target groups. The following information was collected through these efforts.

The average days of employment obtained by the target groups, comparison of the proportion of people who obtained employment among SC/ST, employment obtained between women and others, the duration of employment generated, the season in which employment was obtained, frequency at which wages were received by the target group in the sample districts are tabulated and arranged in the Tables below. (Table 4.11 series)

Table 4.11
The average days of employment obtained under JRY during one year in three sample Districts

Kollam	Palakkad	Kannur
11.12	11.49	12.24

* *Source:* Personal survey.

Of the 300 individual benefeciaries interviewed in the 3 Districts, only 143 stated that they have got employment under the Yojana. Based on it, an average 11 days of employment was generated annually in Kollam, 11.5 days in Palakkad and 12 days in Kannur. This is below the number of days of employment generated as per official statistics. A graphical representation of the same is given in Fig. 4.2. in the appendix.

A close analysis of man-days of employment generated at Grama Panchayat level has revealed that of the 42 persons who got employment in Kollam, 40 per cent belonged to SC/ST and 60 per cent belonged to other communities. In Palakkad, out of the 67 who got employment 39 per cent belonged to SC/ST and 61 per cent belonged to others. In Kannur, of the 25 who got employment, 36 per cent belonged to SC/ST and 64 per cent belonged to others. The details regading this is given below in Table 4.12.

Table 4.12
Total employment obtained under JRY during one year in three sample Districts

	Kollam		*Palakkad*		*Kannur*		*Total*	
	No.	*%*	*No*	*%*	*No.*	*%*	*No.*	*%*
SC/ST	17	40.48	26	38.81	9	36	52	8.81
Others	25	59.52	41	61.19	16	64	82	9.19
Total	42	00.00	67	00.00	25	00	34	100

* *Source:* Personal survey

It is seen that, when compared to Kollam and Kannur, Palakkad was far ahead of the other two districts regarding the number of persons who got employment in the SC/ST. A graphical representation regrding this is given in Fig. 4.1/4.3 in the appendix. Fig 4.3 average employment obtained under JRY per year during 8th Five Year Plan for SC/ST and others.

Table 4.13
Employment obtained between women and others during one year in three sample Districts

	Kollam		*Palakkad*		*Kannur*		*Total*	
	No.	*%*	*No*	*%*	*No.*	*%*	*No.*	*%*
Women	9	21.43	21	31.34	7	28	37	27.61
Others	3.3	78.57	46	68.67	18	72	97	72.39
Total	42	100	67	100	25	100	134	100

* *Source:* Personal survey.

With regard to the employment generated for women, in Kollam, of the 42 who received employment, 21.43 per cent were women and 78.53 per cent were others. In Palakkad out of 67 who got employment, 31 per cent were women and 69 per cent were others. In Kannur, of 25 who received employment, 28 per cent were women, and 72 per cent were others.

When compared to Kollam and Kannur, the employment generated for women is higher in Palakkad (31 per cent). It shows that the performance of Palakkad is better than the other two Districts because more job opportunities were provided for women. Thus, of 134 persons who received employment under JRY, 28 per cent were women and 72 per cent, others. The graphical representation of this aspect is given in Fig. 4.4. in the appendix.

4.9 Duration of Employment Generated

When we analyse the duration of employment created, it is revealed that out of 134 persons, 23 per cent received a full-week employment and only 4 per cent received one month employment. At the same time, the majority (73 per cent) got employment not on a regular basis. When nature of the duration of employment generated is compared District-wise, it was seen that in Kollam, 26 per cent got a full-week employment, in Kannur it was 24 per cent and in Palakkad it was only 21 per cent. Those who received one month employment is more or less the same in Kollam (2.38 per cent) and Palakkad (2.99 per cent). The following Table shows the details regarding the duration of employment generated.

Table 4.14
Duration of employment obtained under JRY scheme in the three Districts

	Kollam		*Palakkad*		*Kannur*		*Total*	
	No.	*%*	*No*	*%*	*No.*	*%*	*No.*	*%*
Whole Week	11	6.19	14	0.90	6	4.00	31	3.13
Whole Month	1	2.38	2	2.99	18	8.00	5	3.73
Irregular	30	1.43	51	6.12	25	8.00	98	3.13
Total	42	100	67	100		100	134	100

* *Source:* Personal survey.

However, in Kannur, 8 per cent received one month employment. It is seen that a majority who received employment did not get it regularly. This category is 71.4 per cent in Kollam, 76.12 per cent in Palakkad and 68 per cent in Kannur. This is graphically represented in Fig. 4.5. in the appendix.

The season in which employment was generated also reveals the fact that the majority of persons did not obtain work in any particular season. Of the 134 persons, 15 per cent stated that they received employment on the lean agricultural season and 26 per cent stated they received work during the harvesting season. The majority, 60 per cent, stated that they received employment not in any particluar season. Details regarding this is given in Table below. The graphical representation of this is shown in Fig. 4.6 in the appendix.

Table 4.15
The season in which employment was obtained under JRY in three sample Districts

	Kollam		*Palakkad*		*Kannur*		*Total*	
	No.	*%*	*No*	*%*	*No.*	*%*	*No.*	*%*
Lean	6	4.29	12	7.91	2	8.00	20	4.93
Harvest	11	6.19	17	5.37	7	8.00	35	6.12
Irregular	25	·9.52	38	6.72	16	4.00	79	8.96
Total	42	100	67	100	25	100	134	100

* *Source:* Personal survey

The figures above reveal that the objectives of the Yojana could not be realised in the the generation of employment. Though it is a target oriented employment generation programme for the rural poor, when we look into its performance in the angle of employment generation, the results are disappointing. All the persons who received employment through JRY stated that they received the wages in cash and not in any other manner. However, from 1989 to 1992, along with wages, food articles were also supplied. Due to various criticisms and anomalies related to the distribution of food articles, it was discontinued. It shows lack of interest on the part of the people of Kerala towards the 'Food for Work' idea. Another important aspect seen was that the wages were not disbursed in time.

Of the 134, only 32 per cent stated that they have received wages in time, while 60 per cent stated that wages were delayed by 15 to 30 days. Details regarding the delay in receiving wages are given in the Table below. The graphical representation of this aspect is given in Fig. 4.7. in the appendix.

Table 4.16
Frequency at which wages were received under JRY in three sample Districts

	Kollam		*Palakkad*		*Kannur*		*Total*	
	No.	*%*	*No.*	*%*	*No.*	*%*	*No.*	*%*
Regular	13	30.95	22	32.84	8	32.00	43	32.09
Late	29	69.05	45	67.16	17	32.00	43	32.09
Total	42	100	67	100	25	100	134	100

* *Source:* Personal survey.

The study reveals that it was primarily due to non-availability of funds and in a few cases, it was due to negligence or irresponsibility of the officers. concerned. The wage-material ratio fixed under JRY was not scientific and not based on real facts. In the State, the wage rate fixed under JRY was lower than the market rate. It has to be pointed out that this was one of the major factors, which adversely affected the performance of the JRY. It is a clear indication that the 'Food for Work' programme will become a success only if it is made attractive by increasing the material cost and wage-rates. Moreover, proper technical supervision is also essential to enhance the quality of the work-force.

The creation of rural employment and durable community assets was a major objective of JRY scheme which would increase the opportunities for sustained development. It was estimated that, generation of supplementary employment for the under-employed poor in the rural areas would be taken up through the programme. Most of the official statistics reveal that the programme was successful and hundreds and thousands of man-days of employment were created. During the 8th Five Year Plan, the target fixed for employment generation under JRY was 516.94 lakh man-days. However, the employment generated under this scheme shows 589.63 lakhs man-days. an increase over and above the target fixed. The employment generated increased to 114 per cent. When we study the problem in its depth, it could be seen that most of these official statements were not based on facts and were not scientific.

From the survey it could be seen that for road widening, earth works, digging wells etc. more local people were employed. But for the construction of buildings, bridges, black topping of roads etc., local labours were not used regularly. This shows the wrong or unscientific execution of the programme. When analysed the execution of the programme objectively, it seemed that giving employment to under-employed in rural areas, did not fugure in the agenda of JRY. It is seen that, contrary to the specific directives, most of the works were done by the contractors who had engaged their regular labourers for the work. If the works were done under the supervision of the Committee, more local workers could have been employed. It also revealed that wherever works were carried out through public participation and under the supervision of the People's Committees, such works were found good. Not only the quality of the works improved but also a lot of local people were employed for the work. Another serious omission found during the survey was that the officials and the convenors did not show much interest in documenting the data like keeping the muster rolls regarding the quantity of employment generated through a work. It can be seen that large-scale infrastructure development had taken place in Kerala during the 8th plan but the developments were not actually in proportion to the amount spent on the programme. It indicates that there were large scale corruption and manipulations at every stage of implementation.

4.10 JRY and Individual Assets Created

Different types of individual assets in a large scale were created under JRY during the 8th Five Year Plan. Individual assistance was given mainly for three purposes such as housing, drinking water wells and latrines. The details of the asets generated are given in the following Table.

Table 4.17
Types of Individual Assets Created

	District				
	Kollam	*Kannur*	*Palakkad*	*Total*	*Percent*
House	82	80	62	224	74.7%
Drinking water Well	10	17	14	41	13.6%
Latrine	8	3	24	35	11.7%
Total	100	100	100	300	100 %

* *Source:* Personal survey.

In Anchal, of the 100 beneficiaries, 82 per cent received assistance for housing and 10 per cent for drinking water wells. However, only 8 per cent got asstistance for latrine. In Taliparamba, of the 100 beneficiaries, 80 per cent received assistance for housing and only 17per cent for drinking water wells.The number of persons who got assistance for latrines were only 3 per cent. In Pattambi, there was a slight variation with regard to the nature of benefeciaries. Of the 100 beneficiaries 62 per cent received assistance for housing and only 14 per cent for wells. However 24 per cent received assistance for latrines.

4.11 The People who Qualified for Benefits

A thorough microlevel investigation has been made to collect relevant information about the implementation of individual projects under JRY. The details pertaining to the people who qualified for the benefits , the nature of the distribution of assistance including sufficiency, utilisation, leakages, technical assistance are furnished in the following pages. Those who qualified for assistance were either people living the below the poverty line or SC/ST. During the survey it was seen that in certain cases though the beneficiaries received the first and second instalments, the work was not started. This sort of situation creates difficulties and problems to the officers who execute the programme. There are instances where, according to the official record of the Panchayat, assistance was given to a particular person and when field visits were made to assess the quality of the assets, there were none. Such instances were seen mostly with regard to the construction of drinking water wells and latrines.

Of the 100 persons who got assistance at Anchal, 37 per cent people were below the poverty line and 63 per cent belonged to SC/ST. But in Taliparamba, out of 100 individual beneficiaries 30 per cent was in the category of people below poverty line and 70 per cent SC/ST. This reveals that the officials who were in charge of the execution of the projects did not show much interest in identifying the individuals who belong to BPL group. However in Pattambi, out of the 100 beneficiaries 35 per cent were below poverty line and 65 per cent belonged to SC/ST. Here the authorities concerned have showed more preference to the BPL groups when compared to other two districts. It is observed that, of the 300 beneficiaries only 34 per cent belonged to BPL group. It indicates that the major portion of the funds were utilised for the upliftment of SC/ST group compared to other categories of people.

4.12 Distribution of Assistance

A large number of the beneficiaries complained that they did not receive the assistance in time. In Pattambi, and Anchal about 54-58 per cent of the people stated that they received the assistance on time. Fifty three per cent stated that they did not get the assistance in time while in Taliparamba, only 28 per cent got the assistance on time. Here, a majority of the people, i.e. 72 per cent, did not get the assistance in time. Thus, it is seen that in Kannur District, there were lapses and failures in the proper and timely implementation of the programme. It is observed that, after completing each phase of work, persons had to run from pillar to post to get the assistance. Problems of this sort were taking place usually, with regard to all programmes aided by the Government. It is obvious that, there is a wide gap between government promise and practice.

There were many reasons, technical as well as official, responsible for the delay. In several cases money had not been credited to the Panchayat account. Treasury ban and other unexpected factors also caused delay in the release of funds. The field visits of officers were also not regular. The frequent transfer of officials also caused a lot of problems and delay in the release of funds. Generally people complained that officials were not very sincere or sympathetic to the needs of the people. Of the 300 beneficiaries 140 (46.7 per cent) received assistance on time and 160 (53.3 per cent) did not receive the assistance on time. The details may be seen from Table 4.18.

Table 4.18

Did you get the financial assistance in time.

	District				
	Kollam	*Kannur*	*Palakkad*	*Total*	*Percent*
Yes	58	28	54	140	46.7%
No	42	72	46	160	53.3%
Total	100	100	100	300	100%

* *Source:* Personal survey.

4.13 Financial Assistance

It is observed that the assistance given to the people was very low compared to the market rate of labour and material cost. Almost all persons who received assistance under the scheme stated that the assistance was insufficient. The details are given in the following Table (See Table 4.19)

Table 4.19
Was the assistance sufficient

	District				
	Kollam	*Kannur*	*Palakkad*	*Total*	*Percent*
Yes	93	98	96	287	95.7%
No	7	2	4	13	4.3%
Total	100	100	100	300	100%

* *Source:* Personal survey.

It could be gathered that the beneficiaries have faced innumerable difficulties and hardships to fulfil the dream of having a house of their own. In most cases they did a lot of manual work by themselves. Moreover, they were forced to use low quality materials for the construction because the amount received was very low. Since the market rate of materials were high, they were forced to use low quality materials. It could be inferred that, many of them borrowed money from moneylenders at high interest, to complete the work.

It is observed that, about 90 per cent received the assistance in 3 to 4 instalments and also that they received the amount by cheques. The survey revealed that more than 96 per cent of the money was spent for the purpose for which they received the assistance. It is also learned that, there had been not much irregularity or misappropriation of fund by the beneficiaries themselves, when they invested it on building a house. The details about this are given in the following Table

Table 4.20
Was the assistance used properly

	District				
	Kollam	*Kannur*	*Palakkad*	*Total*	*Percent*
Yes	1	Nil	Nil	1	0.33%
No	99	100	100	299	99.7%
Total	100	100	100	300	100%

* *Source:* Personal survey.

4.14 Leakages of Assistance

Though the District of Palakkad implemented the JRY scheme comparatively well during the 8th Plan there were irregularity and misappropriation of JRY fund, reported from the district. During the field survey it was observed that many houses were constructed by contractors and handed over to the beneficiaries. This was a serious irregularity and a naked violation of the guidelines. It is likely that such irregularities might have occurred during the implementation of the scheme in other districts too. The guidelines of the JRY scheme clearly stipulate that there could be no contractors or middlemen in the implementation of the project. It was to eliminate middlemen who were likely to make profit. Yet, it is seen that they were employed. This might have occurred due to unholy nexus between the politicians and government functionaries. When contractors and middle-men were engaged in the construction of JRY works, naturally there was corruption. This sort of nexus between officers and People's Representatives at the grassroot level is too dangerous. There were instances in which engineers and extension officers demanded money for preparing projects.

In the construction of drinking water wells and latrines, there had been large scale manipulation and misappropriation. It was seen that, most of the Panchayats did not maintain recodrs like the muster rolls correctly. Since there was no proper system in maintaining records, it caused serious difficulty in finding out the details of the beneficiaries. It has been observed that, the ill -maintenance of records itself indicated likely misappropriation of funds. In Kannur, the maintenance of Registers was not satisfactory but in Palakkad there was a very good system of maintaining the Registers regarding JRY projects. It was learned that there were chances of misuse of funds during the execution of projects owing to ill-maintenance of records. The official statistics shows an exemplary performance of the execution of JRY projects. But the field study shows there were large scale corruption, leakages and misappropriation in JRY implementation.

4.15 Technical Assistance

It was also found that a majority (98.7 per cent) of the beneficiaries did not get any technical assistance when they did the work. The details regarding this is given in Table 4.21, below.

Table 4.21
Did you get any technical assistance

	District				
	Kollam	*Kannur*	*Palakkad*	*Total*	*Percent*
Yes	4	Nil	Nil	4	1.3%
No	96	100	100	296	98.7%
Total	100	100	100	300	100%

* *Source:* Personal survey.

It was seen that, nobody visited the site other than the village extension officer. This was a serious omission on the part of the officers and it weakened the trust put on the officials. The assets created under JRY scheme for individuals were mostly houses, wells, latrines and both latrines and houses.

4.16 Quality of Assets Created

The generation of employment and creation of permanent community assets are the most important goal of JRY. Under JRY, various types of community assets were created all over the State during the 8th Five Year Plan. The quality of the assets and its maintenance are equally important. The details of this vital aspect arranged in Tables are given in the following pages.

The survey reveals that people were not satisfied with the quality of assets created under JRY. Of the 300 beneficiaries only 13.3 per cent stated that they were satisfied with the quality of the assets created and 86.7 per cent stated that they were not satisfied. The details mayb be seen from the Table given below.

Table 4.22
Are you satusfied with the quality of assets created

	District				
	Kollam	*Kannur*	*Palakkad*	*Total*	*Percent*
Yes	24	5	11	40	13.3%
No	76	95	89	260	86.7%
Total	100	100	100	300	100%

* *Source:* Personal survey.

The quality of individual assets created were poor mainly due to insufficiency of the assistance given to the beneficiaries and as a result were forced to use low quality materials for constructions. The average guaranteed life span of the house constructed under

JRY would be 10 years. But it was noted that, many houses which have not completed even five years were in a dilapidated condition. Due to endmic financial constraints, the beneficiaries were also not in a position to maintain the assets properly.

4.17 Maintenance of Assets

Maintenance of assets created is very important when we view the matter from the larger context of the society and the aim to create sustainable development. During the survey, various individual assets were closely examined and views elicited from beneficiaries. Ninety four per cent of the beneficiaries stated that they are not able to maintain the assets properly. Only 5.7 per cent claimed that the assets are being maintained properly. To assess the ground situation regarding the assets and their maintenance, the researcher took special care to study them during investigation. Their responses are shown in the Table below.

Table 4.23

Are the assets created properly maintained

	District				
	Kollam	*Kannur*	*Palakkad*	*Total*	*Percent*
Yes	3	3	11	17	5.7%
No	97	97	89	283	94.3%
Total	100	100	100	300	100%

* *Source:* Personal survey.

It could seen that under People's Planning, the amount given to house construction was Rs.35,000 per person and it was almost sufficient for the construction of a small house. But the amount given under the JRY scheme was not very attractive because it was only Rs. 22,000 in 1996-97. The amount given for the construction of drinking water wells were Rs. 1,500 and for latrine, Rs. 500 only. It is obvious that, the amount given under JRY was insufficient. These deficiencies indicate that when projects are conceived from the national context, the ground situations exisiting in the different states are not taken into account and the scale prescribed does not fit into the matrix of the States with widely varying situations. As a result, the centrally sponsored schemes fail to deliver the goods.

This is a strong cause for reviewing this approach. It could be seen that, most of the houses were in bad shape and needed immediate repair. It was clear that, to maintain the quality of the assets the amount allotted has to be realistic and should be reviewed. Otherwise the amount spent would not produce the desired results and would be nothing but a large scale waste of money and energy. Many houses did not have latrine facility though there was stipulation under JRY for the same. It is not clear as to what indices were employed to estimate the cost of construction and to arrive at this figure. It is important that regional and local variations must be taken into consideration while executing the programme. The Panchayati Raj institutions at each level should be given freedom to select and execute the programme of their choice. Only broad guidelines are to be issued to the Panchayats on the objectives to be achieved. Then only, can these schemes become successful or achieve their goals or objectives. Local conditions and regional disparities must be well considered when introducing and implementing centrally sponsored schemes. It is high time we rectified these distortions and brought rationality and propriety in to fiscal federalism and multi-level planning in the country. District Planning Commttee should strictly analyse the implementation of the CSSs now going on in our State. It is stated that the District Planning Committees are performing well in Kerala. Therefore, DPCs in Kerala should thoroughly examine whether development assistance is being given in accordance with project requirements.

To make the decentralisation process a viable and sustainable part of Indian development agenda, PRIs should be made fiscally autonomous. It is obvious that each area has certain distinctive features with regard to natural and physical conditions. It is therefore obvious that regional development plans meant for a particular region cannot be applicable ipso facto to another region. Therefore, a rethinking on development administration and Panchayati Raj System is essential. Immediate attention is also required in this regard because this is a core or vital field of developmental activity. It is to be remembered that, if villages decay the whole country will decay.

4.18 Community Assets

JRY aimed to create not only additional gainful employment for the unemployed and under employed persons in rural India but also envisaged strengthening the rural economic infrastructure and the creation of durable community assets. This is to improve the quality of rural life and to further the cause of sustainable development. It was seen that, the major chunk of the JRY fund was utilised for community projects in Kerala. Different types of community assets were created under JRY during the period. The extent of community assets created during the period could be learned from the data received from the Rural Commissionerate, Trivandrum, the apex body which maintain the data and scrutinise the same. From the appraisal of the secondary data, it was found that like the individual projects, community projects were also executed well in Palakkad. At the same time Kannur came least in performance and other Districts of Kerala came under the medium range or average in performance.

To collect primary data on the community assets created and their implementation under JRY during the 8th Five Year Plan, a survey was conducted among the beneficiaries of the community projects in three sample Districts. A total of 300 beneficiaries were selected at random and were interviewed. The data collected pertaining to the selection and implementation of projects, usefulness and the maintenance of assets created are arranged in Tables and Figures given in the following pages. The schedule employed for this is given in Appendix II.

The selection and implementation of community projects are very crucial for infrastructure development. There are very clear guidelines regarding the selection and implementation of the community projects. The details of the major aspects with regard to the selection of the projects and implementation of the projects including transparency, maintenance of accounts, financing the project, types of works, quality of the works and assets are given in Tables at approprirate places. The guidelines of the JRY schemes clearly states that the projects which were undertaken must fulfill the felt needs of the people.

Of the 300 respondents, 98.66 per cent stated that the projects completed under the scheme catered to the felt needs of the people. Only a negligible 1.34 per cent stated that the project was unnecessary and they were from Anchal. In Anchal, out of 100 respondents, 98.66 per cent accepted the selection of the project and they stated that it was useful to the community and 1.34 per cent stated that the project was unnecessary, because they did not derive any direct benefit from the project. It was found that the reason for such an opinion from them was mainly on account of the fact that they were staying in front of a main road and did not directly benefit by the construction of a new road, while other beneficiaries stated that it was necessary and useful. But in other two Districts, the respondents fully accepted and supported the selection of projects under JRY.

Table 4.24
Do you consider the projects useful

	Kollam	*Kannur*	*Palakkad*	*Total*
Percentage of those who said Yes	96 98.66%	100 100%	100 100%	296 98.66%
Percentage of those who said No	4 1.34%	Nil	Nil	4
Total percentage	100 100%	100 100%	100 100%	300 100%

**Source:* Personal survey.

From the above data, it can be inferred that the projects undertaken in Kerala were useful in general, except in a few cases. However, it was found that there were political interferences and petty local interests in the selection of projects. This is perhaps inevitable in a State like Kerala with a politically surcharged atmosphere. However, it does not affect the relevance of the projects selected.

4.19 Implementation of the Project

Implementation of projects require special attention. Grama Panchayats are entrusted with the responsibility of the implementation of the programme. According to the JRY guidelines, all the works must be executed through Peoples' Committee and in no circumstance should contractors or middle men employed for a work that costs upto Rs. 50,000. But it could be observed that there were several instances where this directive was ignored and a nominee of the Panchayat President or Ward member did the work preparing falsely a list of committe members and implemented the work on their own.

Of the 100 respondents at Anchal, 81 per cent have stated that the works were executed by contractors and middlemen. Only 19 per cent of respondents have stated that works were executed under the supervision of the committees. In Taliparamba of the 100 respondents 63 per cent have stated works were executed by contractors and 37 per cent have stated it was done under the supervision of the committee. Responses are given in Table 4.25 given below.

Table 4.25
How the projects were implemented

	District			
	Kollam	*Kannur*	*Palakkad*	*Total*
Committees	19	37	54	110
	19.0%	37.0%	54.0%	36.7%
Contractors	81	63	41	185
	81.0%	63.0%	41.0%	61.7%
Middlemen	Nil	Nil	5	5
	----	----	5.0%	1.7%
Total	100	100	100	300
	100.0%	00.0%	100.0%	100.0%

* *Source:* Personal survey.

In Pattambi of the 100 respondents, 54 per cent have stated that the work was done by the Committee and only 41 per cent stated the work was done by contractors or middlemen.

Of the 300 respondents 61.7 per cent stated that the JRY works were done by contractors or middlemen and 36.7 per cent stated that it was done by committees.

From the above, it can be seen that a majority of the community projects were done by the contractors or middlemen. It is also seen that where there were committees, they were neither active nor useful. From the field survey it could be learned that most of the community works were carried out just like routine government work.

The works were executed not according to the prescriptions of the JRY guidelines. The study by Gupta states that in Kerala 95 per cent of the works were done by the beneficiary committees. He pointed out that the reason for such a high percentage in case of Kerala are due to the higher participation of the people at the planning and implementation stage.[9] Data collected by this researcher contradicts the findings of Gupta. More than 60 per cent of the respondents have stated that JRY works were done by and large by contractors. Though there were names of committees on the official record, but most of them existed only on paper. It was found that in actual practice, the work was either carried out by contractors or middlemen of the local political leaders. The observations and findings here are seen reflected in the print media. The Malayala Manorama, the Malayalam newspaper with largest readership, has commented that JRY works were executed not according to the guidelines issued by the centre; but the works were not being executed by the committees and in most cases, a nominee of the Panchayat President or Ward member carried out the work. It is evident that the JRY works were done by the contractors or middlemen as it were a routine government work.[10]

4.20 Transparency

The need for transparency in expending public funds cannot be over emphasised. Transparency in the execution of public works of all kinds is also essential to ensure accountability and quality of the projects. JRY guidelines specifically emphasise this vital aspect with regard to the implementation of the projects. In this study, it was observed that in most cases the Convenor did not start the work at the right time. The convenor neither maintained the accounts nor placed the same for public scrutiny. The keeping of accounts is very important and absolutely essential to maintain transparency in implementation.There was lack of transparency in JRY works and as a result, there were many complaints on the implementation of projects.

Of the 300 respondents, 86 per cent stated that though they were the beneficiaries of the projects they were not aware of the amount spent and were also not much concerned of the same. Only

14 per cent stated that the convenor kept the accounts of the work while the work was done. Table 4.26 gives the details.

Table 4.26
Were there transparency in the implementation of projects

	Districts			
	Kollam	*Kannur*	*Palakkad*	*Total*
Yes	12	20	10	42
	12.0%	20.0%	10.0%	14.0%
No	88	80	90	258
	88.0%	80.0%	90.0%	86.0%
Total	100	100	100	300
	100%	100%	100%	100%

* *Source:* Personal survey.

It can be seen that the beneficiaries generally were not very particular to see that the accounts, of the works were properly maintained. It was mainly because they thought that it was government work. The answer from beneficiaries regarding the maintenance of accounts by the convenor was generally negative.

The above facts clearly reveal that there were opportunities for misappropriation or leakages and manipulation at the time of implementation. Based on the above data, an inference can also made be that this would have been the case with regard to the implementation of other anti-poverty programmes too. From the field survey and interview with officials, it was gathered that many schemes were introduced with vigour and enthusiasm under poverty alleviation programmes, since 1980 such as IRDP, RLEGP, NREP, DWCRA, TRYSEM etc. But the initial enthusiasm and vigour waned and was not seen in the implementation at later stages. Several officers in charge of centrally sponsored schemes stated that none of the projects are functioning well though they were started with good intentions. The opinion of official functionaries emphasise that a stock-taking or evaluation of the schemes is essential and it needs urgent attention of those concerned.

4.21 Financing the Project

The field observations and interview with officials also reveal that the funds allotted for community projects were not distributed in time and utilised properly. In most cases, works had been undertaken at the fag end of the financial year. The aim it would appear was somehow to achieve the targets and to keep in view its quality or usefulness. It would appear that this is the general approach with regard to all developmental works. This inefficency and non-accountability of the officials demonstrates an attitude of indifference. It was found that delayed release of funds adversely affected the quality of the work. The people on their part had the feeling that it is a contract work, and they should not interfere unnecessarily in the execution of the work.

The apathy or passivity of the people pave the way for vested interests to exploit the situation. The untimely release of funds and untimely execution of work lead to misutilization of money on a large scale. The geniuiness of the committee constituted for doing the work also is doubtful. Usually the convenor of such committees collect 25 per cent of the estimated amount in advance and put the same in local private banks and earn huge profits. They deliberately delay the work for petty personal gains. There were several instances in which for the completion of two or three kilometeres of road, money was not being sanctioned in one lot. Huge amounts of money were sanctioned year after year for the same work on the pretext of first reach, second reach and so on. This practice was seen in some other public works also. This is a serious handicap with regard to the implementation of the JRY projects and is a major cause of corruption.

Under the JRY guidelines, there is a stipulation that a project undertaken should be completed with in two years. It is mainly intended to complete the work as early as possible, so that the benefits of the projects should reach the people without delay. For sustainable development, timely completion of work is all the more important and inevitable. But actually what happens is that the politicians and officials make action-plan of projects in such a way as to take maximum undue advantage out of it. It was seen that, there was not much chance for manipulation or exploitation during the execution of the projects, where People's Committees were strong and were involved.

In the survey it was seen that many projects were successfully completed under the strict supervision of the people's committee. The urge and enthusiasm of the people were clearly reflected in the completion of such works. But such works were few compared to the large number of works undertaken under JRY. It was found that many projects were being implemented without proper attention or sincerity. For instance, under the 'Ela' development programme, several bunds and retaining walls were constructed, but most of those bunds were neither strong nor useful. The condition of such constructions are precarious and they may likely to fall down at any moment.

This would also be the case with the construction of several roads, culverts, retaining walls, buildings, markets, bus stands etc. It indicates the poor monitoring and supervision by officials at the time of constructing the work. This is a serious administrative lapse on the part of officials. Another grave aspect is that in several cases the money was thinly distributed for too many activities. This sort of allocation of fund not only affected the quality of the work but also wasted money. Such arrangements are being made mainly for satisfying the Ward members and consoling the public. The thin distribution of funds for many projects in a Panchayat on an yearly basis is a sheer national waste and stringent action against such practice is essential.

4.22 Types of Works undertaken

Different types of works were undertaken in rural areas under JRY. These works were undertaken in order to fulfil the objectives of the programme such as employment generation, and creation of durable community assets.In this study, 73 per cent of the respondents have stated that the JRY works undertaken were durable in character such as black topping of roads, construction of culverts, retaining walls, markets, bus stands, buildings, wells etc. The study by Gupta also substantiate the same in respect of Kerala.

There was a complaint that the scheduled rates for cement, sand, bricks, etc. were lower than the market rates (actual prevailing rates). But it could be learned that, in Kerala, almost all works were done as per the market rates rather than the scheduled rates. So there had been no room for non-availability of sufficient amount adversely affect the quality of the works. However, the quality of the assets created under JRY were not in proportion to the amounts spent for the same and hence the assets created under JRY called for early repair and maintenance.

4.23 Assets and its Quality

About the quality of the work people have responded almost equally in three areas of Kerala. The details are given in Table 4.27.

Table 4.27

Are you satisfied with the quality of the works created

	Districts			
	Kollam	*Kannur*	*Palakkad*	*Total*
Yes	31	42	72	145
	31.0%	42.0%	72.0%	48.3%
No	69	58	28	155
	69.0%	58.0%	28.0%	51.7%
Total	100	100	100	300
	100%	100%	100%	100%

* *Source:* personal survey.

Of the 300 respondents, 48.3 per cent stated that the works were done well and their quality was up to the standard. Meanwhile, 51.7 per cent stated that the quality of the work was not up to the mark.

When the quality of assets created among the three Districts are compared, it is found that in Kollam and Kannur, there is much difference in significance. The quality of assets created in Palakkad is much higher than that of the other two Districts. It was understood that, the quality of the assets were below the standard in several cases, in the other Districts. The reasons attributed for the poor quality of work are lack of availability of sufficient funds and the pressure to achieve the target of 60 per cent wage component. Similarly the thin spread of funds on too many activities was also a major defect. Such arrangements would naturally reduce the quality of the projects. Though the Panchayati Raj rules are being in force, the participation of the people in the selection of projects and its execution are not found to be satisfactory. Moreover, the representatives of Beneficiary Committee did not have adequate resources (money and equipments) for the timely completion of the works. It causes delay in implementation and ultimately a fall in the quality of work.

Usually, under a Block Panchayat, there are only two Junier engineer JEs to supervise the JRY works. These JEs are expected to look after the works of other programmes viz., EAS, MWS and IAY. If we look in to the quality of the works in the three sample Districts, it can be seen that Palakkad performed better. Of the 100 respondents 72 per cent stated that the JRY works were done well with good quality. Only 28 per cent respondents stated that it was poor. At the same time in Kollam out of 100 respondents only 31 per cent respondents stated that the quality of the work was good and 69 per cent respondents stated that the work done under JRY was bad or of low quality. In Kannur also out of 100 respondents 42 per cent stated that the work was good and 58 per cent stated that the work was below average.

This survey proves that the inferences of the secondary data are correct. But slight variation can be seen with regard to the performance in Kollam. According to the secondary data analysis, the District of Kollam gave medium performance. But the sample taken at Anchal disproves the same when we assess the quality of the assets. Here, the quality of assets in most cases is poor or below average. The above findings bring out the fact that JRY programme helped to create a lot of durable community assets in Kerala such as roads, school buildings, markets, health centres, community centers, panchayat ghar, bus stand etc. Though the quantitywise performance is encouraging, the quality of the work is below the standard.

4.24 Maintenance of Assets

The assets created under the scheme was intended to provide better living to the rural poor and as such these warranted regular, adequate and timely maintenance. Keeping this in view, there was clear stipulattion to give a maximum of 10 per cent of the annual allocation of the JRY fund for the maintenance of assets created. It is observed that adequate importance was not given for maintenance of assets by the Gram Panchayats who are responsible for maintenance of assets under their respective jurisdiction. The details are given in the following Table 4.28.

Table 4.28
Whether the assets were properly maintained

	Districts			
	Kollam	*Kannur*	*Palakkad*	*Total*
Yes	18	18	18	51
	15.0%	18.0%	18.0%	17.0%
No	85	82	83	249
	85.0%	82.0%	82.0%	83.0%
Total	100	100	100	300
	100%	100%	100%	100%

* *Source:* Personal survey.

Of the 300 respondents, 83 per cent stated that the assets were not maintained properly. Only 17 per cent of respondents were of the opinion that the assets were maintained properly. (See Table 4.26) The study reveals that, the District of Palakkad performed well with regard to the implementation of JRY. However, the field study conducted there reveals that the assets created were not maintained properly. Many projects which were done earlier under JRY were put under the Action Plan of the People's Planning and done again. Out of 100 respondents in Pattambi 82 per cent stated that the assets created were not maintained properly and only 18 per cent stated that the assets were being maintained properly. The study conducted at Kollam (Anchal) and Kannur (Taliparamba) also reveal the same trend. In Kollam, 85 per cent respondents stated that the assets were not maintained properly. Only 15per cent respondents stated that the maintenance was being done properly. In Kannur, 82 per cent respondents stated that the assets were not being maintained properly while 18 per cent stated that the assets were being properly maintained.

It was observed that though many projects have been completed under JRY it was not being operated well. In Kannur there was an instance where a toilet and a well were constructed few years back, but a pump-set had not yet been installed. So the people are not getting the benefits though money was being spent for it. Similarly, many projects were completed only partly. In another example, in Anchal Block area, in a public market, many works were done for several years under JRY but the condition of the market is still pathetic. The people stated that the new construction work created more problems than solving the existing problems. The poor quality of the assets created necessitate immediate repair and maintenance. This situation proves beyond any doubt that the authorities did not monitor the works properly while they were constructed. There were grave lapses and irresponsibility on the part of the authorities and peoples representative with regard to the maintenance of assets.

The JRY works were expected to be executed by people's committees. But almost everywhere, an unholy nexus between the local political leaders and officials lead exploitation and misappropriation in the implementation of JRY programmes. It is evident that more vigil and enthusiasm of the people are required for the effective execution of anti-poverty programmes. The dictum 'eternal vigilance is the price of liberty', would appear to be apt here, 'mutatis mutandis'.

4.25 Usefulness of the JRY Scheme

A question mooted to the beneficiaries regarding the usefulness of the programme reveals that a majority of them are not satisfied. Generally, the schemes taken up under the programme were good and beneficial for the community. The survey revealed that out of 300 respondents 54.3 per cent stated that JRY was not beneficial to the community and 45.7 per cent respondents stated it was beneficial. In Pattambi out of 100 respondents 70 per cent stated that the scheme was beneficial to the community and 25 respondents, i.e., 30 per cent stated that it was not beneficial.

However in Anchal out of 100 respondents 64 per cent stated that it was not useful and 36 per cent stated it was beneficial to community. In Thalipparambu, 69 per cent stated that it was not useful to the society and 31 per cent stated it was beneficial to the community.

Table 4.29
Do you consider the JRY Scheme useful

	Districts			
	Kollam	*Kannur*	*Palakkad*	*Total*
Yes Count	36	31	70	137
	36.0%	31.0%	70.0%	45.7%
No	64	69	30	163
	64.0%	69.0%	30.0%	54.3%
Total	100	100	100	300
	100%	100%	100%	100%

* *Source:* Personal Survey.

It is evident that the reason for the complaint was not actually with the programme, but with the execution. The objectives of the programme were good, but the pious objectives were not achieved through its implementation. Though it is often complained that certain guidelines and stipulations are not good to all States and regions, it was observed that JRY was a good programme compared to other major centrally sponsored schemes implemented up to the end of the 8th Five Year Plan.

There is a general complaint that the State Governments are reluctant to implement centrally sponsored schemes sincerely. It is also seen that many state governments are implementing central schemes as their own projects or schemes and giving undue publicity. There have been reports to this effect in the media. A report that appeared in the Malayala Manorama daily is an instance in which the Central Minister for Rural Development stated that the centrally sponsored schemes are not being implemented sincerely in Kerala. He severely criticised the Government of Kerala for not showing enthusiasm in implementing centrally sponsored schemes. He further stated that though huge amounts were allotted for the same, it was not utilised properly.[11] There is a wrong notion that the stipulation and guidelines of the central schemes are rigid and difficult to follow. So Grama Panchayats are not showing much enthusiasm in implementing the same like the State schemes. The State machinery is concentrating only on the implementation of the State schemes for general welfare and rural development. Evere under the new Panchayati Raj and this situation has not been changed the Peoples' Planning programmes, Now central schemes are merged into the State Plan without giving due recognition to the central schemes. It created confusion in the minds of the people and they could not distinguish the central and State schemes.

At the inception of the JRY, the authorities concerned had shown greater interest in the execution of the programme. During that period, JRY scheme was projected as a very important progamme for the development of rural areas. The works done under the scheme was known by every one as JRY.

JRY was an ambitious programme for the uplift of the rural poor by providing them supplementary employment opportunities and creation of infrastructure facilities. In terms of coverage, the programme has impressive statistics, but in reality there was not much to be proud of. Irregularities and leakages in implementation of JRY are well known, but were hardly investigated in a systematic manner. This study was an attempt to assess the impact of JRY with regard to employment generation and creation of community assets. The study reveals that, many of the objectives of the programme could not be achieved by implementing the programme. It was also found that the programme failed to mobilise the needed popular participation. In most cases, beneficiary committees neither existed nor functioned effectively. Further, apathy of officers and representatives of the people very often created hurdles for effective implementation of the programe. The field investigation and the interaction with various groups of people reveal that there were large scale irregularities in its implementation. The physical achievement of the programme, when compared with the amount spent for it, is far from satisfactory. The quality of the assets created and maintenance of assets in most cases was found to be either average or poor. Hence, a regular supervision and maintenance of assets have to be ensured. It also sheds light on the relevance of JRY as an anti-poverty programme.

References

1. Government of Kerala, "Economic Review", *State Plannig Board,* Thiruvananthapuram: 1999, 191.
2. Government of India, 'Rural Development', *Ministry of Information and Broadcasting,* New Delhi: 2001, 425-439.

3. Government of India, '8th Five Year Plan Document', *Rural Development and Poverty Alleviation*, New Delhi: 1992, 30-32. Also see, Govt. of Kerala, "Jawahar Rozgar Yojana Manual" (Malayalam), *Rural Information Bureau,* Dept. of Rural Development, 1996, 1-39.
4. Govt. of India, Planning Commission, *Programme Evaluation Organisation,* New Delhi:1992, 54-61. Also see, Gupta D.N., *Rural Development System Policy Issues: International Development and Management of Rural Development,* (New Delhi: Book India International, 2001, 146-175).
5. Kannan K.P. and Shaji K. Francis, *State Assisted Social Security for Poverty Alleviation and Human Development: Kerala Record and Its Lessons,* (ed.) Mahendra, Dev, S.S., Piush Antony, Gayatri V., Mamgain, R.P., Social and Economic Security in India, (New Delhi: Institute for Human Development, 2001) 411-438. Also see, Gupta, 107-112.
6. *Malayala Manorama Yearbook*, (Kottayam: Malayala Manorama (Pvt.) Ltd. 1994) 230-284.
7. *Malayala Manorama Yearbook*, (Kottayam: Malayala Manorama (Pvt.) Ltd. 1994) .
8. *Malayala Manorama Yearbook*, (Kottayam: Malayala Manorama (Pvt.) Ltd. 1994).
9. Gupta,146-175.
10. *Malayala Manorama Daily*, (Kottayam: Malayala Manorama (Pvt.) Ltd. 1994) June 3, 1995.
11. *Malayala Manorama Daily*, June 14, 2000.

5
Panchayats and Welfare Administration

As part of the Five Year Plans, the Panchayati Raj institutions execute a large number of welfare and poverty alleviation programmes. The Jawahar Rozgar Yojana, one of the most important of them, has been studied particulary to evaluate the effectiveness of implementation in Kerala during the 8th Five Year Plan. In order to test the hypothesis, a total of 63 officials and 62 elected representatives of the people to the local bodies, in three sample Districts, were interviewed with a structured schedule.

5.1 Panchayats and their Functions

Since ancient times, local self governments of different types existed in India. The Village Republics of ancient India were self-sufficient autonomous units managed by village elders. They administered customary laws, adjudicated disputes, maintained law and order and performed a variety of other functions. However, the Panchayats of pre-Independent India were not, on the whole, very strong or efficient. The Municipal administration introduced by the British were structurally, as well as functionally, different from the traditional communitarian Panchayats of Indian villages. [1]

After Independence, imbibed by the spirit of Gandhian ideals as reflected in Article 40 of the Constitution of India, Village Panchayats were constituted in the country. But it had serious drawbacks with regard to the quantum of power and authority. The Panchayat Act enacted in Kerala in 1960, for the first time contained provisions pertaining to the functions, powers of Panchayats. The functions of the Panchayats were listed as duties and functions of discretionary nature rather than obligatory or mandatory. The duties included promotion of agriculture, protection of animals, co-operatives, public works, public health, education and some other subjects. Besides, they had to attend to civic activities such as streetlighting, conservancy, management of markets, slaughter houses, ferry services and registration of births and deaths. The Kerala Panchayat Act of 1960 conferred on the Panchayats, large powers.[2]

In many States, the legislation remained only on the statute books. The provisions were not implemented and Panchayats remained inactive. It is pointed out that in Kerala, the powers given to the Panchayats under the Panchayat Act 1960, were only on paper. To strengthen the Panchayati Raj institutions, serious efforts have been made, and high-powered commissions were appointed under eminent persons like Balwanth Ray Mehta, Ashok Mehta, V.K.R.V. Rao and L.M. Singhvi, by the Government to study the Panchayati Raj system and they recommended a uniform pattern of Panchayati Raj system all over the country with wider powers. But it is seen that nothing much could be achieved till 1993 when the 73rd and 74th Constitution Amendments were brought about to revamp the Panchayati Raj Institution (PRI) system. It was the most serious attempt to decentralise political and economic power by eliciting people's participation at the Village, Block and District levels.[3]

In tune with the Constitutional Amendmends, the State of Kerala passed the required legislations on 24 April, 1994. Certain provisions of the amendments were mandatory, while on many, the State legislature could make its own provisions. The first elections to the new three-tier Panchayati Raj set up were held in September 1995. An important step by the Government of Kerala after the elections in 1995, was the transfer of a number of Departments to Panchayati Raj institutions. Another notable event was that a separate document known as Annexure IV was created by which the Panchayats could enhance their economic position even without an Executive Order. Meanwhile, in 1996, the State Government initiated a massive decentralisation programme known as 'People's Planning'. It was a revolutionary step towards harnessing public support for participatory planning at the grassroots. The effect of the programme was quite impressive. It enabled the Panchayats to formalise and institutionalise the paradigm shift in the system of planning. It opened the floodgates of 'bottom-up' approach to planning and development with people's participation. It could play a crucial role in the process of economic development based on the principles of social equality and social justice. The creation of Grama Sabhas in each Ward of the Grama Panchayat become a catalytic agency for decentralised planning and democracy at grassroots.[4]

5.2 Centrally Sponsored Schemes and the Role Assigned to the Panchayats

Welfare and development activities are being undertaken by the Panchayat Raj institutions on the basis of the Annual Action Plan accepted by each Panchayat Samithi. For the Centrally Sponsored Schemes, the Annual Action Plan must be prepared only according to the stipulations of the Central Government.

There are specific rules and regulations for the implementation of each programme. But, the general rules and guidelines are the same for all the projects. When the Centrally sponsored wage employment programmes are being executed, certain conditions like the objectives of the programme, availability of resources, priorities fixed, evaluation of the existing programme etc. have to be observed. Jawahar Rozgar Yojana was the most important wage employment programme implemented for rural development and poverty alleviation under Centrally Sponsored Schemes. The amount allocated for this scheme was to be distributed to Grama Panchayats, Block Panchayats and District Panchayats according to a ratio of 70:15:15.[5]

It was imperative that, every year, each Panchayat should spend at least 85 per cent of the amount allotted to them before the Action Plan for the coming year was prepared . The amount for the current year would be fixed only on the basis of the utilisation of the funds in the previous year. A copy of the Action Plan will be sent to the Project Officer in the District Poverty Alleviation Cell. While undertaking programmes, due preference will be given to infrastructure development of SC/ST colonies, ancillary projects of Sampoorna Grama Samrthi Yojana, agriculture and socio-economic development.

The selection of benefeciaries was the responsibility of the respective Grama Sabha. The list of benefeciaries for the Block

Panchayat Projects are also prepared by the Grama Sabha. The list of benefeciaries prepared by the Grama Sabha will be submitted for the approval of the Panchayat Samiti. It would then be forwarded to the Block Panchayat.

There were different Committees to monitor the progress of various development programmes. In the Block Level Committees, the President of the Block Panchayat would be the Chairman and Block Panchayat Secretary, the Convener. The Members of the Block Panchayat, the Presidents of the Grama Panchayats, a person representing Village Development Council and top officials of the Block Panchayats were members of these Commitees. The functions of the Samiti pertain to monitoring the progress of the projects at least once in a month, examining whether projects are being implemented as per schedule, giving directions to Grama Panchayats, examining whether the beneficiaries are being selected according to the norms of the project, giving assistance to mobilise regional resources and taking necessary steps to make available the funds for the completion of each stage of the project.[6]

5.3 Role of Bureaucracy

Bureaucracy or civil service play a predominant role in the administration of the State. They are the integral part of the permanent executive branch of State administration. It was a system inherited primarily from the Colonial rule. They were entrusted with the task of general administration, collection of revenue and maintenance of law and order. However, serious doubts have been raised regarding its competence to contribute significantly to nation building. This is particularly so in a country like India, with a plethora of problems-abject poverty, unemployment, ill-health, illiteracy, ignorance and superstition, affect the large majority of its population. For achieving economic development and establishing a Welfare State, a well developed, active and efficient civil service has an important role. A Weberian, rule-oriented administration had to be transformed into a development oriented civil service. The concept of development administration has great relevance in the planning process.

Development administration in Kerala is crucial in the wake of the emergence of decentralisation and participatory democracy at grassroot level. To strengthen grassroot level democracy and promote participatory development, a new approach or style in the structure and functioning of the civil service is inevitable. Thus, it is necessary that an administration sensitive to popular needs and aspirations should be evolved to deal with the challenges faced by the country.[7]

5.4 Profile of the Officials

To collect data on the implementation of welfare programmes, it was decided to undertake a survey of functionaries of Panchayati Raj institutions holding various positions in these institutions. The defacto sampling technique was employed for selecting the subjects. From among officials, 63 functionaries were selected. The data collected from them are arranged in Tables and given below.

The profile of the functionaries interviewed pertaining to designation, gender, educational qualifications are given in Table 5.1 to 5.3.

Table 5.1
Designation of Officials

Designation	*Number*	*Percentage*
Secretary	11	17.5
Co-ordinator	1	1.6
Clerk	34	54.0
Head clerk	5	7.9
Extension Officer	4	6.3
Superintendent	3	4.8
Engineer	1	1.6
Block Development Officer	4	6.3
Total	63	100.0

**Source:* personal survey .

Table 5.2
Gender Distribution of Officials

Sex	*Number*	*Percentage*
Male	51	81.0
Female	12	19.0
Total	63	100.0

**Source:* personal survey.

Table 5.3
Educational Qualifications of Officials

Education	*Number*	*Percentage*
10th Standard	29	46.0
P D C	7	11.1
Degree	22	34.9
Post graduate	3	4.8
Diploma	2	3.2
Total	63	100.0

**Source:* personal survey.

The officials selected for the survey, as can be seen from the above Tables, are representative in terms of offices held, gender distribution, and educational qualifications.

A factor that has not been depicted in the Tables is the age group of subjects. The subjects came from an age group of 27-54 and had, as a result, varying periods of experience. In view of the transfer and posting policy governing government servants, it was not considered necessary to arrange them age-wise. Further, it is well known that in government heirarchy, age mostly denote the length of service except in the case of direct recruits or there in All India Services.

Though the development programmes have to be implemented by the elected representatives of the people, the government officials also play a crucial role. This is more so where the elected representatives lack administrative experience and familiarity with rules and procedures. In disbursing financial assistance or grants, the expertise of officials is of substantial importance to them. Their attitudes, commitment, personal philisophy, sincerity and efficiency are bound to influence the process of administration. Well-qualified officials are thus an important segment with regard to the effective implemenation of development programmes. It is axiomatic that efficiency of implementation would improve where the officials are well qualified and experienced. If they are committed to the concept of rapid social transformation through a developmental agenda, the results are bound to be substantial.

Of the 63 persons interviewed, 51 are males and 12 females. As has been mentioned above, they fell into an age group between

27 and 54. Their educational qualification was very revealing especially in the background of a highly literate State like Kerala. Graduates were 25 in number, of whom 3 were post-graduates. Of the rest, 29 were matriculates and 7 had spent 2 years in college to pass the Predegree examination, and 2 had technical training.

These 63 personnel occupied the various rungs of the local self-government institutions from Secretary to clerical staff. The large mass, 34, belong to the clerical category with another five head clerks supervising the work of the clerical staff. Others made up the post of Coordinator, Engineer, Block Development Officer, Extension Officer and Secretary. Thus, on the whole, the subject selected for interview was a representative cross section of the local self-government institutions at the levels subject to the study.

5.5 Implementation of the Programme

The question mooted to the officials with regard to implementation of the JRY programme helped to unearth valuable information. The officials stated that too many programmes were entrusted with them and it created many hurdles, difficulties and bottlenecks. These were, broadly, excess workload, non-availability of funds in time, insufficiency of manpower, lack of communication, unrealistic targets and priorities, improper utilisation of resources and selection of benefeciaries and attitude of the people and lack of proper reward and punishment system.

Tables 5.4 and 5.5 give the details of the number of officials who pointed out that excess workload and other major difficulties were encountered during the implementation of the programme.

Table 5.4
Did Excess Workload Affect Officials in JRY Implementation

	Number	*Percentage*
Yes	48	76.2
No	15	23.8
Total	63	100.0

**Source:* personal survey.

Of the 63 respondents, 76.2 per cent stated that they were overburdened with the execution of too many programmes and functions while 23.8 per cent stated that there was not much difficulty for them with the many programmes entrusted with them. When interacted with officials and Panchayat Secretaries, it could be learned that there was lack of sufficient number of officers to discharge the numerous functions. This was more so because the Village Development Officer and Panchayat Secretary and other officials are supposed to act as change agents by virtue of their involvement in the execution of development schemes along with their routine duties.

Timely implementation of the programme was an important aspect of the scheme. This issue was therefore, taken up with the officials interviewed. Forty officials, 63.5 percent have stated that they experienced difficulties in the timely implementation of the scheme. A smaller number, 23 (36.5 per cent) however, did not experience any difficulty. This is a revealing disclosure covering the attitudes and responses of officials who were to help the elected representatives in the implementation of the scheme. It underscores the earlier assumption, of the crucial role played by bureaucracy in the development agenda of the State.

The respondents were offered 18 options on the difficulties they encountered in the timely implementation of the scheme with the further option to identify other difficulties outside the range suggested to them. This was so done because it would not have been possible for them to identify any specific difficulty in the implementation of the scheme and it was more likely that there were combination of grounds. In interpreting the responses, the researcher has arranged responses to the extent possible where they fell under distinct Tables and have discussed the rest in the appropriate context.

Table 5.5

Whether there were Difficulties in the timely Implementation of JRY

	Number	*Percentage*
Yes	40	63.5
No	23	36.5
Total	63	100.0

**Source:* personal survey.

It was not easy to make the officials respond, as they were inhibited by the status as government servants, subject to rules of conduct and regulations of public behaviour. In fact, some of them were reluctant to express themselves on this issue. Female officials in particular, were found to be reluctant to respond. The reservation they had on the freedom to express their views candidly on the success of the implementation of a project or the difficulties they encountered is an aspect that has to be taken serious note of. It means that the feedback on the implementation of the project is not likely to be reliable and the planners and administrators are unaware of the ground situations. It has to be considered whether government officials working in local self government institutions should not be encouraged to share freely their experience on the implementation of the programmes and their evaluation of the success or failure of a scheme for the benefit of others particularly those engaged in shaping policies. If threatened less by conduct rules, perhaps their evaluations would be more honest and objective.

The difficulties the officials encountered are arranged below in a rough order of priority. It was also pointed out that, there were no personnel with specialisation to execute and supervise JRY works, as a result, accounts were ill maintained and assets created were of poor quality. The respondents observed that the Panchayat staff have to look after a number of duties including poverty alleviation programmes and JRY work schemes, as an additional burden. They sincerely believed that they are overburdened. The need for deployment of staff was strongly suggested owing to this reason.

It would appear that when new responsibilities were passed on to the staff of the Panchayats, the question of exposing them to a required slot of training was lost sight of. Infact, training and re-training should have received the attention of the concerned, so that required skills and attitudinal changes could have been attempted. The assumption that the existing staff would adjust to the changing situations and pick up the skills on the job were not found well-based. This also led to bickerings and complaints and eventually affecting the quality of their performance.

5.5.1. Non Availability of Funds

Among the respondents, 28.57 per cent have stated that the most important problem was non-availability of funds in time. It was pointed out that, many earlier studies in this country on the performance of rural development have identified this as an issue affecting the programme. One of the reasons for this situation, was that the works were started even before funds were made available. There was also delay in the release of funds from the central and the state governments. There was also delay in paying for work performed. Such delays, it was argued, was owing to under-staffing in the accounts branch of the concerned offices such as DRDA, Block Office etc. It was also found that as more works were undertaken, more delays evolved. Besides, non availability of funds in time also adversely affected a timebound implementation of the programme.

These issues point out to the fact that financial management at this level is rather weak, and the linkages with the relevant administrative departments are not as strong as it ought to be. If local self-government institutions were in a position to raise and manage their revenues themselves, such situations would not have arisen or could have been avoided.

5.5.2 Insufficiency of Manpower

Yet another reason for the failure to implement JRY programme in time, was in sufficient manpower. This was the view expressed by 19.05 per cent officials.

Another serious problem related to the availability and use of technical experts. Of the total respondents, 28.57 per cent stated that there is insufficiency of technical experts. The engineering staff from the District administration had to execute and supervise all the works. In many cases except for the occasional visit by technical staff, no proper technical guidance and supervision were available. Unskilled labourers were required to do the work of engineers and technicians. The relationship between the JRY staff and the engineering staff was also not cordial, which adversely affected the quality of works. In the absence of designing facilities, they normally used the standard type of design with minor modifications for all similar type structures. A serious criticism raised by 14.29 per cent of respondents from among the officials was that the guidelines were vague and not fully relevant. As a result, in many States, and sometimes, even in a region within a State, financing and execution of JRY suffered. It could be inferred therefore, if the Panchayats were given freedom to make necessary changes in the guidelines, the implementation would have been more effective.

Among the respondents, 17.46 per cent stated that the frequent transfer of officers caused difficulty and delay in the implementation of the projects. It is observed that, the officials involved in developmental works were transferred frequently without adequate justification leading to dislocation of work. They hardly get an opportunity to concentrate on their work. It is noted that, frequent transfers of officials was a major problem which affected the smooth functioning of the programme. It was strongly suggested that to obviate this problem, officers must be retained in the same post atleast for three years. It was also seen that a Panchayat Secretary was transferred 4 times within eighteen days without any valid reason. It sheds light on a situation in which there should be a clear cut mechanism to look into the matters concerned with transfers and postings. Obviously, the personnel management policies need a revision. A proper arrangement of reward and punishment system also is found to be necessary. The productivity of the personnel, the quality of their performance and their commitment invariably depend on sound personnel management practices.

5.5.3 Communication Blocks and Lack of Coordination

One of the startling disclosures from the respondents was that there was lack of communication even between the different levels of the local self government institutions like Grama panchayat, Block Panchayat, and District organisation. It was also hinted that there was a hiatus among the personnel at different levels on account of diverse value systems and perceptions borne out of institutional impacts. For instance, officials from the lower level often thought that those at the District organisation, maintained altogether a different perception about the work and working condition of those at the Panchayat and at the Block levels. As a result, it was felt, that a communication gap existed among the different levels of bureaucracy itself. Such a situation contributed to a widening of communication gap between the bureaucracy and the community. It was pointed out that one of the reasons for the failure to meet the targets and to complete projects in time was this gap in communication and identity of interest.

It was also pointed out by the respondents that there was lack of coordination among the different District development agencies hindering the achievement of the objectives of the programme. Co-ordination is basic and essential for good administration and good administration in effect is good coordination. Lack of coordination necessarily leads to delays in the execution of programmes. Coordination is of utmost importance when too many programmes are being run simultaneously and when there is unequal distribution of workload among various agencies, causing hindrances in achieving targets. The responses from officials strongly indicate that there is a pressing need for evolving a satisfactory mechanism for coordination between the district Planning Board and the DRDA on the one hand and DRDA and Zilla parishad on the other. Infact, the whole question of coordination needs to be re-examined

An interesting finding from the responses of officials was about procedures with regard to implementation. According to 15.87 per cent respondents, time consuming procedures adversely affected the timebound implementation of the programme. Thus, there is a case for the simplification of procedures. It is conceded that, the bureaucratic system is inherently rigid, rule-bound, precedent-oriented and dilatory. The aim of decentralisation of powers and responsibility to the local level institutions is simplification of procedures. It also meant de-bureaucratisation. The responses clearly indicate that the essential characteristics of bureaucracy have remained the same even at the local self-government levels. Some respondents have stated that the District bureaucracy often appeared helpful, but it was otherwise in practice. There were also officials who felt that the Panchayati Raj system would hamper development activities. A question that has to be raised here is whether the Weberian model of bureaucracy is suited for grassroots level development activities. It would appear that a new civil service structure with a development oriented outlook would have to be found to make developmental efforts especially at sub-district levels a success. In fact, the need to make the administration people-oriented, change-oriented and result oriented call both for structural and functional changes.

5.5.4 Unrealistic Targets and Priorities

One of the questions administered to the respondents was regarding targets and priorities of the programme. There is a general criticism that Plan programmes often fail because of unrealistic targets and priorities assigned to them. This was perhaps inevitable when Plans were structured for India, which is a sub-continent, with enormous diversities. The demand for decentralised planning has its roots in this situation. Since the JRY was for a specific purpose, the officials as respondents were pointedly asked regarding their appreciation of targets and priorities. It is significant that those who opted to respond to this question came to about 16 per cent only and they have stated that a mismatch of targets and priorities was one of the reasons which affected the implementation of the projects and consequently the failure to achieve the targets.

The results of the field investigation disclose that when JRY scheme was introduced, the Panchayats initially showed much interest and enthusiasm. This was because it was for the first time that the Grama panchayats were entrusted with such an important responsibility. It may be recalled that JRY programmes were target oriented and were to be completed within a fixed time-frame. The number of people who sought assistance from the scheme were large and there were specific needs like reconstruction and repair of houses, for which each had great urgency. In such circumstances, funds were allotted for such purposes and in most cases, officers aimed at completing the targets assigned to them irrespective of the constraints. The economic viability of the projects was, often, not considered while finances were made available to achieve the targets. Thus, it was seen that the approach to the implementation of the programme was based on unrealistic targets and priorities. It has to be observed that a better mechanism could have been conceived, to make the programme scientific and result-oriented and the Grama panchayats given the freedom to complete the work according to the action plan already prepared by them. It was also seen that most of the programmes were target oriented and not people oriented.

It has also been found that unscientific methods were employed to fix priorities. It has come to the notice that priorities were wrongly placed and frequently changed. Further, a nexus developed between the officials and the elected representatives leading to many unhealthy practices in the selection and implementation of projects. It was found that funds were allotted to the Panchayats on ward basis to satisfy the interests of influential ward members. Besides, being unscientific and resulting in loss, it also created unhealthy competition and imbalances. Nearly 13 per cent of the respondents have stated that in the development activities of the panchayats, this was a common phenomenon. It has been observed that even under the Panchayati raj system all was not going well [8] Therefore, the data here strongly indicate that targets have to be realistic, priorities attainable within the timeframe, selection of beneficiaries objective, allotment of resources realistic and on the whole the management of the programme professional and scientific. Thus, the data offers very valid grounds for redesigning the very approach towards poverty alleviation and welfare oriented projects.

5.5.5 Improper Utilisation of Resources and Selection of Benefeciaries

It has been found that targets and priorities have been unrealistic and there has been violation of the guidelines regarding the execution of the work, eliminating contractors and middlemen. It has been found that these lapses led to improper utilisation of resources, mismanagement and misappropriation and wastage. All these call for corrective action. But it has to be admitted that such measures would have only post-mortem impact as the project would have been completed under the disabilities and disadvantages mentioned above. This is a serious lapse and if the feedback is not properly employed while redesigning new projects, the situation would continue to be the same in respect of future projects also.

It has been observed that excessive politicisation and political competition lead to mismanagement of projects, both in terms of allotment of funds and selection of beneficiaries. Very often, it is seen that, assistance is extended to the underserving at the cost of the deserving and the needy. It is reasons of political advantage that often influence such decisions. Nepotism, and political patronage are seen influencing the selection of beneficiaries under the Grama Sabha. Among the respondents,. 6.35 percent have stated that there are instances where assistance was given to undeserving people, rather than deserving, on account of political preferences and nepotism.

It may be mentioned here that the core concern of the project is the development of the rural areas and rendering assistance to uplift the poor and the weak who have not benefited from the general growth programmes. The benefits of such programmes are bagged by the richer sections of the society. Therefore, the identification of beneficiaries assumes critical importance. When the deserving are eliminated on account of nepotism or patronage, the situation becomes tragic as the benefits of the targeted programme elude the deserving again rendering all national efforts at development, reconstruction, poverty alleviation and welfare meaningless. There has been bold experiments elsewhere in the selection of beneficiaries. One such effort was to resort to a lot system when the number of applicants were large.[9] It is obvious that such a system, though unscientific, would help to eliminate allegations of favouritism, political nepotism and the possibility of the resources going to the underserving.

The data here has very important implications to both the projects under study and to the projects to be designed in future for the benefit of the marginalised.

5.5.6 Poverty of the Beneficiaries

In many cases poverty of the beneficiancies acted as a hindrance for the timely and successful implementation of the JRY programmes, Of the three objectives of JRY, two were sharply focussed on povery alleviation and employment generation. The third objective asset generation was to follow the other two objectives. It has to be pointed out that neither income generation nor poverty alleviation can be fully achieved by one or two projects. Poverty is the inability to attain a minimum standard of living as defined in the World Development Report, 1999 and is a relative concept. Poverty is the result of unequal distribution of resources among the people. In India, poverty is measured on household basis and the Indian planners put those below the poverty line as around 37 per cent according to the 1997 NSS data. There has been substantial reduction in povery in this country in recent years and the credit should go to the massive intervention by the national and state government agencies. There has also been a very positive shift in the attitude of various agencies in government towards elimination of poverty in the country. The decisions of the apex court on food security is a telling development. Yet, the press reports on starvation death meant that even the most sympathetic policies fail to eliminate the basic problem of access to facilities. Poverty is a major road block even to the deserving access to alleviatory measures and government help and subsidies. Infact, in this country, empowerment is a qualifying process and the qualifying process is not without strings. Therefore, it was interesting to find that poverty factor is a constraint in the timely implementation of JRY projects under study. Among the respondents, 19.05 per cent have stated that poverty of the beneficiaries was a factor that created hurdles in the timely implementation of the programme. Even when the benefits given under the projects were substantial, it did not cover the entire cost of the project related to a beneficiary. There was a contribution to be made by him in terms of certain man hours committed to the projects. Otherwise, the gap had to be filled by contribution from the public through the Beneficiary Committee. It was very often found that this gap remained as one to be filled up by the beneficiary. In his search for employment for livelihood, a beneficiary who was in abject povery would assign a lower priority to his contribution to projects. Between the demands for meeting the needs for the day, and the needs for the timely implementaton of the projects, the latter was likely to take the back seat. The responses show that this has happened in respect of JRY schemes and poverty has been a serious hindrance to the timely implementation of the programme which was targetted to benefit the poor.

This finding suggests that a participatory role assigned to the poor, while conceptually flawless is likely to create a problem of choice and therefore alternate options will have to be considered when the beneficiaries are in a hand to mouth situation. Here, is thus a valuable lesson for our planners.

5.5.7 Non-recognition

One of the complaints that surfaced from government functionaries in charge of the projects at different levels was that their hard and dedicated work was hardly recognised by the people or by the government. When it came to criticism or fixing responsibility for failures they were almost always targetted. It has been pointed out earlier that a sound personnel management policy would have helped the functioning of the local self government institutions and the implementation of the projects, better. Designing a realistic reward and punishment system strongly emerges from the responses. It has also came out that the quantum of funds allocated for several development programmes underwent rapid increase. There has not been a corresponding increase in the number of personnel to look after the projects. It is necessary to point out that this has been a bane on India's development efforts. Most projects are assumed to be for the benefit of the bureaucracy, which grows disproportionately for each project and gets absorbed in the corpus of the civil service even after the conclusion of the projects. In other words, the personnel inducted for a project continue to be part of the government service even after the project is wound up. The demand for additional staff for implementation of the project has to be therefore evaluated carefully so as to avoid the staff eating away funds meant for the projects. There is also the need to develop an awareness that government is not anymore the universal job giver and the emerging concepts of limits to government, downsizing of the states, e-governance and so forth envisage a lean governmental structure and not proliferation of government functionaries, in the wake of every project. A healthy and viable approach therefore would be to design every project, defining the different components.

5.6 Panchayati Raj and Implementation of Welfare Projects

In the background of the emerging new design for local self government, after the constitutional amendments, a question was asked to the officials whether the JRY schemes would have been more effectively implemented under the Panchayati Raj systems. The responses are tabulated in Table 5.6.

Table 5.6
Are Panchayati Raj Rules Effective in Implementing JRY Programmes

	Number	*Percentage*
Yes	38	60.3
No	25	39.7
Total	63	100.0

**Source:* personal survey.

It can be seen from the Table that while 60.3 per cent of the respondents from among officials believed that the quality of implementation of the programme would be better, if implemented under the Panchayati Raj rules. Among the same group of officials, 39.7 per cent have stated that it would not have made any difference on the implementation. These diverse responses have very significant implications. It indicates that a substantial percentage of officials do not accept the merits of decentralisation and the involvement of people's representatives in the process of project implementation at the grass root levels. It is likely that there is also an ideological divide between these officials representing the bureaucracy and the elected representatives of the people on different issues at various stages. What augurs well for the future of local self government institutions is that above 60 per cent of the respondents support decentralisation and people's participation and the basic and important assumptions of the Panchayati Raj system. What is important here is to examine whether it should be possible to broaden this support base among officials, by sympathetic and intelligent handling of their preferences. It may also be necessary in the future to screen officials on the basis of their views on decentralisation, de-bureaucratisation and people's participation, before they are deployed for duties in the local self government institutions. It also points out the need to train the officials assigned to work in local bodies on developing appropriate attitudes and sympathies. It is clear that any government servant would not do where issues concerning development and peoples' participation are central.

But it has to be a group of people properly selected and trained to fit into the new dispensation. This is all the more necessary because in Kerala, a bold experiment was initated through people's involvement at the planning process. Though the experiment has yet to be subjected to a performance audit, the message that people would be associated with the planning process at the village level has caught the imagination of the public and it would appear that the trend cannot be reversed. Therefore, there is an additional dimension to the role of officials working in local self government institutions. They have to accept people and their participation as a reality. People are not henceforth intruders into the bureaucratic domain, but partners and stake-holders in the governing and planning process. There has to be therefore, a shift in the mindset of officials earmarked to work in local government institutions. The success of poverty alleviation programmes and other schemes for rural development need a close knit association of all the stake-holders, officials, elected representatives and the people to make the best out of the projects. Table 5.7 testifies to their role in implementing the JRY schemes.

Table 5.7

Are the Role of Representatives of the People Effective in Implementing JRY Schemes

	Number	*Percentage*
Yes	45	71.4
No	18	28.6
Total	63	100.0

**Source:* personal survey.

The above proposition has received the support of a substantial percentage of respondents as can be seen from the Table above. The respondents were asked whether the role of representatives of the people is effective in implementing the JRY programmes. Of the 63 respondents, 45 (71.4 per cent) was emphatic in their response that involvement of the people's representatives is crucial for executing projects for the local people. There was of course a voice of dissent from 18 respondents (28.6 per cent) who felt that any role played by the representatives of the people would not help the effective implemenation of programmes. It has been found that the same percentage of respondents have consistently held the view that development programmes should be exclusively made the preserve of bureaucracy and not an area where the people and their representatives play any role. One of the revealing facets of the present study is that bureaucratic resistance is a factor to be reckoned with in conceptualising and implementing development projects. However, 71.4 percent of the respondents have said that the association of people's representatives help to make implementation of projects a success. Since the people have a close access to them, it is possible for them to ventilate their grievances and the peoples' representatives can intitiate appropriate corrective measures. Such a close working relationship between the people and their representatives eliminates conflicts and makes the wheel of governance at the local level move faster. It is evident that under the new Panchayati Raj system, peoples' representatives would have a much more important role to play than they had during the early years. It would appear that the people's planning process itself is a reflection of this emerging reality. One of the points stressed by the respondents was that government employees should not be permitted to contest elections to the local bodies. They argue that they would be hurdled in view of their bureaucratic past and slow transformation to be true represntatives of the people. The respondents have suggested that the relevant rules have to be amended for this purpose. As such, we do not have empirical data to conclude whether associaiton of government servants as elected representatives would be beneficial for local government institutions or not. In fact much can be said in support of both views. A truly service conscious government servant, shorn off the bureaucratic mould would be an asset to the local bodies due to their office familiarity and admnistrative capabilities. It is also likely that a public servant can get elected only with the support of political party and the policy of the party cannot but regulate his conduct and style of funtioning.

The large number of teachers who have taken up the role of peoples' representatves in West Bengal, it is reported, contributed significantly to the development of grassroot level democracy and more effective implementation of development projects.[10] Therefore, the question whether government servants should or should not be permitted in local government administration as elected representatives merit a comprehensive study.

5.7 Public Participation and Implementation of JRY Projects

One of the moot issues today, is the role of the people and their participation in developmental efforts. Democracy at the grassroot level envisages peoples' participation. Deccentralised planning contemplates planning at micro level taking into account the needs of each locality. Infact, it has been accepted that a planning agenda shaped for a country like india with its many diversities from distant Delhi would be a misfit for larger areas of the country. The shift to micro-level planning was the result of such a realisation. Besides, association of people with local government institutions would help to develop local leadership unless there is direct participation shouldering responsibilities in planning and executing programmes at micro level, a new breed of leadership cannot be built in the country[11]. Association of people in the governing as well as development process is therefore essential to nurture involvement of the people in nationbuilding activities and the process of self-government. The Korean experiment of village development committess with opportunities of people to plan and shoulder responsibilites is pointed out as a sucess story in peoples' participation.[12] Only through the active participation and involvement of the people, can the socio- political system be made conducive to the attainment of economic development with a greater degree of social justice. The responses of officials regarding public participation and effectivenss in the implementation of JRY schemes may be seen in Table 5.8 given below.

Table 5.8
Was Public Participation Effective in Implementing JRY Programme

	Number	*Percentage*
Yes	55	87.3
No	8	12.7
Total	63	100.0

**Source:* personal survey.

Of the 63 respondents, 87.3 per cent stated that public participation is inevitable in the sucessful implementation of rural development programmes. However, we find that 12.7 per cent of responding officials have reservations. They did not believe that the people, by and large, are not yet to be associated with developmental projects. It may be pointed out that this view is extant among some officials despite the volumnous material produced by national level commissions like the Balwant Ray Mehta Committee (1957), Ashok Mehta Commitee (1977) and other Committes and the novel experiment initiated by S.K. Dey, viz., Community Development Programme, as early as 1957. However, a redeeming feature is the increasing awareness among a majority of government officials that peoples' participation would contribute to increasing the efficiency in the implementation of poverty alleviation programmes and developmental programmes.

5.8 Assets Created

JRY was a major wage employment and rural infrastructure development programme that aimed to create large scale community assets all over the State. However, there are apprehensions with regard to its quality and usefulness. The following Table (Table 5.9) shows the number of officials who expressed their views on this question.

Table 5.9
Whether the Assets Created Under JRY are Useful

	Number	*Percentage*
Yes	61	96.8
No	2	3.2
Total	63	100.0

**Source:* personal survey.

About the usefulness of the assets created under JRY, of the 63 respondents 96.8 per cent have stated that they were useful. Only 3.2 per cent have stated that they were not useful. It may be recalled that, it was a wage-employment and rural infrastructre development programme started in 1989 at the fag end of the 7th Plan and continued under the 8th and 9th Plans.

Though 96.80 per cent of officials have stated that the assest created under JRY are useful, it would not appear to be the actual position. During the field survey and interaction with the public, the researcher could learn that neither the respective departments nor the Panchayats was taking genuine interest in the timely maintenance of assets. Moreover, the local initiative and participation were also found to be lacking. The major reason attributed to the ill-maintenance of assets has been administrative delays and lack of funds. Therefore, a proper and scientific mechanism has to be developed urgently for the maintenance of assets. It would be essential to get continuous benefits from the assets and also to promote the welfare of the poor. It has to be realised that any negligence with regard to this vital aspect would be disastrous, as the assets created would perish fast.

To stimulate popular enthusiasm in programmes of planned change, government functionaries can play a positive role. It has been observed that the best use of scarce resources takes place when officials and politicians work together with a clear understanding of their goals and agree upon procedures for reaching them. The crucial test of efficiency and effectiveness of administration lies in the accomplishment of the objectives stipulated in policy decisions. Generally one sees that, although the policy is good, its implementation is poor or bad. In a democratic set up, administration is a vehicle or tool for implementing public policy. The administration must be development oriented and thus, necessary steps will have to be taken to strenghten the administrative structure and adapt viable administrative processes, a task which requires a very human and sympathetic approach towards all people and not an approach which is geared for fault finding. The attitude of the administrator, at whatever level he is, should be that of service and of rendering help.[13]

6. Representatives of the People and Welfare Administration

It has been observed that, unless power and responsibility are shared with the people, developmental goals would not be achieved. This is true of all underdeveloped countries, and particularly of rual India. Village or rual development can be made real only when the community understands its problems, realizes its responsibilities, exercises the necessary power through its chosen representatives and maintains a constant and intelligent vigil on local administration.

Local leadership is an effective mechanism for mobilization of the villagers and also for building up of organizations within them. An effective leadership can build a group of followers and can transmit through them any idea or carry out any action and thereby diffuse the same to a larger section of the society. Thus, the gap between the idea for social change and the actions required to implement them need to be bridged. The leaders can play an exemplary role in the development process under the Panchayati Raj system as, they are proficient in conflict resolution and crises management. It is only the leader in a crisis situation who can galvanize the isolated and dissenting members into a cooperative group. If rural development programmes are tested as movements for socio-economic change, then leadership can be treated as the most effective instrument for interest identification, interest articulation and interest aggregation.Leaders also act as experts by popularizing innovations and techniques for development. Moreover, they can act as agents for modernization, social change and social mobility. Therefore, for speedy and smooth identification of a development programme, there is need for identification and proper utilization of the local leaders. A basic attribute of leadership is motivation. Leadership means, ability to influence group activities towards goal-setting and goal achievement. Thus, leadership is not only a technique but an art by itself.[14] It has been observed that ideologies have great impact in shaping the social attitudes of leaders. Leadership is an effect and the physical, spiritual and social backgrounds are the causes that produce that effect.

With the introduction of decentralised system of administration, a large number of local leaders are emerging from the grass root levels. There are specific guidelines regarding representation of SC/ST and women. Their representation and involvement in the administration of the local bodies have largely increased. The initial taboos and bottlenecks have almost gone with regard to representation of women in local government institutions. Women representatives are found to be very active and take active interest in the day to day administration. It could be inferred that if larger responsibilites are entrusted with them, the face of our villages would change.

To know the attitude and opinion of the elected representatives in local bodies on various issues of welfare and developmental programmes, an interview among them was conducted with a structured schedule.The de-facto sampling technique was employed for selecting the subjects. A total of 62 representatives of the people were interviewed to elicit their opinion on welfare administration. The data colleted from them are arranged in Tables given below.

6.1 Profile of the People's Representatives

A profile of the Representatives of the People of the Panchayati Raj institutions interviewed pertaining to designation, gender, age, marital status and educational qualifications are given in Table to 6.5.

Table 6.1
Designation of Representatives of the People

	Number	*Percentage*
President	17	27.5
Member	40	64.5
Chairman standing Committee	5	8.0
Total	62	100.0

**Source:* personal survey.

Table 6.2
Gender Distribution of Representatives of the People

Sex	*Frequency*	*Percent*
Male	36	58.1
Female	26	41.9
Total	62	100.0

**Source:* personal survey.

Table 6.3
Age Distribution of Representatives of the People

Age group	*Number*	*Percentage*
25-35	18	29
36-50	34	54.9
51-71	10	16.1
Total	62	100

**Source:* personal survey.

Table 6.4
Marital Status of Representatives of the People

	Number	*Percentage*
Married	54	87.1
Unmarried	7	11.3
Widow	1	1.6
Total	62	100

**Source:* personal survey.

Table 6.5
Educational Qualifications of Representatives of the People

	Number	*Percentage*
Below 10th Standard	11	17.7
10th standard	26	42.0
Pre-degree	9	14.5
Degree	13	21.0
Post Graduate	1	1.6
Diploma	1	1.6
LLB	1	1.6
Total	62	100.0

**Source:* personal survey

It can be seen from the above Tables that, the subject population has in it representatives of the people holding various positions in Panchayati Raj institutions from that of President and Members to that of Chairman of the Standing Committees.

Of the 62 representatives, 26 (41.9 per cent) are females. It is evident that, the reservation of seats for women attracted a large number of women to the elected offices. It is likely that a number of them would have come to hold office without any previous experience.

The educational qualification of the subjects differ widely. among the respondents, 26 (42 per cent) have studied upto the 10th standard, while 11 (17.7 per cent) did not complete the 7th standards and 14. 5 per cent have studied upto PreDegree. Those who hold a Degree constitute 21 per cent and there is one Post Gaduate, a Dilploma holder and one holding a Law Degree. It can be seen that the largest group (26) belong to those who have studied upto the 10th standard. When those who have studied upto Pre Degree are also added to this number, it makes 56.5 percent. It is therefore, clear that, persons who have been attracted to the lur of office in local government institutions are not the most brilliant or well educated among the people, but those who opted out of the educational process quite early either due to lack of interest or due to other constraints. However there are no illiterates and the least educated have put in atleast 7 or 8 years of schooling. It is evident that they are all political activists who have drifted into one or other political party after discontinuing school education. It further shows that the representatives of the people by and large have had political education and are not sheer novices.

The age-wise distribution of the sample gives an interesting picture. The samples are from different age groups, between 25 and 71. Those who are in the age group of 36-50 are 54.9 per cent and those in the age group of 25 and 35 constitute 29 per cent, together making a percentage of 83.9. Those who are above 51 and below the age of 71 are 10 or 16 per cent clearly indicating that a large majority of elected representatives are of an active age group of between 25 and 50. It is evident that, the local government offices have attracted the young and the active. This obviously means that an active political profile and familiarity with ploitical process are essential for getting elected to the local government institutions. The fact that a younger age group have been elected to the local government institutions indicate that the innovations through decentralisation and development with peoples' participation have attracted the younger generation. This is a very encouraging development.

6.2 Awareness of the Programme

Awareness of Panchayati Raj rules and welfare programmes initiated at grassroot level is a necessary condition for an elected representative to discharge his duties well. To a question regarding the awareness of the programme, the majority of the peoples' representatives stated that they are familiar with poverty alleviation programmes, especially JRY schemes.

Table 6.6
Are you Aware of the Welfare Programmes

	Number	*Percentage*
Yes	55	88.7
No	7	11.3
Total	62	100.0

**Source:* personal survey.

Of the 62 respondents, 88.7 per cent stated that they are familiar with the JRY and 11.3 per cent have however revealed their unawareness. Though the majority has given a positive answer, it cannot be taken for granted. It has to be remembered that mere knowledge of such programmes is not sufficient for a responsible leader. They should acquire a thorough knowlwedge of the various welfare programmes and the modalities of its execution. It would be essential in getting a command over the officials, to guide and correct them while executing such vital programmes. Therefore, the peoples' representatives need to equip themselves not only with the content of various programmes, but also should have the enthusiasm to serve the people sincerely. It also points out the vital aspect of giving up lethargy and passivity by the representatives of local bodies, which usually hinder the welfare programmes.

6.3 Implementation of the Programme

To a very important question to the representatives of the people regarding the timely implementation of the programme, the majority pointed out to the drawbacks of the programme. Of the respondents, 77.4 per cent have stated that there were drawbacks in the implementation of the programme and have identified drawbacks as unscientific selection of programmes, defective execution and beneficiary selection, rigid administrative procedures, lack of training, apathy of officers and poor education of the people. These drawbacks, it may be pointed out, are not insurmountable and can be rectified through a number of local initiatives. This is an aspect to which pointed attention has to be paid by planners and administrators. The following Tables 6.7 & 6.8 give the details.

Table 6.7
Presence of any Drawbacks in Implementation of JRY

	Number	*Percentage*
Yes	48	77.4
No	14	22.6
Total	62	100.0

* *Source:* Personal survey

6.3.1 Selection and Execution of the Programme

Among the respondents, 20 have stated that, the selection of programme was unscientific. They have also stated that in the implementation of the programme there were serious flaws. Unscientific selection of programme and defective implementation, would no doubt, destroy the very objectives of the programme. About 22 respondents have stated that the programmes were not suited to local conditions. As a result, they caused serious setbacks in the effective implementation of JRY programme. Defective execution was pointed out as a drawback by 19 respondents. This was mainly due to lack of coordination between different agencies, set up to implement the programme. Of the respondents, 27.0 per cent found this to be a serious problem. There was also a general complaint that the programmes lack flexibility, forward and backward linkages and there was a shortage of well trained officers. It is obvious that these are very serious defects and a mere increase in expenditure under various anti poverty programmes would not yield the desired results.

6.3.2 Selection of Beneficiaries

It need not be emphasied that, identifying the right beneficiary is central to any poverty alleviation programme. This is so because the projects are targetted towards a finite group. Therefore, the selection of benefeciaries and whether the right beneficiaries were selected in the JRY programme was put to the respondents, both from the officials and elected representatives. The responses from the elected representatives expressed almost identical views as those from the officials. 31 per cent respondents from elected representatives stated that selection of benefeciaries was not done properly. We have earlier found that 6.3 per cent of respondents from officials had stated that assistance was given to undeserving rather than deserving on account of political preferences and nepotism. When both groups, elected representatives and officials, state that the selection of benefeciaries was flawed, a serious question arises as to who is responsible for selecting the wrong beneficiary. It is obvious that, in the selection of beneficiaries, the methods employed were not fool proof and there must have been an agonising amount of bargaining and squabbles among the representatives of the different political parties holding office. A system which distort does not produce the right result and does not satisfy neither the officials nor the elected representatives and is therefore, one that has to be replaced. This is very essential for the success of the scheme. It is a sad commentary on the implementation of such projects that the schemes and funds for the uplift of the underpriveleged and the deprived do not reach the deserving. This is an aspect that is to be looked into under the Panchayati Raj system. The selection of beneficiaries have to be made scientific and transparent, perhaps involving the Grama Sabha itself.

Another inference that can be drawn from the data in this Table is that 17.74 per cent of respondents stated that non cooperation and pulls and pressures at cross purposes in fact a constant tug-of-war existed between the officials and peoples' representatives. Such a situation is bound to retard the implementation of various projects, identification of deserving beneficiaries and the very implementation of the programe. As a result, the objectives of the programme would get derailed. This has to be, therfore, one of the important concerns of the Panchayati Raj administration. In any case, the officials and elected representatives have to function as part of a team and not as participants in a conflict.

6.3.3 Rigid Administrative Procedures

Forty four per cent of respondents have highlighted the problem of lengthy and rigid administrative procedures leading to red tapism. It is axiomatic that the development process has to be simple and short with the least amount of paper work. There has to be ruthless axing of delays that lead to corruption and misuse of powers and resources. It has come out from various studies that, corruption is the bane of national development in the underdeveloped world. [15] There is a need to evolve a new administrative and political culture, especially in local self government institutions, which would set its face against corruption, nepotism and redtapism. This is an aspect of administration that needs to be taken seriously.

6.3.4 Lack of Training and Apathy of Officers

It has to be admitted that projects like JRY aimed at employment generation and poverty alleviation are new intiatives involving local government institutions. The implementation of such programmes indicates a shift in the approch of the government, from relying entirely on the civil service machinery to putting its trust on the people and their elected representatives. While this is conceptually very laudable, it has to be admitted that such projects call for a certain amount of administrative expertise and familiarity. Both the officials and elected representatives have to be therefore put through appropriate training modules. Lack of training would create hurdles and training has to be focussed and purposive. There is no doubt that training prior to assumption of an office and while in the office and familiarity with the job on hand would improve the quality of work undertaken. Training is both a process of learning and unlearning, unlearning what is irrelevant, archaic, and learning what is relevant and topical. About 19.35 per cent of the respondents have stated that incompetent and untrained officials affected the quality of work and caused delays. This is a serious deficiency which requires special attention. It is seen that the government is aware of the need for such training as is evident from the various training programmes offered by the Institute of Management in Government (IMG) and also Kerala Institute for Local Administration (KILA). However, it has to be examined whether all concerned have been put through the required amount of training and whether the reach of the training programmes has been sufficiently wide, so as to include all concerned. Twenty percent of respondents, have also stated that apathy and indifference of officials put severe contraints on timely execution of the programme. Apathy, indifference or passivity on the part of officials, indicate the need for remedial training. There has also to be better standards of accountability and audit of performance. The wealth of experience of the civil service and their administrative ability have to be shared with the people at the grass root level and infused into the projects concerning them. An administration that is irresponsive, inefficient and unsympathetic cannot serve the people efficiently and faithfully.[16] Thus, a lesson that comes out from the responses here is that there is compelling need to re-educate and re-cycle the officials and the official machinery to vibe well the local government institutions and their functionaries.

6.3.5 Poor Educational Standards of the People

Educational backwardness of the people has been found to be a problem that adversely affect the success of the anti-poverty programmes. Kerala has a higher rate of literacy and adult education programme has been successful in carrying out the message of literacy to the people. In fact, mass literacy programmes have been very successful in Kerala. However, it is doubtful whether literacy had led to attitudinal transformation on the part of the people or increased motivation to take part in government programmes and projects. It is often assumed that the more the people are educated, the more would be their participation in development activities and projects. It is true that in comparison, the participation of the people is quite encouraging in Kerala. However, it has been pointed out that such participation is not emerging at most required or expected levels.The very concept of local self government, and the projects for development, and reconstruction, involve active participation of the people. The 'Grama Sabhas' and the 'Neighbourhoods' are two institutions conceived under the Panchayati Raj to make the participation of the people, meaningful. A special feature of the life of the people in Kerala, is the extreme invasion of politics at all levels. Every programme, every initiative of the government in power is viewed, seen and evaluated with political overtones. It is bound to affect the success of the development programmes, if they are also evaluated through political standards. It is therefore, necessary that the people themselves discourage the influx of politics and approcah projects and programmes for rural reconstruction and development from a different prespective. It would appear that the success of local self-governmemt to a very great extent depends on non political response of the people at large rather than divisive political considerations.

6.4 Panchayati Raj and Implementation of Welfare Programmes

The implementation of welfare programmes through the Panchayati Raj institutions provide a new dimension to local self government activities. The new Panchayati Raj rules have been in operation since 1993. Article 243-G clearly lays down that only the legislature of a State can endow Panchayats with powers and authority so as to enable them to function as institutions of self-government. Unfortunately, many State Governments have neatly bypassed the spirit, and often the letter of this Article by enacting laws empowering themselves to assign or withdraw any power and function to and from Panchayats.[17]

It is seen that Kerala has faithfully implemented the provision of Article 243-G of the Constitution. In Kerala, the welfare programmes of the Panchayats are being executed through peoples' participation and Grama Sabhas. It is pointed out that many of the State governments have refused to act according to the constitutional provisions. In many States, the Panchayats are still functioning as mere extension agencies of the central administrative machinery. The elite groups in the society are obstructing the move for decentralisation and participatory democracy at grass root level [18]

Panchayats are institutions of self-government. A basic feature of any such institution is autonomy, autonomy in matters of resources, autonomy in decision making, in respect of powers and functions assigned and autonomy in implementing decisions through its own functionaries. One can say that there is a 3-F formula, viz., Functions, Finance, Functionary.[19]

It seems that, decentralisation as visualised in the Panchayati Raj system is simply an illusion in several parts of the country. The Panchayati Raj System is being used by the Government functionaries as a condition for poverty alleviation and other welfare programmes, namely, Integrated Rural Development Progamme (IRDP), Jawahar Rozgar Yojana (JRY), Employment Assurance Scheme (EAS), Special Area Programmes, etc. But, there is a wide spread complaint with regard to the execution of the programmes, even under the new Panchayati Raj system. It is argued that the Government, through the officials, has found it convenient to use the Panchayati Raj System in various degrees to implement such programmes without devolution of authority. This type of arrangement is termed as 'deconcentration'. It does not generally include decentralisation of power or authority. It can be considered an illusory process of transferring some functions to the lower levels to decrease the work-load of the main authority and to facilitate its functioning without the participation of lower levels in formulating programmes and granting them authority.[20] People have great expectations in the effective functioning of the Panchayati Raj system. They believe that the welfare programmes would be executed effectively through the Panchayati Raj institutions. Tables 6.8 and 6.9 show the opinion of the representatives of the people on this vital aspect and the level of its significance.

Table 6.8
Whether Panchayati Raj Rules are Effective in Implementing JRY

	Number	*Percentage*
Yes	51	82.3
No	11	17.7
Total	62	100.0

* *Source:* Personal survey.

Of the 62 respondents, 82.3 per cent has stated that if the Panchayati Raj rules are followed strictly, the scheme will become more successful. At the sametime, 18 per cent were not accepting the effectiveness of the Panchayati Raj in implementing JRY system. With regard to the effectiveness of the Panchayati Raj system in implementing development programmes in proportion of persons who favoured amongst the people's representatives, it is found that there is much difference in signifance (Z = 6.46) as z-value is greater than 1.96 at 5 per cent level of significance.

Table 6.9
Proportion of Representatives of the People who Stated that the Implementation of the Programme was a Success through Panchayati Raj

P	N	Z
82.3	100	6.46

P is the proportion of the people and
N is the number of sample population
* *Source:* Personal survey.

Rajiv Gandhi, in one of his public addresses, had expressed the view that out of a rupee spent on various anti-poverty programmes, only 15 paise reached the beneficiaries, the rest 85 paise were being eaten up in the process. Recent evaluation of such programmes bear testimony to these tendencies, of vast cracks in the delivery system. The recent evaluation on IRDP also indicates this malady.[21]

It is seen that, more than 83 per cent of respondents supported and accepted the effectiveness of the Panchayati Raj in solving the drawbacks associated with the implementation of the poverty alleviation porgrammes. The new Panchayat Raj System envisages 'bottom up' planning and participation of the people. The participation of the people can be ensured at all stages of the programme such as articulating the felt needs of the people through the Grama Sabha, making policies and projects, implementing the projects and maintaining the assets created.

The study reveals that, the People's Representatives can play a crucial role in co-ordinating the programmes effectively in their respective wards. Corruption, nepotism and such drawbacks may be reduced to the maximum through this system. The system contains provisions for making the officials accountable and responsible to the people. There is also an advantage that implementation of the projects can be evaluated at all stages. Public participation and monitoring of projects are an added advantage. If the programmes are implemented according to the guidelines and stipulations of Panchayati Raj, it may produce the best results. For it, the people must be vigilant and responsive.

The present set up does not allow the local bodies to select suitable projects of their choice when they implement poverty alleviation programmes. There is no provision for the Panchayats to alter the scheme according to the local conditions or considering regional variations. Therefore it adversely affects the effectiveness of the programme. There is a serious complaint pertaining to Central schemes that they are target oriented and rigid. Many people hold the opinion that if sufficient freedom is given to the Panchayats in the execution of the programmes, it will become more effective and useful. Table 6.10 shows the opinion of the representatives of the people on this vital issue.

Table 6.10

Will More Freedom for Panchayats in the Selection of Projects Improve the Welfare Programmes

	Number	*Percentage*
Yes	48	77.4
No	14	22.6
Total	62	100.0

* *Source:* Personal survey.

Of the 62 respondents, 77.4 per cent respondents have stated that in order to get the best result out of its implementation, more freedom has to be given to Panchayats to make appropriate alterations as and when required. However 22.6 per cent of respondents are not in favour of the idea of giving freedom to Panchayats to alter the scheme to suit their requirements while implementing them.

At present, Panchayats are facing several constraints with regard to the implementation of projects due to the rigid guidelines. Since the three-tier constitutional institution exist at the local level, there is no harm in giving freedom to select appropriate projects by the Panchayats themselves. However, the use of the discretionary power by the Panchayat should be within the core limit of the programme. Now the programmes are not capable enough to reflect the real needs of the people. The design of specific schemes, within the realm of guidelines of the programmes, also gets upset due to restricted options or limited resources. The funds provided under a scheme to the Panchayats could be diverted to other important needs such as the programmes for population control, literacy, public health and welfare of the disabled and the destitute. Since these programmes have direct impact on poverty, it is better to link such programmes with the strategy of anti poverty programmes.

6.5 Public Awareness and Participation

Introducing various programmes under the poverty alleviation scheme without adequate ground work, discussion or propaganda, creates a lot of problems to the implementing agencies and local bodies. Many ongoing programmes are remodelled and put together to make new ones by the Central Government, all of a sudden. This is an attempt to get popularity and attract the attention of the people towards the Government. However, such tendencies must be avoided because rural development is a crucial area where much attention is required. The mechanism of trial and error method should be avoided with regard to the policies and programmes of rural development. Before introducing such programmes, prior discussions must be held at all levels and all the concerned departments and line agencies should be informed about it. Thorough preparation or ground work should be done before announcing such vital schemes by the Central government because such schemes have far reaching consequences or impact on the people and the society. In such circumstances, the officials and the Peoples Representatives at local levels should be given training concerned with all aspects of the project.

The rules and guidelines must be made simple and easy to follow. The majority of the respondents (97 per cent) favoured the view that proper prior knowledge and training about a particular programme will improve the quality of execution. This opinion of the peopless' representatives should be considered seriously. The present practice of announcing unscientific programmes may be viewed as equivalent to grabbing the genuine rights of the local bodies. The very concept of Panchayati Raj is based on decentralisation and participation of the people at all levels. It should be racalled how the successful implementation of rural development programmes depend upon mass support and participation. Table 6.11 depicts the opinion of the representatives of the people.

Table 6.11
Whether Participation of the People will Make the Programme More Effective

	Number	*Percentage*
Yes	56	90.3
No	6	9.7
Total	62	100.0

* *Source:*Personal survey

About 90.3 per cent of the respondents emphasised the need for public participation. Many programmes were introduced by the Central Government for poverty alleviation earlier but they did not produce the desired result due to non participation of the people. The JRY scheme announced in late 1980s was primarily intended to stimulate welfare activities in our villages and contained provisions for ensuring better public participation. It was a programme that contained the spirit of the Panchayati Raj system and People's Planning. To ensure public participation to the maximum possible extent was one of the basic objective of the scheme. In that sense, it was also considered as the forerunner to the People's Planning because the guidelines and modalities of the programmes resemble People's Planning. A programme announced by the government and implemented with the participation of the people, automatically becomes a programme by the people for the people and of the people. The participation of the people at all stages such as planning implementation and maintaining the project would be evolved properly.

The panchayati raj system contains several provisions for the direct participation of the people in rural development. The presence of Grama Sabha is the foremost instance.

6.6 Assets Creation and its Maintenance

Different varieties of assets were created under the JRY programme throughout the length and breadth of the State during the 8th Plan period. But the assets created are not being maintained properly, which would lead to a great national waste. A poor country like India cannot afford such a wastage. So a better mechanism to maintain assets created is essential. People's representative in suggested various measures for the proper upkeep and maintenance of assests created under JRY (see Table 6.12)

Table 6.12

Do you have any Suggestions Regarding the maintenance of assets created under JRY

	Number	*Percentage*
Yes	52	83.9
No	10	16.1
Total	62	100.0

* *Source:* Personal Survey.

Of the 62 respondents, 83.9 per cent stated that they have better mechanism to suggest. The measures suggested by them include (1) formation of peoples committees to look after the assets (2) release of sufficient maintenance grants (3) field visits by peoples representation and (4) appointment of expert staff.

During the field survey, it has been found that the assets created are not being properly maintained. In this context, the opinion of the people's representatives deserves serious attention. Therefore, the Panchayati Raj System should take earnest and practical steps to maintain the assets created.

People always criticise the local body authorities for their passive or negative attitude towards the people's genuine needs. It is obvious that people are expecting genuine assistance from the Panchayats, but they are not getting the service as they expect. A vibrant grass root level democracy is the need of the hour, and for it the present system must be changed. A new rural life must emanate from the present crisis which would be capable enough to solve the problems of the people to a great extent.

From the above analysis, it could be inferred that rural development is a subject that requires much more serious approach. The Panchayati Raj system and the decentralisation process initiated in the State should be strengthened by devolution of more power and authority. Inorder to materialise the dreams of Mahatma Gandhi and other national leaders to build a new society based on social justice and egalitarianism, a new system of administration must be developed. We need officials and representatives of the people who could work together for saving the country from the present disaster and distortion. The structural arrangement visualised in the decentralised system of planning must be strengthened because, the forces against devolution of powers to the Panchayats are still powerful. Thus, its is high time to realize those forces and make strong campaigns to make the Panchayats an integral part of people's lives. Strengthening and extending the basis of welfare programmes at grassroot level require work of great magnitude. Needless, to say that, those concerned with the Panchayati Raj system should be ready to harness all human energy as well as utilize fully the administrative genius available.

References

1. Govt. of India, India 2001, New Delhi: Publication Division, Ministry of Information and Broadcasting, 2001, 425-426.
2. Raphael, Jose, *Decentralised Planning in India,* (New Delhi: Anmol Publications (Pvt.) Ltd., 2000) 171-174.
3. Ramachandran V., *Panchayati Raj in Kerala,* (ed.) Mathew, George, Status of the Panchayat Raj in the States and Union Territories in India, (New Delhi: Institute of Social Sciences, 2000) 155-163.
4. Ramachandran V., 155-163.
5. 'Gramangalil Mattathinte Shankholi' (Malayalam) *Village Development Department*, (Thiruvananthapuram: Rural Information Bureau, 1999) 8-33.
6. Government of Kerala, 'Panchayati Raj' Vol. 6, (ed.) Thiruvananthapuram: Sept. 2001, 32-37.
7. Heady, Ferrel , *Public Administration: A Comparative Perspective* (London: Prentice Hall) 1966, 16.

8. Kannan, K.P., "People's Planning", 'Kalacku Munnil Kettiya Vandi' (Malayalam) *The Mathrubhoomi Weekly,* (Kozhikode: September 2000) 14-16.

9. Narayanswamy, Raju , Malayalam Weekly, September 27, 2002.

10. Banerjee, Surabhi, *Jyoti basu: An Intimate Biography, (*Calcutte: Viking Penguin Ltd., 1997).

11. Markandam, *Designing Development Plans: A Bottom-up Process,* (ed.) J. Palanidurai, Dwaraki D.R., Swami, Narayana, New Panchayati Raj System, (New Delhi: Kanishka Publishers, 1997) 65.

12. Dwarakanath H.D., 'Rural Development Policy and Programme Implementation: An Evaluation', New Delhi: *Social Action*, October-December, 1995, 454.

13. Chaturvedi, T.N., 'Administrative Performance and Accountability', International Training Programme on Audit of Rural Development Programmes, Selected Readings, Vol. I, New Delhi: September 1 to December 3, 1988, 1-21.

14. Stogdill, R.M., 'Leadership Membership and Organisation', Psychology Bullettin, Vol. 47, No. 1, January 1950.

15 Sharma R.D., *Administrative System of Developing Societies* (New Delhi: Mittal Publications, 2000) 33.

16. Bandhopadhyay D., 'Panchayats and Democracy: Elites Versus Dalits', Chandigarh: *Man and Development*, Vol. 4, December 1999, 77.

17. Mathew, George*, Status of the Panchayati Raj in the States and Union Territories in India,* (New Delhi: Institute of Social Science, 2000, 4).

18. Bandhopadhyay D., 71.

19. Randhawa, S, Narendra, 'Panchayati Raj System Decentralised Planning: Myths and Realities, Chandigarh, *Man and Development,* Vol. 13, September 1996, 38-39.

20. Bandhopadhyay, 75-76.

21. Mohanlal, Morley, G., *Rajiv Gandhi and Panchayati Raj,* (New Delhi: Konar Publishers, 1994) 20-50.

6
Conclusion and Suggestions

Justice and equality are the basic principles that guide the democratic governments. In order to make these principles meaningful and effective, most of the governments have incorporated suitable provisions in their constitutions. Adoption of the concept of welfare state has been a national outcome of these efforts. With the welfare objectives in mind, adequate provisions were included in our constitution. Poverty, unemployment and inequality have been haunting Indian polity for decades. Suitable socio-economic policies are essential for the eradication of these evils. Since independence, several legislations were enacted to that effect by the central and state governments. Planning has been introduced in India in 1951 for the speedy execution of the various socio-economic development programmes. Under the planning process, several measures have already been initiated. to uplift the masses. These measures were mainly centered on two realms - protective and promotional. The protective measures are largely for the organized sectors, such as medical care and benefits relating to sickness, maternity, old age etc. The promotional measures are primarily for the unorganised, in terms of self-employment, wage employment and provisions of basic needs.

Though several programmes were launched to ameliorate the basic problems of the poor and the marginalised, they did not bring about any significant changes in their socio-economic conditions. Therefore, a number of special employment and poverty alleviation programmes were introduced during the 6th and 7th Five Year Plans. These programmes continued during the 8th Five Year Plan also. The major strategies adopted in the implementation of these programmes were to ensure a high level of growth with emphasis on employment generation in all sectors. Besides, special efforts have been taken to protect the interest of the poor and vulnerable groups. Such an effort has been mainly on the realisation of the fact that the incidence of poverty in India is the highest among the agricultural labours in rural areas and casual labours in urban areas. It is among this category of people that non-availability of work from time to time would be a major cause of low income and high incidence of poverty.

The major poverty alleviation and employment generation programmes introduced since the inception of the 6th Plan included the Integrated Rural Development Programme (IRDP), Development of Women and Children (DWCRA), Training Rural Youth for Self-Employment (TRYSEM), National Rural Employment Programme (NREP), Rural Landless Employment Guarantee Programme (RLEGP), Jawaher Rozgar Yojana (JRY) and Employment Assurance Schemes (EAS)

The NREP and RLEGP are the most popular measures intended for generation of employment and rural infrastructure development. But these programmes did not produce returns commensurate with the investment in terms of creation of useful and durable community assets. Even on the employment generation front, the administrative procedures were not cost effective and thus a sizeable part of the funds got utilised on overheads. With a view to removing these defects, a new Programme, JRY was launched on 1 April, 1989 by merging NREP and RLEGP.

The basic objectives of the programme were (i) creation of additional employment opportunities for the unemployed and under employed (ii) the creation of sustained employment by strengthening rural economic infrastructure and also that of assets in favour of the rural poor (iii) and overall improvements in the quality of life in rural areas.

In addition to the above, secondary objectives of JRY aimed at popular involvement in development planning. It was intended to ensure the active support and participation of the rural poor in project implementation and assets maintenance. An outstanding feature of the programme was that the projects would be executed without contractors.

Since the inception of JRY, 17596.16 million man days of employment have been created and an amount of Rs. 30,900 crores were spent for the programme till March 1998. The programme was introduced in Kerala in 1989. During the 8th Five Year Plan about Rs. 400 crores were spent for JRY in the state.

The official report on the performance of JRY gave an impressive picture. But it has been pointed out that the programme did not produce the expected benefits to the rural poor as claimed in the official reports. JRY was a programme for the rural poor and the responsibility for executing the programme was entrusted with the village Panchayats. Since it was an important programme, an objective assessment of the effectiveness of its implementation was necessary to identify the merits and demerits if any, for restructuring such programme, and their effective implementation in future. The study aimed at an objective evaluation of the JRY in Kerala with a view to assessing the benefits derived by the target groups, and where it fell short and why.

In the process of analysing the usefulness of the JRY as a welfare programme for the rural poor, secondary as well as primary data have been utilised. Secondary data were obtained from published and unpublished sources. The secondary data were mainly collected from the Report on JRY from the Commissionerate of Rural development and State Planning Board, Thiruvananthapuram. It has been processed systematically and statistically analysed district-wise and programme-wise to assess critically the effectiveness of its implementation, and the benefits accrued there under to the concerned.

Primary data were collected through a field survey conducted among the individual and community beneficiaries in selected Block Panchayats and Grama Panchayats by using suitable interview schedules. Besides, a sizeable number of officials and elected representatives of the people from Panchayati Raj bodies were interviewed with a structured schedule. The primary data, so collected sheds light into the various unknown contours of the JRY implementation in the State.

It has been observed that the JRY has not created adequate employment opportunities to the target groups. Out of the 100 days of employment that ought to be created annually, on an average, only 10 to 12 days of employment could be generated. It was also found that the programme was neither productive nor a succour to the target groups. Local workers were invariably avoided from the JRY because most of the works were executed by the contractors or middlemen.

With regard to the nature of execution of the programme, it has been found that many works were done either by contractors or middlemen. The committees formed for the execution of JRY were found to be neither active nor useful. Lack of transparency was evident in the work done under the programme that resulted in several complaints. It was seen that most of the works were carried out just like routine government works. There was no proper technical supervision or assistance provided for the execution of the projects. The amount sanctioned for various projects were insufficient to meet the expenses. The amount sanctioned for the projects were not only insufficient but also not received at the right time. It could be seen that funds were being allotted only at the fag end of a financial year. Besides, public participation did not come up to the expected level. All these factors adversely affected the performance of JRY.

The major lapses identified in the implementation of the programme include unrealistic targets, untimely release of fund, lack of coordination, frequent transfer of officials, lack of training, time consuming procedure, improper selection of projects and beneficiaries, poverty of the people etc. It was seen that the mismatch of targets and priorities was one of the reasons that affected the implementation of projects and consequently the failure to achieve the targets. The economic viability of projects was often not considered while finances were made available to achieve the targets. It has been observed that better mechanisms could have been conceived to make the programme scientific and result oriented.

Lack of coordination also adversely affected the implementation of projects. Co-ordination is basic and essential for administration and good administration in effect is 'good coordination'. Lack of coordination necessarily led to delays in the execution of the programmes. It has been observed that there was no proper coordination amongst different functionaries from DRDA to village Panchayats. A sizeable number of Panchayati Raj officials stated that the frequent transfer of officers caused difficulty and delay in the implementation of projects. It has been observed that, the officials involved in development works were transferred frequently without adequate justification. It is clear that there should be a clear-cut mechanism with transfers and postings. A proper system of reward and punishment is also found to be necessary.

It has been admitted that projects like JRY, aimed at employment generation and poverty alleviation, are new initiatives involving local government institutions. The implementation of such programmes indicates a shift in approach of the government, from relying entirely on the civil service machinery to putting its trust on the people and their elected representatives. Both the officials and elected representatives have to be therefore put through appropriate training modules. It has been observed that lack of training created hurdles on the smooth execution of the scheme. There is no doubt that training prior to assumption of office and while in the service would improve the quality of the work undertaken. Training the representatives of the people is also equally important in the discharge of their functions effectively. Training is both a process of learning what is relevant and topical and unlearning what is irrelevant and archaic.

The time consuming procedures was another serious factor that adversely affected the time bound implementation of the programme. Thus, there is a cause for simplification of procedures. It is conceded that, the bureaucratic system is inherently rigid, rule-bound, precedent oriented and dilatory. The study emphasised the need for a new civil service structure with a development oriented outlook and work culture. Such a service needs to be evolved, to make local self-government institutions work better.

It could be seen that with regard to the selection of SC/ST beneficiaries there was not much irregularity or nepotism. But, the selection of other beneficiaries selection of community projects and the methods employed for such selection were not foolproof. There had been an agonising amount of bargaining and squabbles among the representatives of the different political parties holding office. This is an aspect that is to be looked into under the Panchayati Raj system. The selection of projects and its beneficiaries have to be made scientific and transparent.

One of the difficulties that have been identified in the timely implementation of the programme was the poverty of the beneficiaries. This has prevented them from assigning adequate priority to their contribution to the projects.

The Panchayati Raj functionaries and representatives of the people have reposed great faith in the emerging new design for local self-government. As a response for the relevance of the Panchayati Raj rules in implementing community development projects, sixty percent of officials and large majority of the representatives of the people stated the quality of the programme would improve if rules were strictly adhered to. However, forty per cent of the officials have the view that it would not have made any difference in the implementation. It vindicates that a substantial percentage of officials does accept the merits of decentralisation and involvement of the representatives of the people. Therefore, a change in the attitude of the officials is essential. How this change can be brought about is also important.

Adequate public participation is a pre requisite to the effective implementation of any programme intended for the benefit of the poor. The shift from macro to micro planning is a positive development towards that direction. Unless there is direct participation, shouldering responsibilities in planning and executing programmes at micro level a new breed of leadership cannot be built in the country. The officials and representatives of the people have strongly advocated the urgent need for public participation. They have expressed the hope that under the emerging Panchayati Raj system, public participation would come into operation in a big way.

Assets on a large scale were created under JRY during the 8th Plan in Kerala. But, it has been observed that grave negligence had taken place from the officials and public in maintaining the assets properly. This is mainly due to administrative lacuna and non-availability of funds. A viable mechanism to maintain the assets created has to be evolved. The representatives of the people have suggested several measures for the proper maintenance of assets including the constitution of People's Committees. Improper maintenance of assets is seen as a major issue that retarded the prospects of JRY as an effective community development programme.

Thus, the important findings of the study substantiate the hypotheses that, though large-scale community assets were created under JRY, it was inadequate to provide employment opportunities to the target groups. The people's participation and involvement could not be mobilised at the expected level. There have been serious defects and irregularities in the execution of the programme. There was no provision for proper maintenance of assets created under the programme. The official apathy and administrative incompetence in implementing JRY projects has emerged as a serious system deficiency. It has also come out that the evolving Panchayati Raj institutions should plan and provide for plugging the loopholes in the programmes by strictly adhering to the rules and designs of the programme concerned. Overall, it was found that the deficiency and lapses are part of the present administrative culture and are not unsurmountable or irremediable. Poverty alleviation programmes need to be conceived and implemented with an appropriate design and guideline and should not be taken as part of the regular administrative developmental agenda.

Suggestions

The wage employment infrastructure development programmes should be strengthened and integrated by adopting suitable mechanisms. When projects are conceived from the national context, the ground realities in the different states are to be taken into account. In the absence of such considerations, the centrally sponsored schemes are bound to fail to deliver the goods. Therefore there is a strong cause for reviewing this approach. The areas that have the maximum potential for employment in each Grama Panchayat have to be identified and the projects suited for each locality may be selected and prioritised so that the available resources can be exploited to the maximum.

Measures should be adopted to enhance the skills and capabilities of the vulnerable workers. a proper blend of education and training would be extremely appropriate. A fact that has to be accepted is that skill development and training are the most important factors in increasing the employability in productivity of the workers in the wake of ongoing globalisation, which has a tendency to push the less-skilled out of the market.

To ensure the availability of funds for development projects a proper financial management at local level is urgently needed. The local governments themselves should get power to raise and manage their revenues for the smooth governance of the PRIs. There should be a clear-cut mechanism to look into matters concerned with the transfer and posting of Panchayati Raj personnel. A proper reward and punishment system is also found to be necessary.

The target fixed for a particular programme has to be made realistic and affordable within this time frame. Measures have to be adopted to reduce excessive politicisation and political competitions in the functioning of the local government institutions. Without a peaceful and congenial atmosphere, the projects cannot be executed in time.

The institution of Grama Sabha needs to be strengthened. They must be made a substantial stakes-holder in the process of micro level planning and implementation of projects. It would help develop public support and participation, most essential at the grass root level for socio-economic development. It would also be an exercise to develop local leadership. Measures are to be adapted to give proper training for officials and elected representatives of the people on a permanent basis in order to strengthen administrative expertise and familiarity is another finding of the study. There are also grounds to suggest that the three tier system of Panchayti Raj may not be suitable for Kerala and that the Block Panchayat system can be abolished, if Grama Panchayats could be made strong and powerful. The office of DRDA could be merged with the District Panchayat for evolving effective coordination in rural administration.

There is need to think of putting all the resources for local development under the PRI institutions. Under such a system, multiplicity of agencies can be eliminated. A suggestion that could be made in the present context is that, the vistas of information technology should be properly exploited by the local bodies for improving governance and for maintaining transparency in administration.

To establish self-sufficient 'village republics' as visualised by Gandhiji require sincere and adrent efforts from all concerned. Fulfilling the task, a viable mechanism should be adopted and pursued consistently at the grass root level. It is accepted that, strengthening the process of decentralisation would be the most effective step towards that direction. It would help to reduce a top-heavy central and state administration and enable democracy to be brought within the reach of the common man. It would certainly open the floodgates of a total revolution silently in the villages of India. A root and branch change in the structure and functioning of the Panchayati Raj system would follow, no doubt and that would be the harbinger for making poverty alleviation programmes deliver the desired goals.

Appendix. I

Among Spent for Various Programmes Among SC/ST and Others Under JRY During 8th Five Year Plan in Kerala

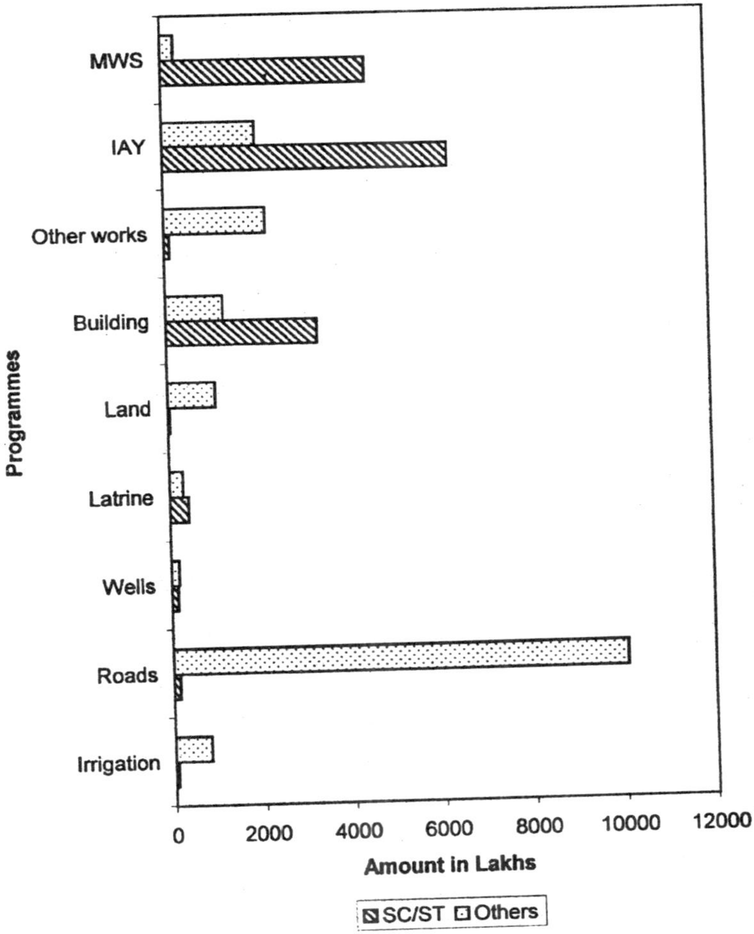

Appendix. II

Amount Spend for Irrigation in Various Districts under JRY during 8th Five Year Plan.

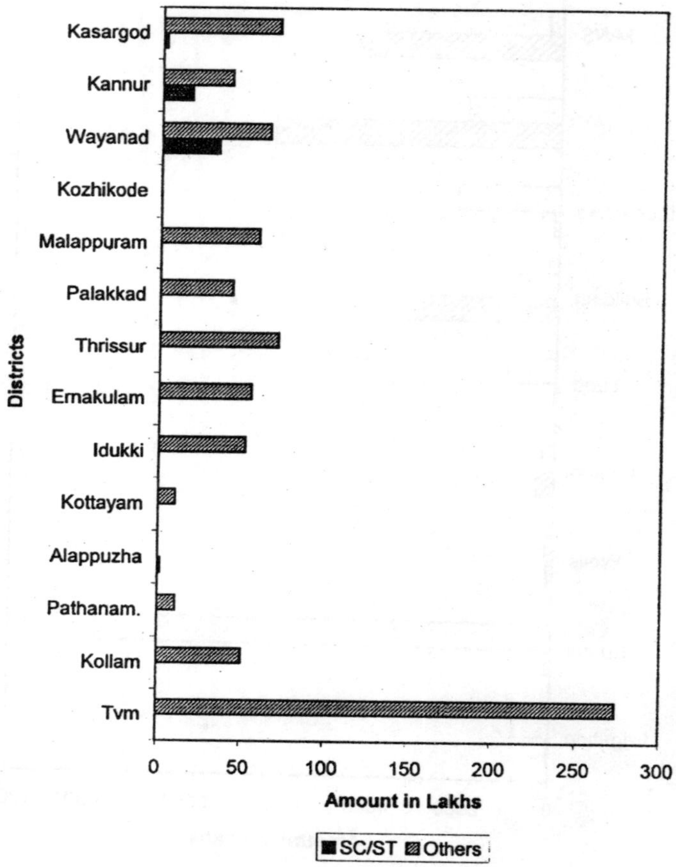

Appendix. II (i)

The percentage of amount spent for irrigation out of the total amount utilised for SC/ST and others under JRY during the 8th Plan in Kerala (1992-93 to 1996-97)

District	*SC/ST*		*Other*		*Total*	
	Amount	*%*	*Amount*	*%*	*Amount*	*%*
Trivandrum	0.00	0.00	273.73	21.62	273.73	10.60
Kollam	0.00	0.00	50.21	3.19	50.21	1.90
Pathanamthitta	0.00	0.00	10.68	1.21	1068.00	0.67
Alappuzha	1.12	0.14	0.00	0.00	1.12	0.07
Kottayam	0.00	0.00	10.24	1.10	10.24	0.65
Idukki	0.00	0.00	51.75	4.10	51.75	2.03
Ernakulam	0.00	0.00	54.69	4.73	54.69	2.66
Thrissur	0.00	0.00	70.56	4.50	70.56	2.37
Palakkad	0.00	0.00	43.06	2.07	4306.00	1.11
Malappuram	0.00	0.00	58.67	3.21	58.67	1.88
Kozhikode	0.00	0.00	0.00	0.00	0.00	0.00
Wyanad	34.10	3.92	64.55	7.14	98.65	5.56
Kannur	17.71	2.86	41.64	4.88	59.35	4.03
Kasaragod	2.10	0.15	69.88	4.62	71.98	2.48
Total	55.03	0.37	799.66	4.39	854.69	2.57

* Amount in lakhs.

** *Source:* Estimated from the respective data of JRY from the Rural Commissionerate.

Appendix. III
Amount Spent for Irrigation Among SC/ST and Others under JRY During 8th Five Year Plan

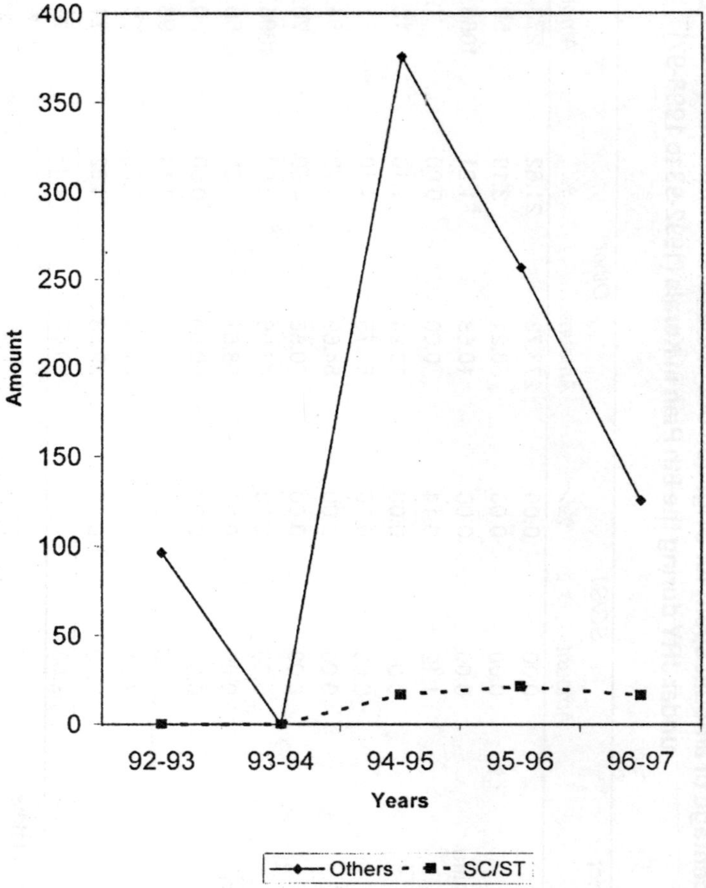

Appendix. IV
Amount Spent for Roads in Various Districts under JRY during 8th Five Year Plan

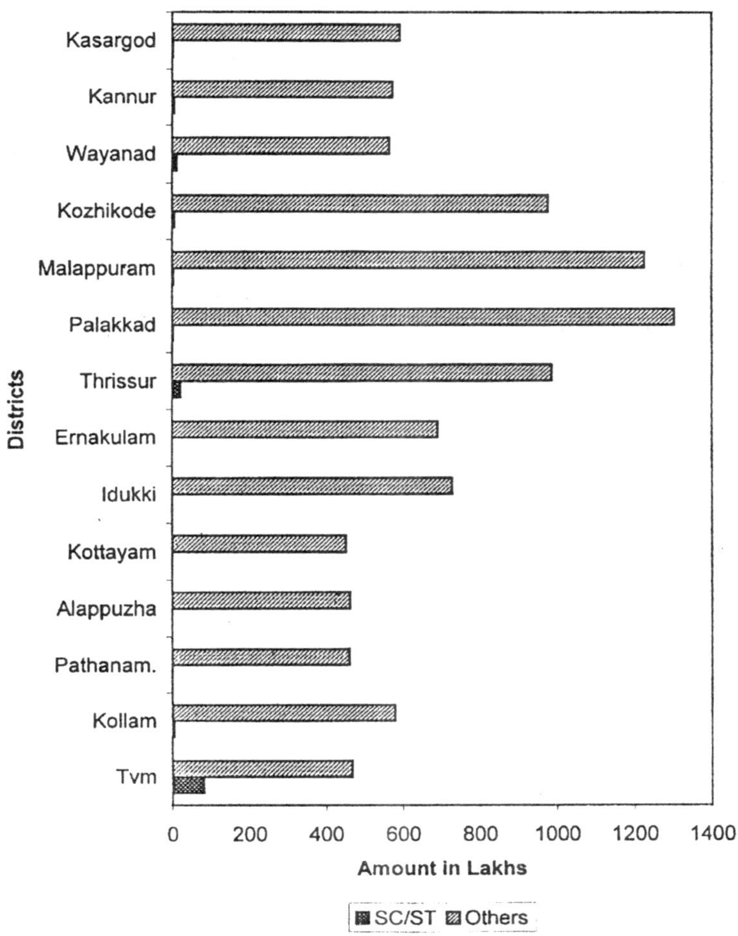

Appendix. IV (i)

The percentage of amount spent for roads out of the total amount utilised for SC/ST and others under JRY during the 8th Plan in Kerala (1992-93 to 1996-97)

District	*SC/ST*		*Other*		*Total*	
	Amount	*%*	*Amount*	*%*	*Amount*	*%*
Trivandrum	81.16	6.16	467.09	36.89	548.25	21.22
Kollam	3.96	0.37	578.37	36.80	582.33	22.00
Pathanamthitta	0.00	0.00	460.26	52.23	460.26	29.04
Alappuzha	0.00	0.00	462.68	55.78	462.68	28.07
Kottayam	0.00	0.00	452.23	48.75	452.23	28.75
Idukki	0.16	0.01	729.02	57.81	729.18	28.63
Ernakulam	0.00	0.00	690.61	59.67	690.61	33.54
Thrissur	22.42	1.60	987.39	62.99	1009.81	33.97
Palakkad	1.70	0.09	1303.19	62.58	1304.89	33.64
Malappuram	3.12	0.24	1226.43	67.17	1229.55	39.50
Kozhikode	5.50	5.59	978.01	62.83	983.51	39.58
Wyanad	11.16	1.28	565.26	62.54	576.42	32.48
Kannur	4.51	0.73	573.55	67.17	578.06	39.27
Kasaragod	2.01	0.14	592.61	39.18	594.62	20.47
Total	135.70	0.90	10066.70	55.32	10202.40	30.69

* Amount in lakhs.

** *Source:* Estimated from the respective data of JRY from the Rural Commissionerate.

Appendix. V
Amount Spent for Roads among SC/ST and Other under JRY during 8th Five Year Plan

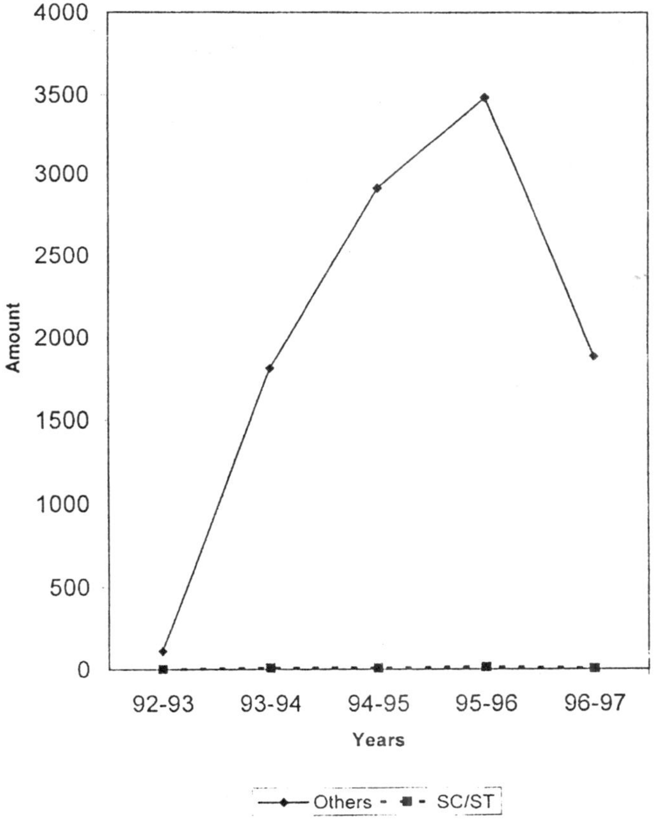

Appendix. VI
Amount Spent for Drinking Water Wells in Various District under JRY during 8th Five Year Plan

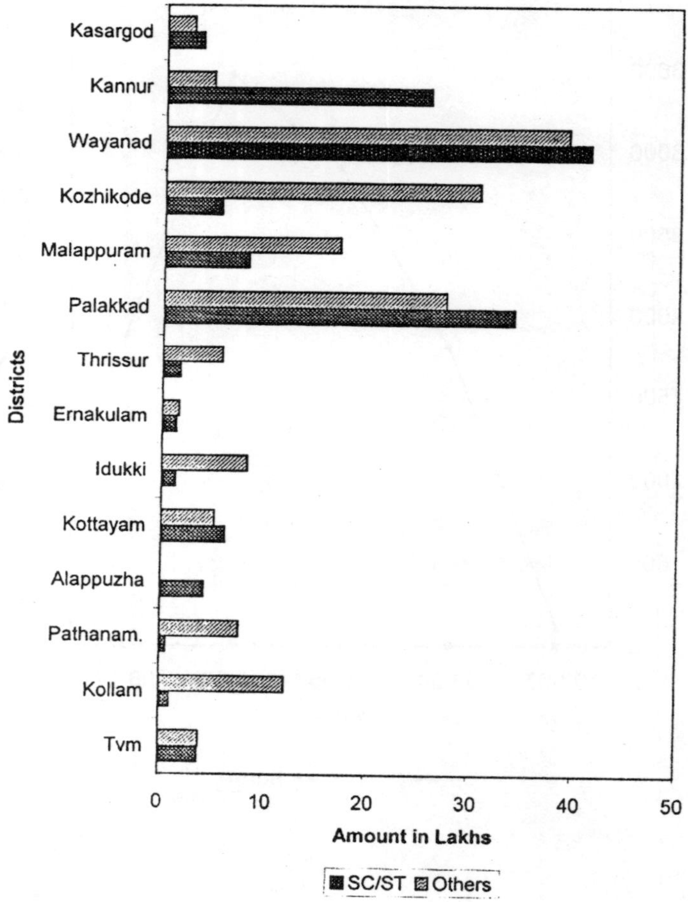

Appendix. VI (i)

The percentage of amount spent for drinking water wells out of the total amount utilised for SC/ST and others under JRY during the 8th Plan in Kerala (1992-93 to 1996-97)

District	*SC/ST*		*Other*		*Total*	
	Amount	*%*	*Amount*	*%*	*Amount*	*%*
Trivandrum	3.80	0.29	3.87	0.31	7.67	0.30
Kollam	1.00	0.09	12.14	0.77	13.14	0.50
Pathanamthitta	0.60	0.09	7.63	0.87	8.23	0.52
Alappuzha	4.20	0.51	0.00	0.00	4.20	0.25
Kottayam	6.19	0.96	5.133	0.55	11.32	0.72
Idukki	1.35	0.10	8.28	0.66	9.63	0.38
Ernakulam	1.38	0.15	1.57	0.14	2.95	0.14
Thrissur	1.71	0.12	5.74	0.37	7.45	0.25
Palakkad	34.11	1.90	27.53	1.32	61.64	1.59
Malappuram	8.20	0.64	17.12	0.94	25.32	0.81
Kozhikode	5.47	0.59	30.65	1.97	36.12	1.45
Wyanad	41.34	4.75	39.22	4.34	80.56	4.54
Kannur	25.80	4.17	4.61	0.54	30.41	2.07
Kasaragod	3.53	0.25	2.65	0.18	6.18	0.21
Total	138.68	0.92	166.14	0.91	304.82	0.92

* Amount in lakhs.

** *Source:* Estimated from the respective data of JRY from the Rural Commissionerate.

Appendix. VII

Amount Spent for Drinking Water Wells among SC/ST and Others under JRY During 8th Five Year Plan

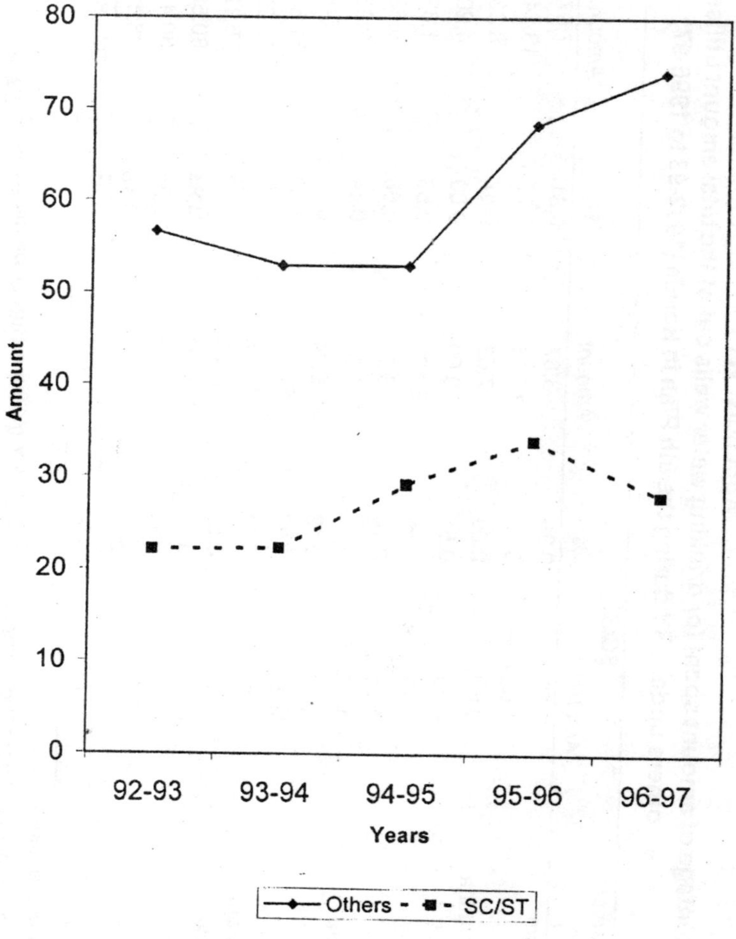

Appendix. VIII
Amount Spent for Million Wells in Various Districts under JRY during 8th Five Year Plan

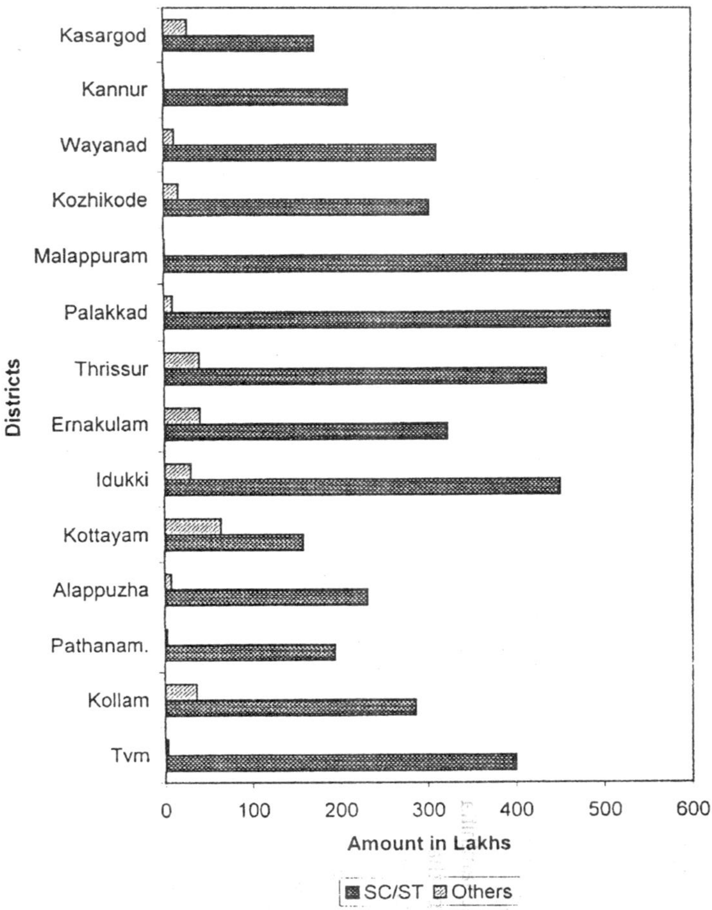

Appendix. VIII (i)

The percentage of amount spent for Million Wells out of the total amount utilised for SC/ST and others under JRY during the 8th Plan in Kerala (1992-93 to 1996-97)

District	*SC/ST*		*Other*		*Total*	
	Amount	*%*	*Amount*	*%*	*Amount*	*%*
Trivandrum	399.37	30.32	3.07	0.24	402.44	15.58
Kollam	286.02	26.60	35.86	2.28	321.88	12.16
Pathanamthitta	194.10	27.58	2.37	0.27	196.47	12.40
Alappuzha	231.26	28.26	7.54	0.91	238.80	14.49
Kottayam	158.00	24.49	64.13	6.91	222.13	14.12
Idukki	450.76	35.05	29.69	2.35	480.45	18.86
Ernakulam	323.10	35.84	40.40	3.49	363.50	17.66
Thrissur	435.72	31.01	39.71	2.53	475.43	15.99
Palakkad	508.20	28.29	9.41	0.45	517.61	13.34
Malappuram	526.74	40.94	1.00	0.05	527.74	16.95
Kozhikode	303.08	32.65	16.74	1.08	319.82	12.87
Wyanad	311.70	35.80	11.86	1.31	323.56	18.23
Kannur	2102.49	34.37	0.93	0.11	213.42	14.50
Kasaragod	172.25	12.37	27.33	1.81	199.58	6.87
Total	4512.80	29.99	290.04	1.59	4802.83	14.45

* Amount in lakhs.

** *Source:* Estimated from the respective data of JRY from the Rural Commissionerate.

Appendix. IX
Amount Spent for Million Wells among SC/ST and Other under JRY during 8th Five Year Plan

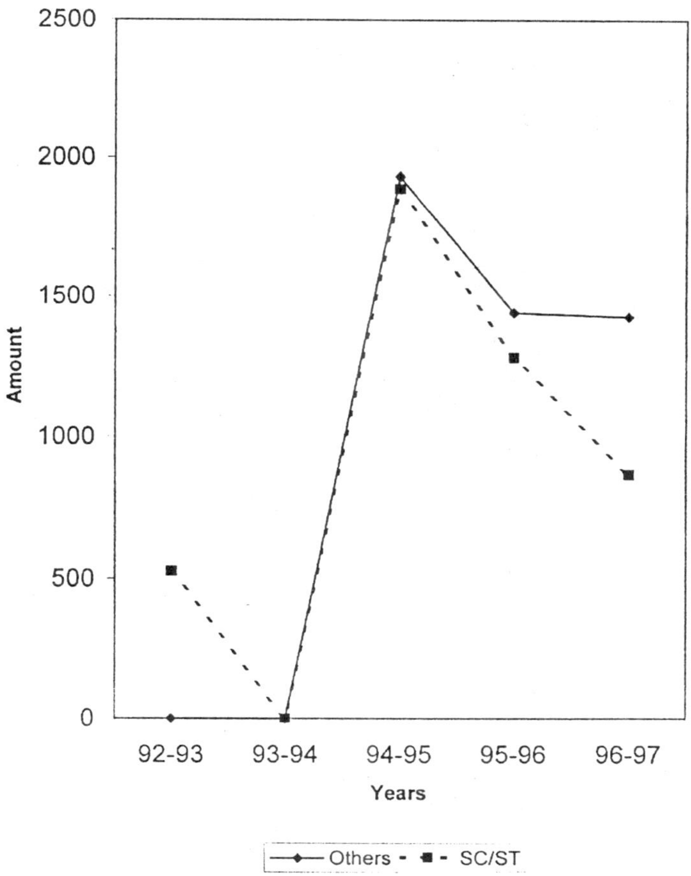

Appendix. X
Amount Spent for Latrines in various Districts under JRY During 8th Five Year Plan

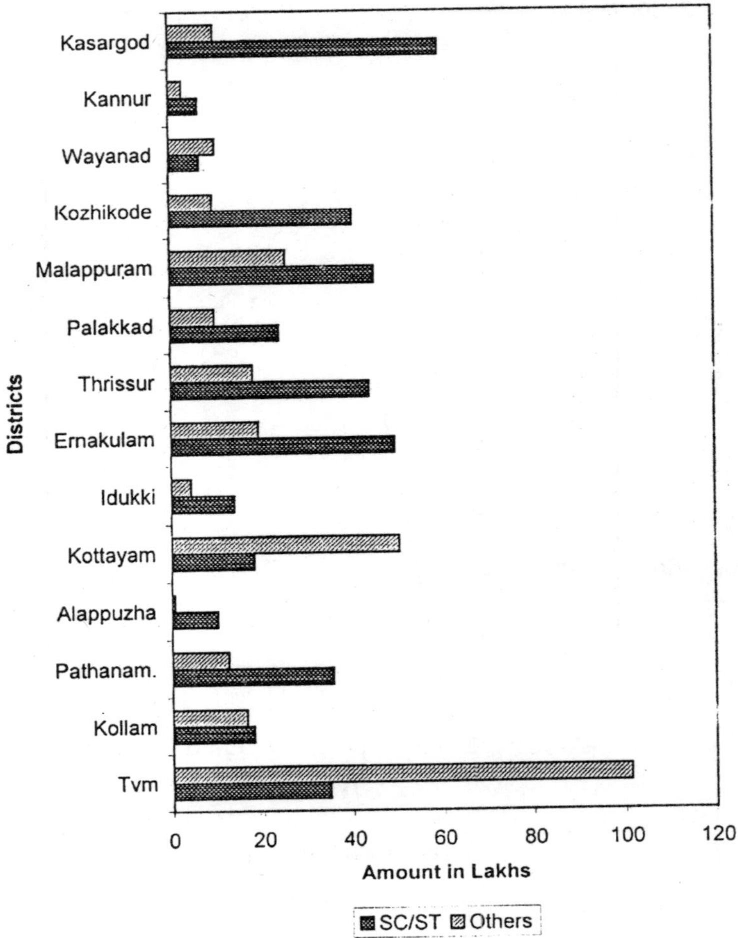

Appendix. X(i)

The percentage of amount spent for Latrines out of the total amount utilised for SC/ST and others under JRY during the 8th Plan in Kerala (1992-93 to 1996-97)

District	*SC/ST*		*Other*		*Total*	
	Amount	*%*	*Amount*	*%*	*Amount*	*%*
Trivandrum	34.77	2.64	101.33	8.00	136.10	5.27
Kollam	17.94	1.67	16.38	1.04	34.32	1.30
Pathanamthitta	35.62	5.06	12.43	1.41	48.05	3.03
Alappuzha	10.12	1.24	0.60	0.07	10.72	0.65
Kottayam	18.26	2.83	50.42	5.44	68.68	4.37
Idukki	13.97	1.09	4.41	0.35	18.38	0.72
Ernakulam	49.55	5.50	19.32	1.67	68.87	3.34
Thrissur	43.95	3.13	18.15	1.16	62.10	2.09
Palakkad	23.99	1.34	9.77	0.47	33.76	0.87
Malapuram	45.21	3.51	25.44	1.39	70.65	2.27
Kozhikode	40.47	4.36	9.48	0.61	49.95	2.01
Wyanad	6.81	0.78	10.19	1.13	17.00	0.96
Kannur	6.53	1.06	3.03	0.35	9.58	0.65
Kasaragod	59.76	4.29	10.05	0.66	69.81	2.40
Total	406.95	2.70	291.00	1.60	697.95	2.10

* Amount in lakhs.

** *Source:* Estimated from the respective data of JRY from the Rural Commissionerate.

Appendix. XI

Amount Spent for Latrines among SC/ST and Other under JRY During 8th Five Year Plan

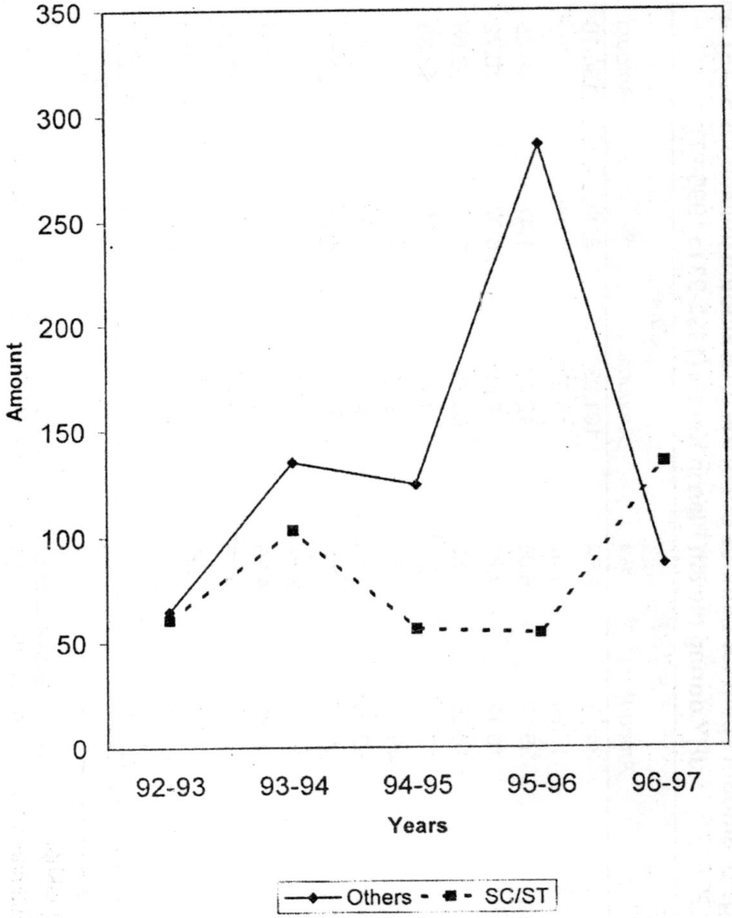

Appendix. XII
Amount Spent for Land Development in Various District under JRY During 8th Five Year Plan

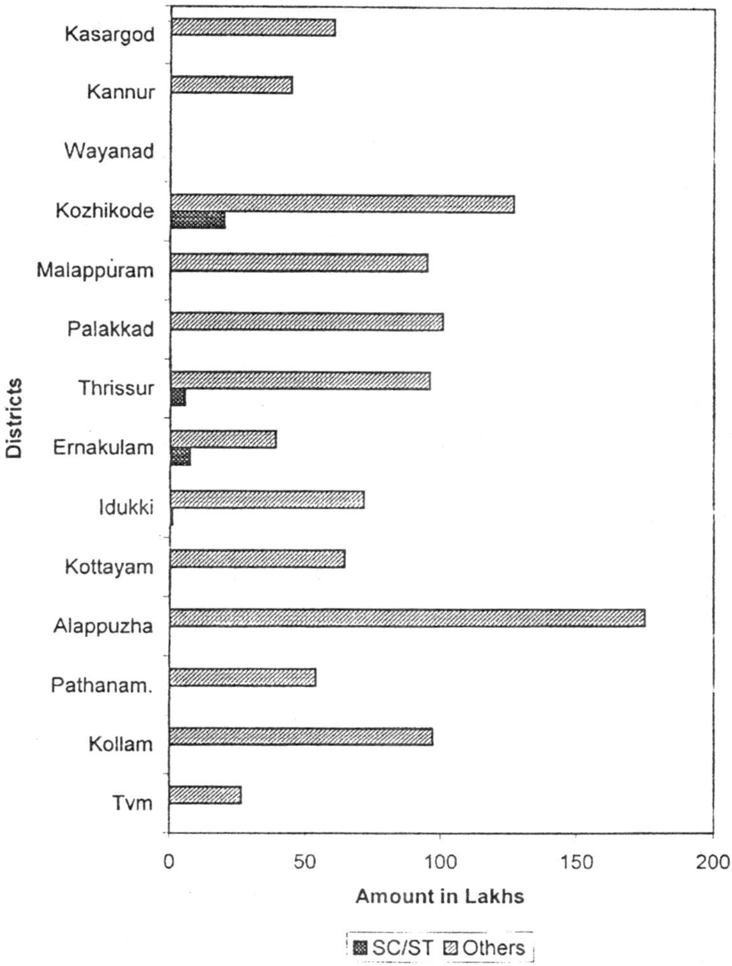

Appendix. XII (i)

The percentage of amount spent for Land Development out of the total amount utilised for SC/ST and others under JRY during the 8th Plan in Kerala (1992-93 to 1996-97)

District	*SC/ST*		*Other*		*Total*	
	Amount	*%*	*Amount*	*%*	*Amount*	*%*
Trivandrum	0.00	0.00	26.44	2.09	26.44	1.02
Kollam	0.00	0.00	96.97	6.17	96.97	3.66
Pathanamthitta	0.00	0.00	53.94	6.12	53.94	3.40
Alappuzha	0.00	0.00	174.86	21.08	174.86	10.61
Kottayam	0.00	0.00	64.58	6.96	64.58	4.11
Idukki	0.82	0.06	71.70	5.63	72.52	2.85
Ernakulam	7.35	0.82	38.96	3.37	46.31	2.25
Thrissur	5.59	0.40	95.71	6.11	101.30	3.41
Palakkad	0.00	0.00	100.54	4.83	100.54	2.59
Malapuram	0.00	0.00	94.83	5.19	94.83	3.05
Kozhikode	20.00	2.15	126.78	8.14	146.78	5.91
Wyanad	0.00	0.00	0.00	0.00	0.00	0.00
Kannur	0.00	0.00	44.60	5.22	44.60	3.03
Kasaragod	0.00	0.00	60.28	3.99	60.28	2.07
Total	33.76	0.22	1050.19	5.77	1083.95	3.26

* Amount in lakhs.

** *Source:* Estimated from the respective data of JRY from the Rural Commissionerate.

Appendix. XIII
Amount Spent for Land Development among SC/ST and Other under JRY During 8th Five Year Plan

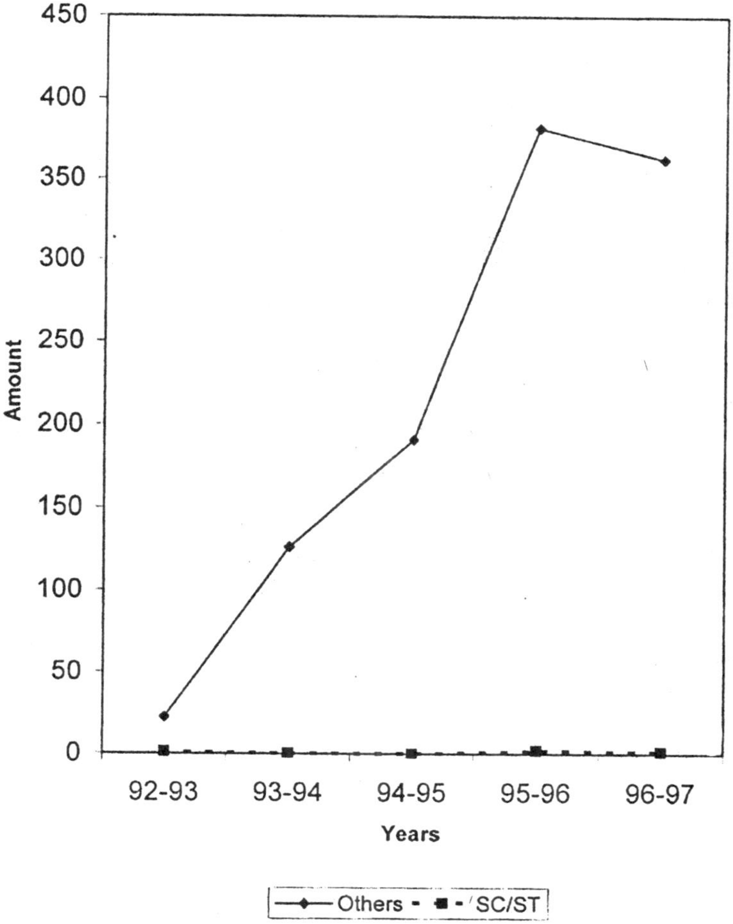

Appendix. XIV
Amount Spent for Building in Various Districts under JRY During 8th Five Year Plan

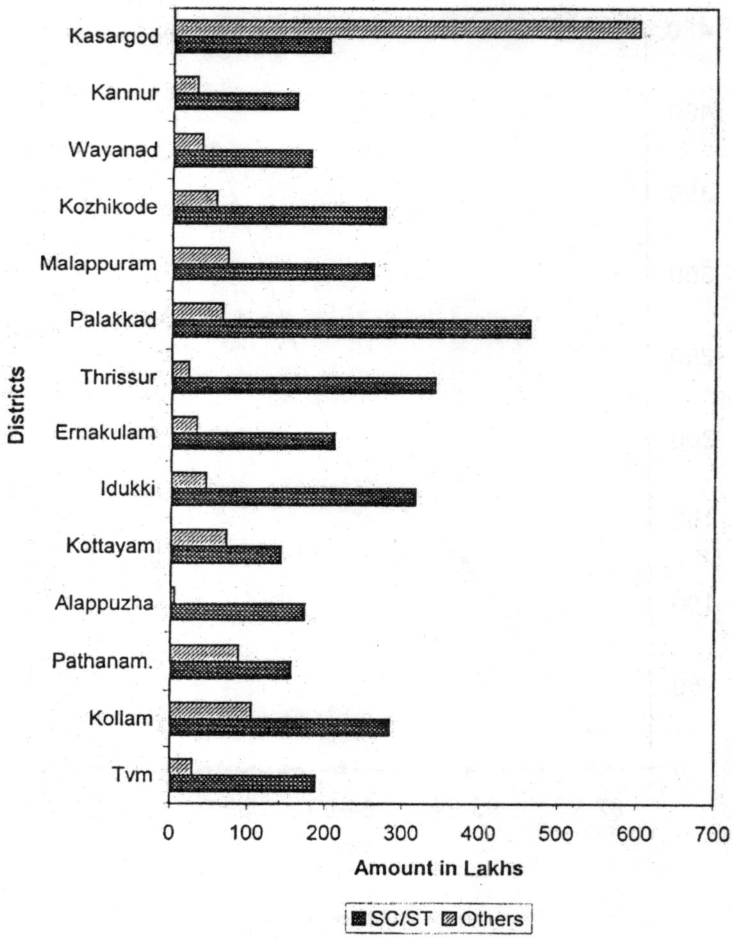

Appendix XIV (i)

The percentage of amount spent for Buildings out of the total amount utilised for SC/ST and others under JRY during the 8th Plan in Kerala (1992-93 to 1996-97)

District	*SC/ST*		*Other*		*Total*	
	Amount	*%*	*Amount*	*%*	*Amount*	*%*
Trivandrum	187.52	14.24	28.71	2.27	216.23	8.37
Kollam	283.50	26.37	104.63	6.66	388.13	14.66
Pathanamthitta	155.86	22.15	88.05	9.99	243.91	15.39
Alappuzha	172.54	21.08	4.56	0.55	177.10	10.75
Kottayam	141.93	22.00	71.68	7.73	213.61	13.58
Idukki	315.06	24.50	45.27	3.59	360.33	14.15
Ernakulam	210.11	23.30	32.76	2.83	242.87	11.80
Thrissur	340.51	24.23	21.87	1.40	362.38	12.19
Palakkad	462.22	25.73	65.23	3.13	527.45	13.60
Malappuram	259.48	20.17	71.80	3.93	331.28	10.64
Kozhikode	274.30	29.55	56.41	3.62	330.71	13.31
Wyanad	177.78	20.42	38.07	42.21	215.85	12.16
Kannur	159.44	25.79	31.10	3.64	190.54	12.94
Kasaragod	201.96	14.50	600.41	39.69	802.37	27.62
Total	3342.20	22.21	1260.55	6.93	4602.76	13.85

* Amount in lakhs.

** *Source:* Estimated from the respective data of JRY from the Rural Commissionerate.

Appendix. XV
Amount Spent for Building among SC/ST and Other under JRY During 8th Five Year Plan

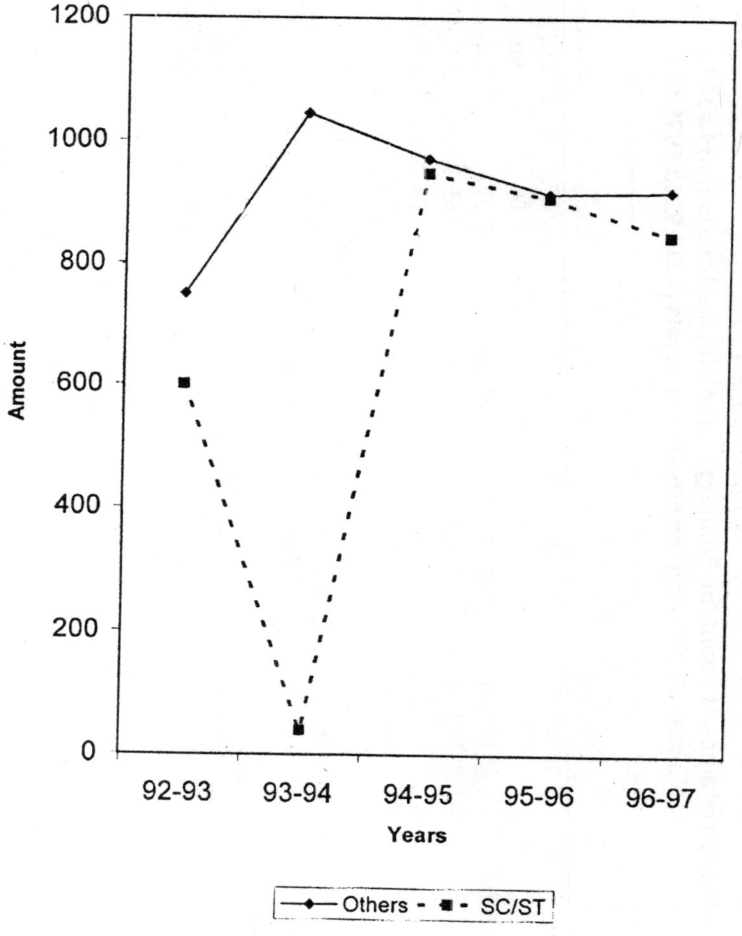

Appendix. XVI
Amount Spent for IAY in Various Districts under JRY During 8th Five Year Plan

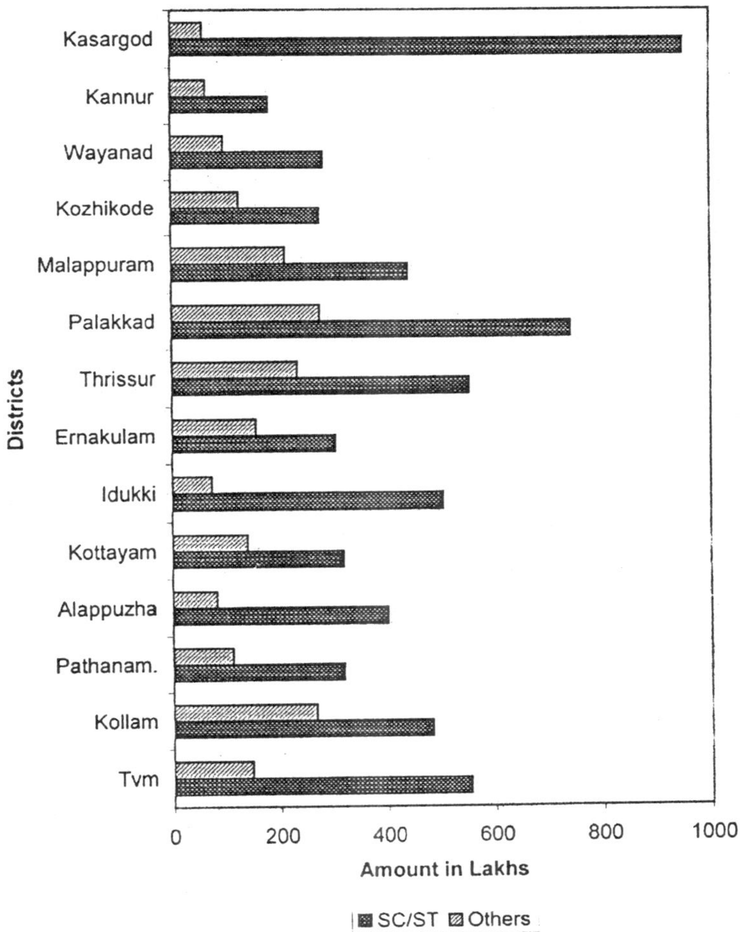

Appendix. XVI (i)

The percentage of amount spent for Indira Awaz Yojana out of the total amount utilised for SC/ST and others under JRY during the 8th Plan in Kerala (1992-93 to 1996-97)

District	*SC/ST*		*Other*		*Total*	
	Amount	*%*	*Amount*	*%*	*Amount*	*%*
Trivandrum	553.14	42.00	146.32	11.55	699.46	27.07
Kollam	482.82	44.90	265.97	16.92	748.79	28.29
Pathanamthitta	317.52	45.12	110.82	12.58	428.34	27.02
Alappuzha	399.43	48.79	82.04	9.89	481.47	29.21
Kottayam	317.33	49.18	139.32	15.02	456.65	29.03
Idukki	503.85	39.18	73.30	5.81	577.15	22.66
Ernakulam	304.00	33.72	155.99	13.48	459.99	22.34
Thrissur	553.74	39.41	233.13	14.87	786.87	26.47
Palakkad	742.06	41.31	275.09	13.21	1017.15	26.22
Malappuram	439.90	34.19	210.69	11.54	650.59	20.90
Kozhikode	275.35	29.66	125.22	8.04	400.57	16.12
Wyanad	283.58	32.57	96.96	10.73	380.54	21.44
Kannur	181.85	29.41	65.10	7.62	246.95	16.77
Kasaragod	951.00	68.29	58.80	3.89	1009.80	34.76
Total	6305.60	41.91	2038.75	11.20	8344.32	25.10

* Amount in lakhs.

** *Source:* Estimated from the respective data of JRY from the Rural Commissionerate.

Appendix. XVII
Amount Spent for IAY among SC/ST and Others under JRY During 8th Five Year Plan

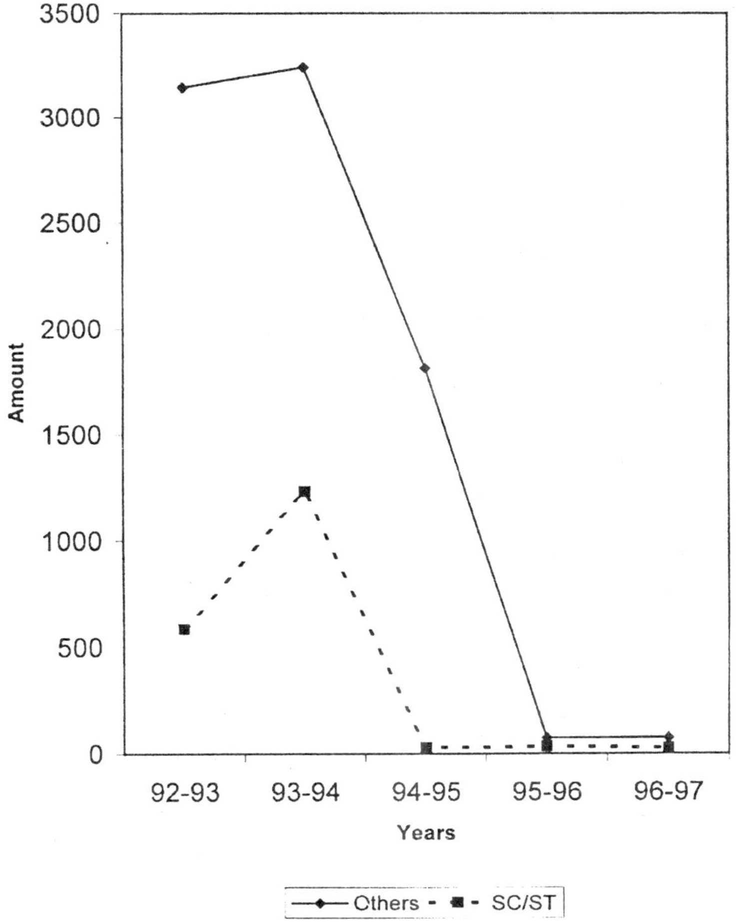

Appendix. XVIII
Amount Spent for Others Work in Various Districts under JRY During 8th Five Year Plan

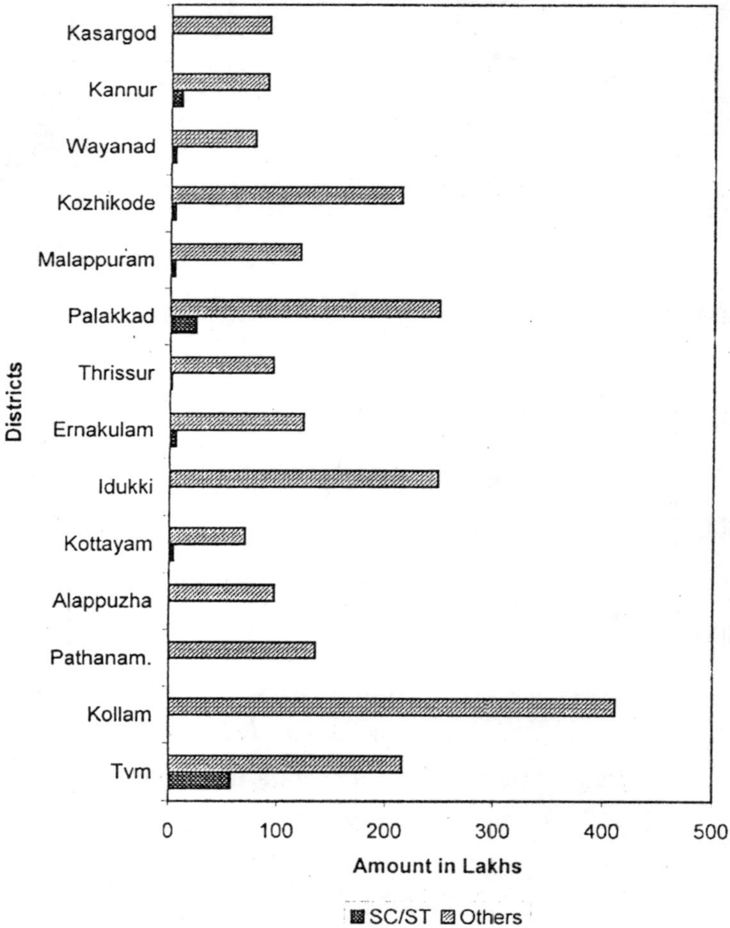

Appendix. XVIII (i)

The percentage of amount spent for Other Works out of the total amount utilised for SC/ST and others under JRY during the 8th Plan in Kerala (1992-93 to 1996-97)

District	*SC/ST*		*Other*		*Total*	
	Amount	*%*	*Amount*	*%*	*Amount*	*%*
Trivandrum	57.37	4.36	215.74	17.04	273.11	10.57
Kollam	0.00	0.00	411.01	26.15	411.01	15.53
Pathanamthitta	0.08	0.01	135.07	15.33	135.15	8.53
Alappuzha	0.00	0.00	97.10	11.72	97.18	5.90
Kottayam	3.56	0.55	69.95	7.54	73.51	4.67
Idukki	0.00	0.00	247.68	19.64	247.68	9.72
Ernakulam	6.09	0.68	123.02	10.63	129.11	6.27
Thrissur	1.49	0.11	95.24	6.08	96.73	3.25
Palakkad	24.12	1.34	248.75	11.94	272.87	7.03
Malappuram	4.06	0.32	119.97	6.57	124.03	3.98
Kozhikode	4.11	0.44	213.42	13.71	217.53	8.75
Wyanad	4.25	0.49	77.78	8.61	82.03	4.62
Kannur	9.90	1.60	89.36	10.46	99.26	6.74
Kasaragod	0.00	0.00	90.66	5.99	90.66	3.12
Total	115.03	0.76	2234.83	12.28	2349.86	7.07

* Amount in lakhs.

** *Source:* Estimated from the respective data of JRY from the Rural Commissionerate.

Appendix. XIX
Amount Spent for Others Work among SC/ST and Other under JRY During 8th Five Year Plan

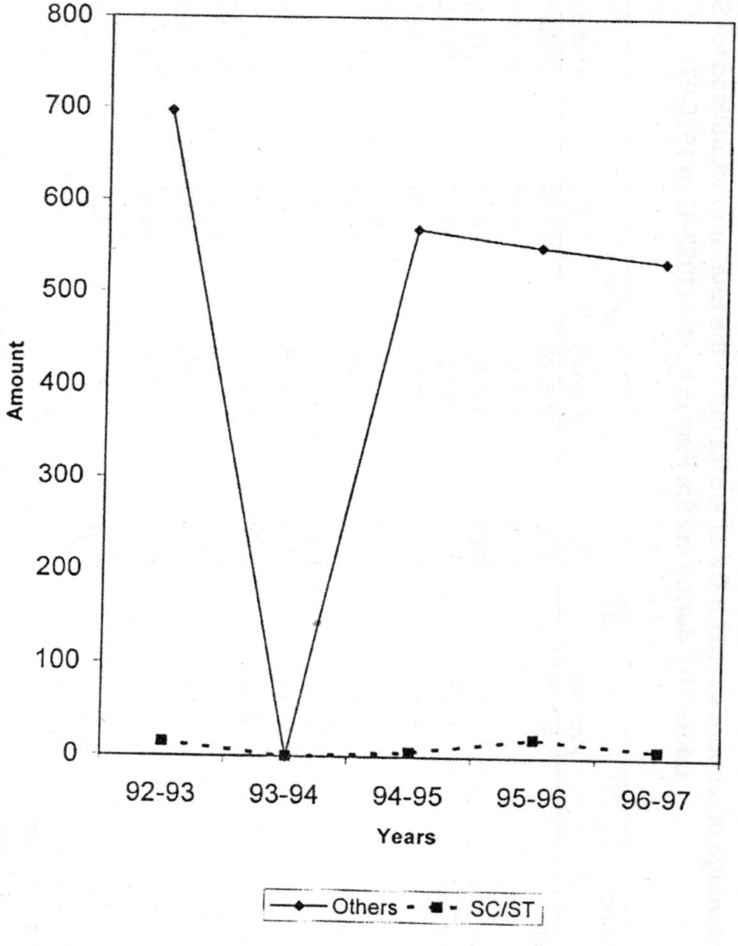

Appendix XIX (i)

The percentage of amount spent for Other Works out of the total amount utilised for SC/ST and others under JRY during the 8th Plan in Kerala (1992-93 to 1996-97)

District	*SC/ST*		*Other*		*Women*		*Total*	
	Amount	*%*	*Amount*	*%*	*Amount*	*%*	*Amount*	*%*
Trivandrum	18.18	10.11	31.10	2.4	13.55	1.81	49.29	3.35
Kollam	18.77	12.12	26.38	2.51	11.05	1.8	45.15	3.75
Pathanamthitta	13.75	16.67	17.92	3.5	11.52	3.76	31.57	5.33
Alappuzha	10.15	10.51	20.85	2.31	10.86	2.12	31.00	3.1
Kottayam	10.77	14	17.79	2.13	8.48	1.85	28.56	3.12
Idukki	24.21	23.37	24.31	5.59	14.34	5.39	48.55	9.01
Ernakulam	14.14	11.47	21.53	1.68	10.17	1.44	35.67	2.53
Thrissur	18.74	11.07	32.76	2.73	18.01	2.53	51.50	3.76
Palakkad	27.89	13.47	44.57	4.52	23.44	3.82	72.40	6.08
Malappuram	20.34	15.28	32.86	2.32	15.47	1.95	53.20	3.44
Kozhikode	9.18	9.66	27.42	2.26	7.47	1.13	36.60	2.79
Wyanad	14.61	20.46	16.28	6.15	12.28	7.44	30.99	9.22
Kasaragod	10.70	19.24	15.01	3.12	8.73	3.22	25.71	4.8
Total	221.62	13.82	348.56	2.69	173.17	2.34	570.18	3.92

* Amount in lakhs

** *Source:* Estimated from the respective data of JRY from the Rural Commissionerate

Appendix. XX
Total and Average Employment Generated in Various Districts During 8th Five Year Plan Under JRY in Kerala

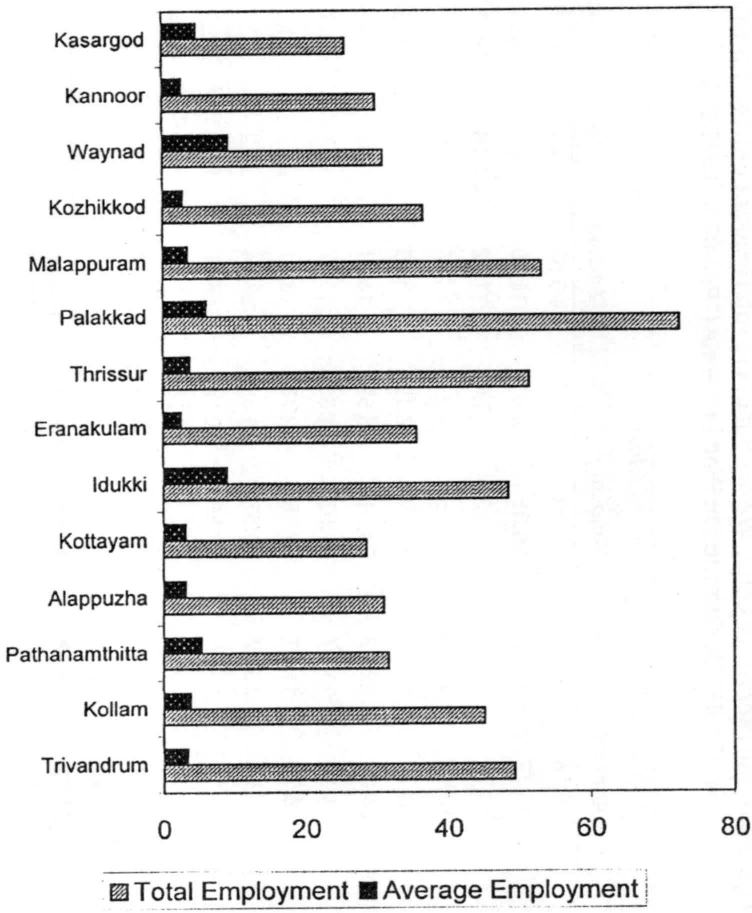

Appendix. XXI

Total and Average Employment Generated for Women in Various Districts During 8th Five Year Plan Under JRY in Kerala

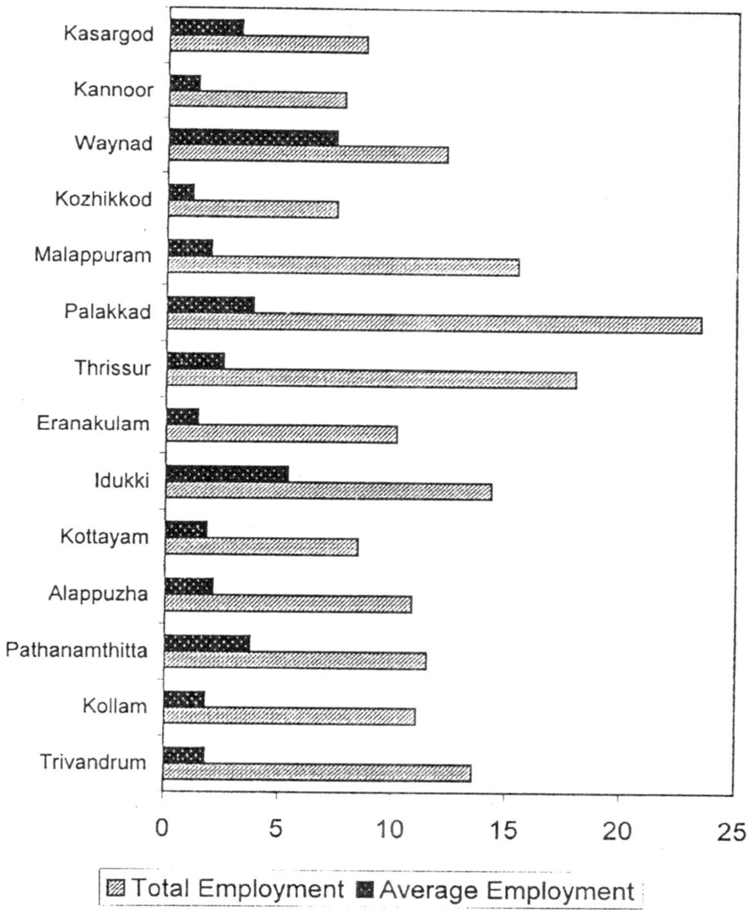

Appendix. XXII
Average Days of Employment Obtained under JRY During the 8th Five Year Plan

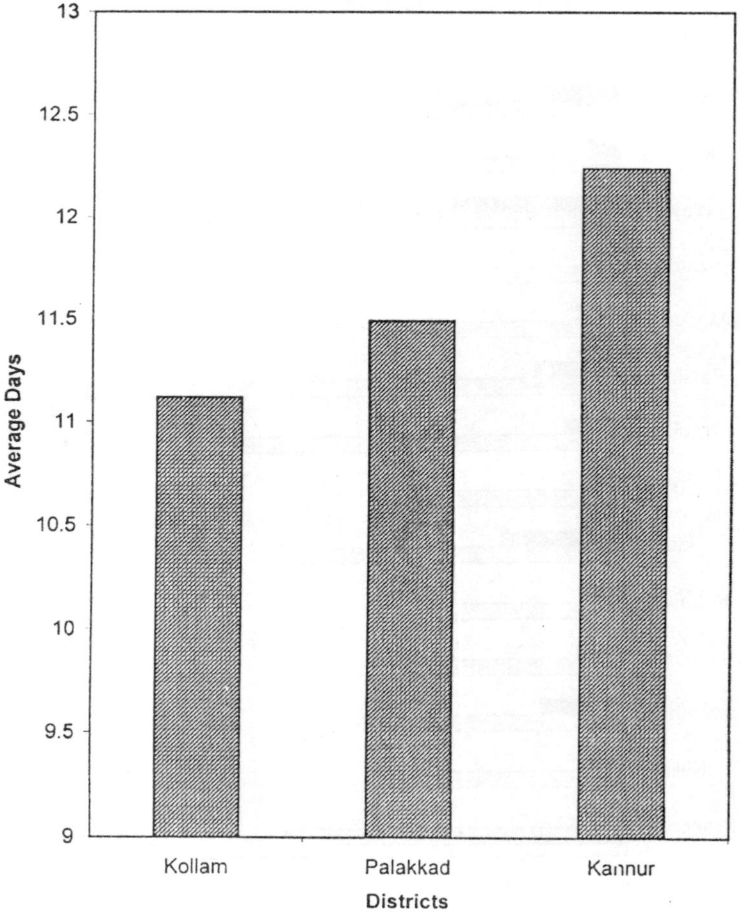

Appendix. XXIII
Average Employment Obtained Under JRY Per Yeare During 8th Five Year Plan for SC/St and Others

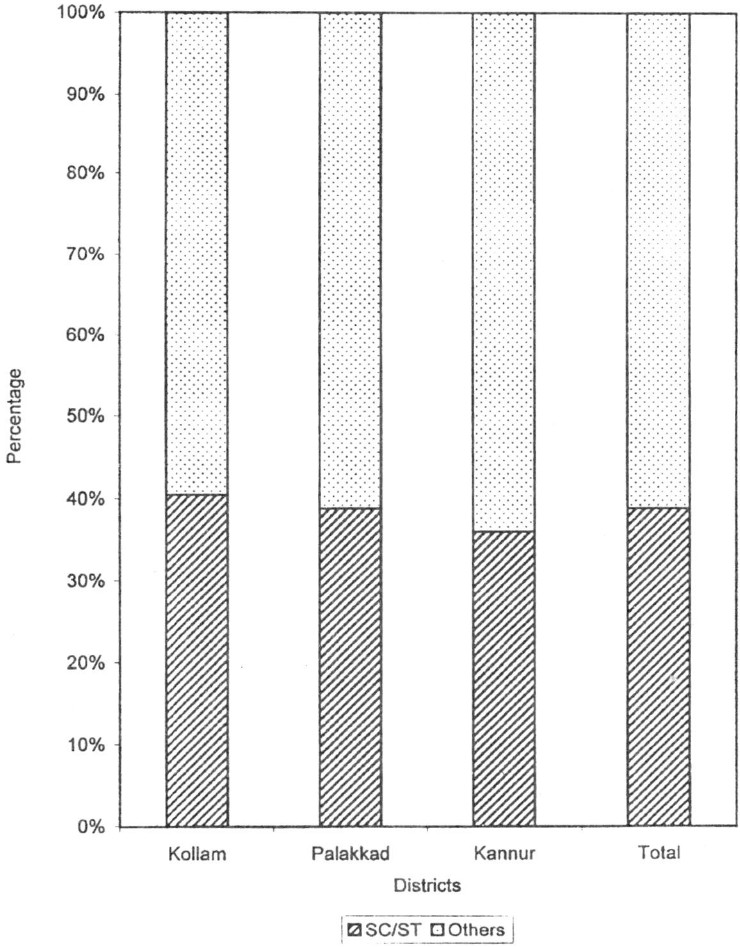

Appendix. XXIV
Average Employment Obtained Under JRY Per Yeare During 8th Five Year Plan for Women and Others

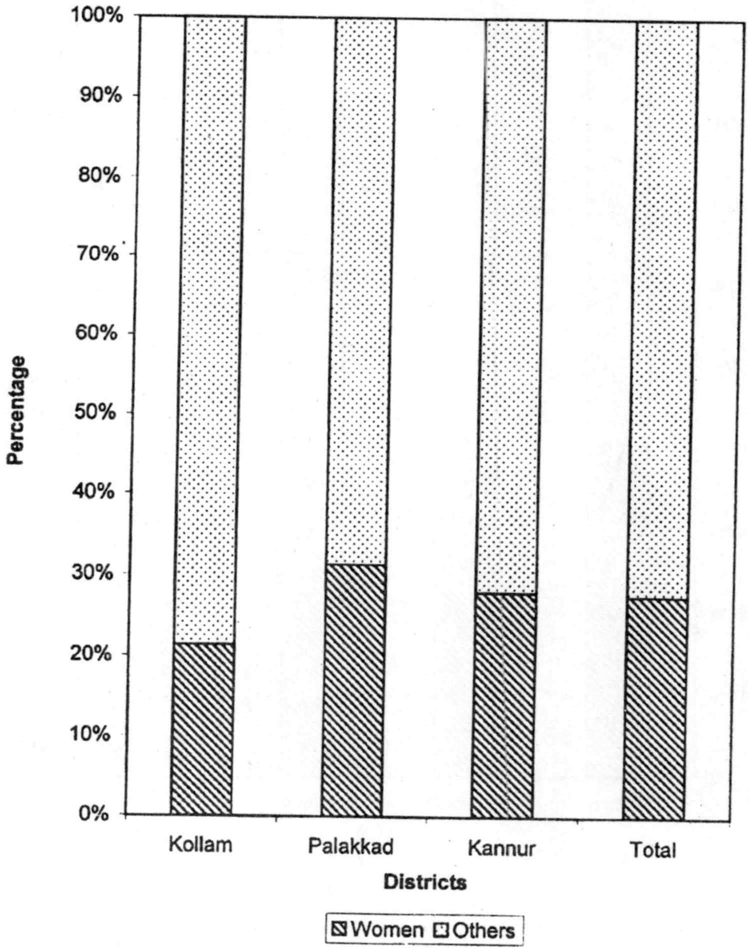

Appendix. XXV
The Nature of Employment Under JRY During 8th Five Year Plan

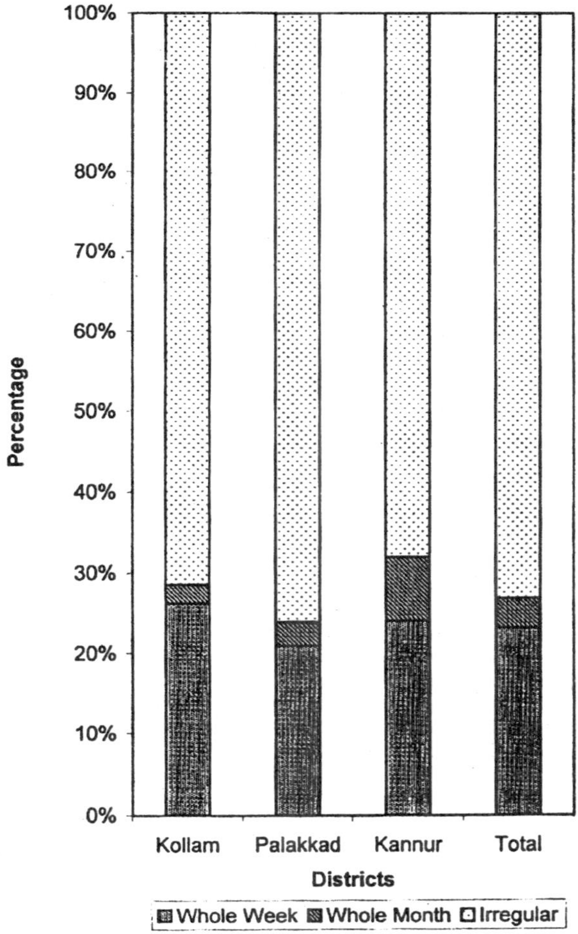

Appendix. XXVI
Season in which Employment Obtained under JRY Per Year During 8th Five Year Plan for Women and Others

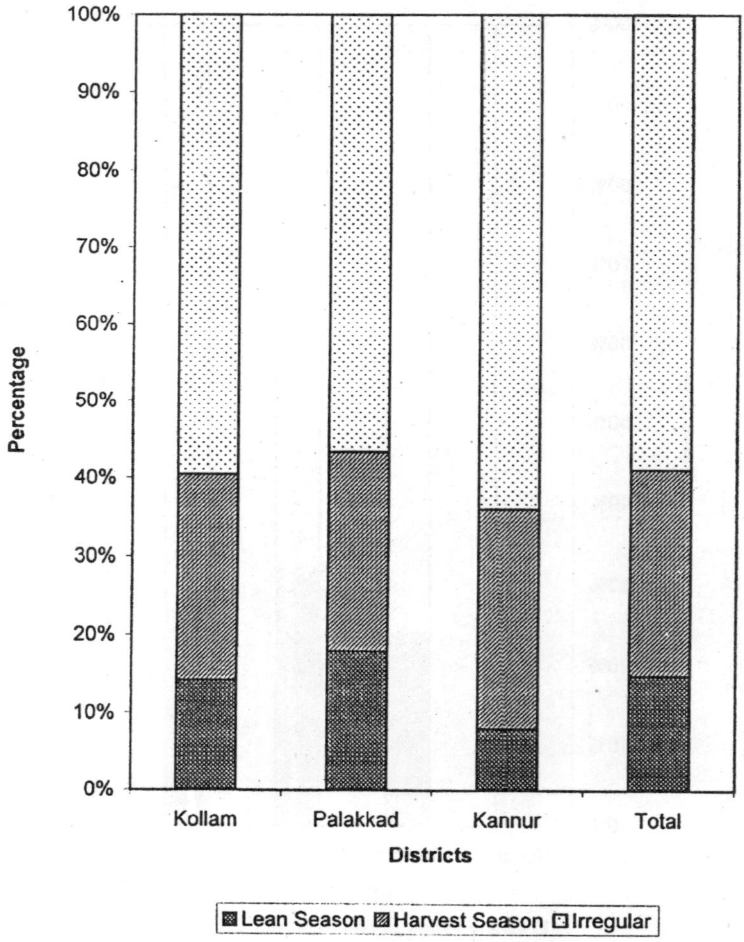

Appendix. XXVII
Pattern of Wage Obtained Under JRY Per Year During 8th five Year Plan

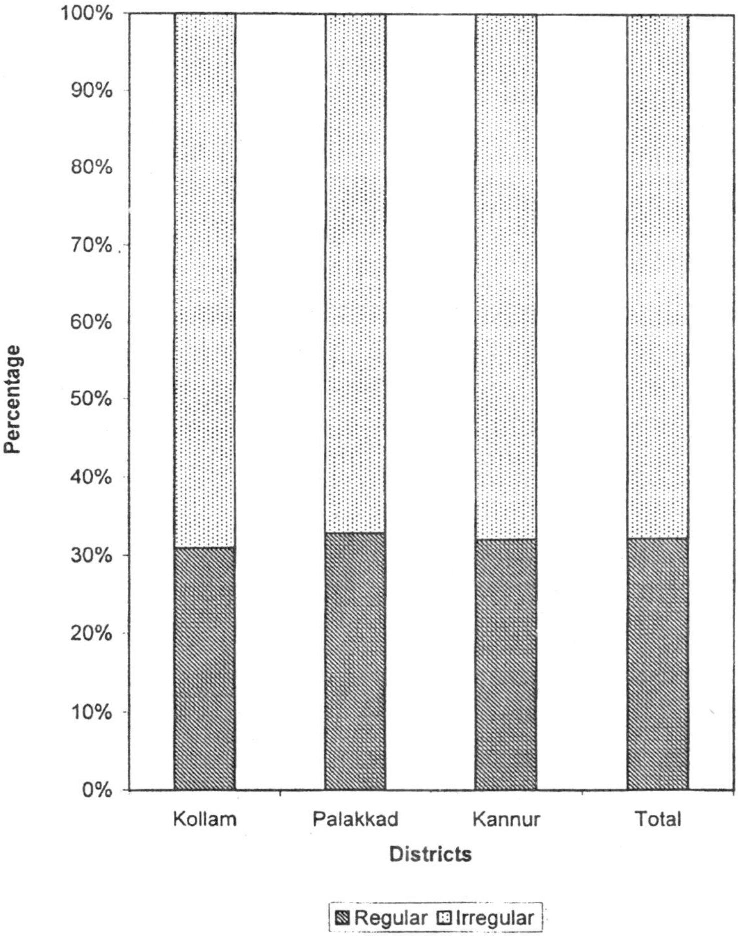

Bibliography

1. Adarkar, B., *Planning of Social Security in India*, (Allahabad: Kitabistan, 1994).
2. Adishesaiah, Malcolm, S., *Some Thoughts on the Seventh Five Year Plan*, (New Delhi : Dialogue Publishers, 1985).
3. Ahluwalia, Isher Judge; I.M.D. Little, *India's Economic Reforms and Development Essays For Manmohan Singh*, (New Delhi. Oxford University Press, 1998).
4. Ahmed, Furquan, *Bureaucracy and Development Administration*, (New Delhi: Manak Publishers, 1995).
5. Ahuja, Ram, *Social Problems in India*, (Jaipur : Rawat Publishers, 1997).
6. Alcock, Peta, *Social Policy in Britain Schemes and Issues*, (England: Macmillan Press Ltd, 1996).
7. Allmendinger, Philip, *Planning in Post Modern Times*, (London: Routledge Publishers, 2001).
8. Aravind, S., *Indian Administration*, (Bombay : Himalaya Publishers, 1992).
9. Armstrong, J; Armstrong, P., *Theorising Women's Work*, (Toronto:Garamond Press, 1990).
10. Arora, Ramesh K; Sangeeta Sharma, (eds.), *Comparative and Development Administration* : Ideas and Action, (Jaipur : Arihant Publishers, 1992).
11. Arora, Ramesh K., *Indian Administration: Perceptions and Perspectives*, (Jaipur : Aalekh Publishers, 1999).
12. Asavaraj, M.N; Rudra, *Global Human Growth Model Millennium Edition -2000*, (New Delhi : Himalaya Publishers, 2000).
13. Asirvatham, E., *Political Theory*, (New Delhi : Upper India Publishing House Ltd., 1965).

14. Baisya, K.N., *Financial Administration*, (New Delhi : Osmos Publishers, 1992).
15. Banerjee, Ajith M; Rekaran Chandra, K. A; *Renewing Governance Issues and Options*, (New Delhi: Tata Mc Graw Hill Publishing Company Ltd., 1996).
16. Banerjee, Surabhi, *Jyoti Basu: An Intimate Biography*, (Calcutta, Viking Penguin Ltd., 1997).
17. Bardan, Pranab, Poverty, *Agrarian Structure and Political Economy in India*, (New Delhi: Oxford University Press, 2003).
18. Basu, Durga Das, *Shorter Constitution of India* (12th Edn.), (New Delhi: Prentice Hall of India, 1996).
19. Basu, K. Dilip; Richard Sisson, (eds.), *Social and Economic Development in India*, (New Delhi: Sage Publications (Pvt.) Ltd., 1986).
20. Basu, Rumki, *Economic Liberalization and Poverty Alleviation*, (New Delhi : Deep and Deep Publishers, 2000).
21. Beveridge, Sir William, *Report on Social Insurance and Allied Services*,(London : Allen and Unwin M D D 6404, HMSO, 1942).
22. Bhadourie, B.P.S., Dua, S.C., *Rural Development Strategy and Perspective*, (New Delhi:Anmol Publications, 1986).
23. Bhandari, Anant, *Public Administration & Responsible Governance*, (New Delhi: Kaniska Publishers, Distributors, 1988).
24. Bhattacharya, Vivek, *Social Security Measures in India*, (New Delhi: Metropolitan Book Co. (Pvt.) Ltd., 1970).
25. Bihari Prasad Sing, Rash, *Social Welfare For Rural Development*,(New Delhi: Inter-India Publishers, 1985).
26. Biju, M.R., *Politics of Democracy and Decentralisation in India* : A Case Study of Kerala, (New Delhi : Atlantic Publishers, 1997).
27. Bramhmanda, P.R., Panchamuki, V.R., *Development Process of the India Economy*, (Bombay : Himalaya Publishers, 1987).
28. Bruce, Maurice, *The Coming of the Welfare State* (London : B.T. Batsford,1966).
29. Byres, Terencel, (ed.), *The State and Development Planning in India*, (New Delhi: Oxford University Press, 1993).

30. Chandra, Ashok, Kabra, Shilpa, (eds.), *Human Resource Strategy- Architecture For Change*, (New Delhi, Saga Publication, 2000).
31. Chathukulam, Jose John, M.S., *Sen Committee and Panchayati Raj*, (Kottayam : Current Books and Publishers, 1998).
32. Chellaih, R.J., and Sudarshan, R, (eds.), *Income, Poverty and Beyond; Human Development in India*, (New Delhi: Social Science Press, 1999).
33. Chowdhry, Paul, *Social Welfare Administration,* (New Delhi : Alma Ram and Son Publishers, 1992).
34. Dev, S. Mahendra, Antony, Piyush, Gayatri, V., Mangain, R.P., (eds.), *Social and Economic Security in India*, (New Delhi: Institute for Human Development, 2001).
35. Devi, Laxmi, *Planning For Employment and Rural Development,* (Lucknow: Institute For Sustainable Development, Anmol Publishers, 1997).
36. Dobb, Maurice, *An Essay on Growth and Planning,* (London : Routledge and Kegan Pant, 1960).
37. Dreze, Jean; Sen, Amartya, *India Development Selected Regional Perspectives,* (Delhi : Oxford University Press, 1998).
38. Dreze, Jean, Sen, Amartya, *Hunger and Public Action: Human Development in India*, (New Delhi:Oxford University Press, 1989).
39. Dubashi, P.R., *Grammar of Planning*, (New Delhi: Indian Institute of Public Administration, 1983).
40. Dube, S.C., *India's Changing Villages: Human Factors in Community Development*, (Mumbai : Allied Publishers, 1958.).
41. Dutt, Ruddar; Sundaram, K.P.M., *Development Issues of Indian Economy*, (New Delhi : S. Chand and Company Ltd., 1995)
42. Dwivedi, P. Onkar, Jain, R.B., Vajpayee, K. Dhirendr (eds.),. *Governing India, Issues Concerning Public Policy: Institutions and Administration*, (New Delhi: RR Publishing Corporation, 1998).
43. Fatia, B.L.; Menaria, P.K. (eds.), *Sarkariah Commission Report and Center State Relations,* (Agra : Sahitya Bhawan, 1990).
44. Forder, Antony, Terry Caslin, Geoffrey Pontoon and Sandra Walklate (eds), *Theories of Welfare*, (London: Routledge & Kegan Paul, 1984).

45. Gangopadhyay, Shubhashis and Wadhwa, Wilma, (ed.), *Economic Reforms For the Poor*, (New Delhi : Konark Publishers, 2000).

46. George, K.K., Nair, Sankaran and Jacob, George, *Economic Development and Quest For Alternatives*, (New Delhi: Concept Publishers, 1997).

47. Ghosh, S., *H. R. D. in the Third World : Quest For Empowerment*, (New Delhi: Vikas Publishing House and Lal Bahadur Shastri Nation Academy Mussorie, 1996).

48. Gibaldi, Joseph, *The Modern language Association of America*: Handbook for Writers of Research Papers, (New Delhi: East West Books (Pvt.) Ltd. 5th Edn, 1999).

49. Goel, S.L., *Advanced Public Administration*, (New Delhi : Sterling Publishers, 1994).

50. Gore, M.S., *Social Aspect of Development*, (Jaipur : Rawat Publishers,1985).

51. Government of India, *A Concurrent Evaluative Study*, (New Delhi : Planning Commission 1992).

52. Government of Kerala, *Jawahar Rozgar Yojana* (Manual), (Thiruvananthapuram: Rural Information Bureau, 1996).

53. Griappa, S., *Evaluation of Rural Development Programmes*, (New Delhi: Mohit Publication, 1998).

54. Grower, Verinder, *Political Process, Government Structure and Administration*, (New Delhi : Deep and Deep Publishers, 1997).

55. Gulati, I.S., George, K.K. (eds), *Essays in Federal Financial Relations*, (New Delhi: Oxford and IBH Publishing Co. (Pvt) Ltd., 1988).

56. Gupta, D.N., *Rural Development System*, (New Delhi : Books India International, 2001).

57. Halder, Srinath, *Indian Economy Challenges Beyond 9th Plan*, (Jaipur: Book Enclave Publishers, 2000).

58. Haragopal, G., *Administrative Leadership and Rural Development in India,* (New Delhi : Light and Life Publishers, 1980).

59. Heady, Ferrel, *Public Administration : A Comparative Perspective*, (Michigan: Institute of Public Administration, 1966).

60. Howard, Jones, *Social Welfare in Third World Countries,* (London: Macmillan, 1999).
61. Isacc, Thomas and Franke, W. Richard, *Local Democracy and Development, People's Campaign for Decentralised Planning in Kerala*, (New Delhi: Leftward Book, 1999).
62. Jain, M.P., *Indian Constitutional Law* (4th Edn.), (Nagpur : Wadhwa and Company, 1993).
63. Jhunjhunwala, Bharat, *Welfare State and Globalisation : Critique of Amartya Sen*, (New Delhi: Rawat Publishers, 2000).
64. Kirit, S. and Parikh, (ed.), *India Development Report*, (New Delhi: Indira Gandhi Institute of Development Research. Oxford University Press, 1997).
65. Krishnan, K.C., Sivarama, *Power to the People: The Policies and Programmes of Decentralization,* (New Delhi : Konark Publishers, 2000).
66. Krishnaswamy, O.R., *Methodology of Research in Social Sciences*, (Mumbai: Himalaya Publishing House, 1999).
67. Kumar, Nagesh, (ed.), *Indian Economy Under Reforms: An Assessment of Economic and Social Impact*, (New Delhi: Bookwell, 2000).
68. Kurup, K.K.N, *Modern Kerala : Studies in Social and Agrarian Relations*, (New Delhi: Mittal Publication, 1998).
69. Lassen, A. Cheryl, *Reaching the Assetless Rural Poor*, (New Delhi: India Social Institute, 1983).
70. Maheshwari S.R., *Rural development in India,* (New Delhi: sage Publications, 1985).
71. Mathew, E.T. , *Employment and Unemployment in Kerala: Some Neglected Aspects*, (New Delhi : Sage Publishers, 1997).
72. Mathew, K.K., *Impact of Welfare Programmes on the Life of Scheduled Castes of Kerala: A Caste Study of Pulayas,*(Unpublished PhD. Dissertation, University of Kerala, Thiruvananthapuram, 1992).
73. Mathew, N.T., *A Development Monitoring Service At the Local Level: Socio Economic Observation Areas in Kerala*, (Geneva : Wolf Scott. U. N. Research Institute For Social Development, Vol. 1,1980).

74. Mathur, Kuldeep, *Development Policy and Administration*, (New Delhi : Sage Publishers, 1996).

75. Mehta, R., Shiva, *Rural Development Policies and Programmes. A Sociological Perspective,* (New Delhi : Sage Publishers, 1984).

76. Menon A., Sreedharan, *A Survey of Kerala History*, (Kottayam: National Book Stall, 1976).

77. Mukerji, B., *Community Development in India*,(Bombay: Orient Longman Ltd; 1961).

78. Mukherjee, Subrata; Sushila Ramaswamy, (ed.), *Political Science Annual 1999 : Focus on Theory*, (New Delhi : Deep and Deep Publishers, 1999).

79. Myrdal, Gunnar, *Asian Drama : An Inquiry Into the Poverty of Nations,* (Vol, 1 & 2) England Penguin Books, 1968.).

80. Nair, A. Balakrishnan, *Landmarks in the Administration of Kerala.,* (Trivandrum : Indian Institute of Public Administration, 1996).

81. Nair, N. Ayyappan, *Gramavikasanavum Panchayati Rajum,* (Malayalam) (Thiruvananthapuram: The State Institute of Languages, 1997).

82. Nampoothiripad, E.M.S., *"Kerala thinte Vikasana Prassnangal",* (Malayalam) (Thiruvananthapuram: Desabhimani Book House, 1999.).

83. Oommen, M. A., (ed.), *Rethinking Development: Kerala's Development Experience,* (New Delhi : Institute of Social Sciences, Concept Publishers, Vol. 1, 2, 1999).

84. Osmani, Rahman, Siddique, *Economic Inequality and Group Welfare. A Theory of Comparison With Application to Bangladesh*,(Oxford : Clarendon Publishers, 1982).

85. Oyen, Else, Miller, S.M; Abdus, Sayed, Samad, *Poverty: A Global Review,* (Jaipur: Rawat Publications, 2003).

86. Palambara, Joseph La, (ed.), *Bureaucracy and Political Development,* (Princeton: N. J. Prinston University Press, 1963).

87. Panandikar, V. A.; Kshirsagar, *Bureaucracy and Development Administration*, (New Delhi : 1978).

88. Panikkar, K.K., *Community Development Administration in Kerala,* (New Delhi : S. Chand and Co. Publishers, 1974).
89. Parayil, Govindan, (ed.), *Kerala : The Development Experience,* (London: Zed Books 2000).
90. Pherson, Christopher, *Beyond the Welfare State,* (London: Blackwell Publishers Ltd., 1998).
91. Phillee and Cohin, Raban, *Welfare Theory and Social Policy : Reform or Revolutions,* (New Delhi : Sage Publishers, 1998).
92. Pillai, Balachandran, P.G., *Political Process of the Cooperative Sector: A Study on the Primary Cooperative Banks in Kerala,* (Unpublished PhD. Dissertation, University of Kerala, Thiruvananthapuram, 1999).
93. Pinto,R, Marina; Srinivasan R., *Development Administration,* (Bombay : Himalay Publishers, 1990).
94. Prasad, K.N, *An Outline of Growth Development and Planning,* (Bombay: Himalaya Publishers, 1992).
95. Prasad, Kamta, *Planning For Poverty Alleviation,* (New Delhi : Agricole Publishing Academy 1985).
96. Pulparambil, John, *Panchayat Raj: Oru Management Sameepanam* (Malayalam), (Thiruvananthapuram: Institute of Management in Government, EGMI Services, 1995).
97. Purushottam, D. Vashisht, *Raj to the Indian Raj,* (New Delhi: RNC Print and Publishing Co., 1989).
98. Quibrin, M.G., (ed.), *Rural Poverty in Developing Asia (Vol. 1) Bangladesh, India and Srilanka,* (Asian Development Bank, 1994).
99. Rahim P., Abudu; Kumar Suresh, *Perspectives on Human Rights,* (New Delhi: Manak Publishers, 1999).
100. Ramachandran, Padma; Oommen M. A.. (eds.), *Some Issues in Development Administration,* (New Delhi: Oxford and IBH Publishing Company, 1987).
101. Ramachandran, Padma, *Public Administration in India,* (New Delhi : National Book Trust of India, 1995).
102. Ramadas, Bhatkal, (ed.), *Alternative Strategies and India's Development,* (Mumbai: Popular Prakashan, 1999).
103. Ramnatha Aiyar, Sundara, Stewart Ashgate and Macpherson, *Social Development in Kerala: Illusion or Reality,* (USA. 2000.).

104. Rao C. N., Bhaia, *Administration, Politics and Development in India,* (Bombay: Lavani Publishing House, 1972).

105. Rao M., Sankara, *Public Administration and Management, Special Reference to India,* (New Delhi : Deep and Deep Publishers, 1991).

106. Raphael, Jose, *Decentralized Planning in India,* (New Delhi : Anmol Publications, 2000).

107. Rath, S.N., *The Development of the Welfare State in Orissa,* (New Delhi:Chand and Chand Company, 1977).

108. Ray, Biswanth, (ed.), *Welfare Choice and Development : Essays in Honor of Professor Amartya Sen,* (New Delhi : Kanishka Publishers, 2001).

109. Reddy S., Mahendra, Reddy, Reddy, Yadava, K.S. Upadhyay and C.L.Reghuiam (eds.), *Seventh Five Year Plan: Performance and Perspectives,* (New Delhi :Sterling Publishers, 1989.

110. Robson, William A; *Welfare State and Welfare Policy. Illusion and Reality,* (London : George Allen and Unwin Ltd. 1976).

111. Roll, Eric; *A History of Economic Thought,* (London: Faber and Faber Ltd, 1953).

112. Sachdeva, D.R., *Social Welfare Administration in India,* (Allahabad : Kitab Mahal Publishers, 1993).

113. Sachs, Ignacy; *Understanding Development,* (New Delhi : Oxford University Press, 2000).

114. Sainath, E.N., Payananan, *JP on Village Autonomy,* (Chennai: Compiled by Gandhibai Shah, 203).

115. Sainath, *Everybody Loves a Good Drought,* (New Delhi: Penguin Books, 1996).

116. Saini, R.C; Gupta, R.K., *Peoples Power Indian Reality,* (New Delhi: Commonwealth Publishers, 1994).

117. Sapru, P.K., *Development Administration,* (New Delhi : Sterling Publisher, 1994).

118. Sathish, S.; Gawati, *The Impact of Economic Development and Rural Participation - A Case Study,* (New Delhi : Himalaya Publishers, 2000).

119. Seervai, H.M., *Constitutional Law of India: A Critical Commentary,* (Bombay: NM Tripathi (Pvt) Ltd., 4 Vols, 1996).

120. Sharma, Aruna; Rajagopal, *Planning For Rural Development Administration,* (New Delhi : Rawat Publications, 1995).

121. Sharma, B.A.V., Prasad, Raveendra, D., Satyanarayana, P., (eds.), *Research Methods in Social Sciences,* (New Delhi: Sterling Publishers (Pvt) Ltd., 1989).

122. Sharma, B.R., *Socio-Economic Justice Under Indian Constitution.*, (New Delhi: Deep and Deep Publishers, 1984.).

123. Sharma, S.C., Prakash, Jai and Gupta, Anitha, *Decentralized Planning in India*, (New Delhi : Mohit Publishers 1997).

124. Sharma, S.K., *Dynamics of Development : An International Perspective* (Vol. 2) (New Delhi : Concept Publishers, 1997).

125. Sharma, S.K.., (ed.), *Administrative Systems of Developing Societies*, (New Delhi : Mittal Publications, 2000).

126. Shastri, Siddharth, *Financing of State Five Year Plans in India*, (New Delhi : Mittal Publishers, 1992).

127. Singh, Anhimanya, *Strategy For Economic Development of Backward Region*, (New Delhi: Anmol Publishers, 1997).

128. Singh, Hoshiar, Singh, Mohinder, *Public Administration in India: Theory and Practice*, (New Delhi : Sterling Publishers, 1995).

129. Singh, Mohinder, (ed.), *Rural Development in India :Current Perspectives*, (New Delhi : Intellectual Publishers, 1992).

130. Singh, Yogendra, *Social Change in India: Crisis and Resilience,* (New Delhi: Har Anand Publications, 1996).

131. Sinha, R.K., (ed.), *Economic Development Planning and Policy in India*, (New Delhi : Deep & Deep Pulishers, 1989).

132. Sinha, R.K., Har Anand, (ed.), *Planning and Development in India*, (New Delhi : Indian Economic Trust For Research and Development, 1994).

133. Sundaran, K.U., *Decentralised Multilevel Planning Principles and Practice: Asian and African Experience*, (New Delhi : Concept Publishers, 1999).

134. Tax Research Institute, *Fifty Years of Economic Planning in India 1950-2000*, (New Delhi : Indian Tax Services 2000).

135. Thevaraj, M.J.K., *Financial Administration of India*, (New Delhi: Sultan Chand and Sons, 1978).

136. Titumuss, M. Richard, *Esays On The Welfare State,* (3rd Edn.), (London:George Allen and Unwin Ltd., 1976).

137. Varma, Ram K., *Rural Development and Anti – Poverty Programme,* (Jaipur : Print Well Publishers, Vol 6, 1995).

138. Varma, S.C., *Millions in Poverty Grip. India's Rural Works Programme,* (New Delhi : Kunju Publication House, 1984).

139. Visalakshi, N. R., *Administration of Village Panchayats in Kerala,* (Thiruvananthapuram. Educational Supplies Dept. 1967.).

140. Vyshalu, Vinod, *Panchayats, Democracy and Development,* (Jaipur: Rawat Publications, 2003).

141. Walker, Alan, *Social Planning: A Strategy For Socialist Welfare,* (Oxford : Basil Blackwell, 1984).

148. Waterston, Albert, *Development Planning-Lessons of Experience;* (Baltimore: John Hopkins Press, 1965).

Articles

1. Bagshi, Amaresh ; "Rethinking Federalism, Overview of Current Debates With Some Reflections in Indian Context", *Economic and Political Weekly* 19 Aug. 2000, 3025-35.

2. Bandopadhyay, D., "Panchayats and Democracy Elites Versus Dalits", *Man and Development* Vol XXI, 4, December 1996, 69-84.

3. Fan, Shenggen, Hazel, Peter; and S.K.Throat, "Impact of Public Expendi ture on Poverty in Rural India", *Economic and Political Weekly* 30 Sept. 2000, 3581-3588.

4. Franco, Fernando "Poverty Reduction: Challenges and Opportunities", *Social Action* Vol. 49. October – December 1999, 355 –370.

5. Ghatak, Maitreesh and Maitreya Ghatak, "Recent References in the Panchayat System in West Bengal Towards Greater Participatory Governance", *Economic and Political Weekly,* Januray 2002, 45-58.

6. Jain, Kamal; "Social Justice in Indian Constitution", *Prashasanika,* Vol. XXII Number 2 July – Dec 1995, 35-40.

7. Jaya Kumar, E.C., "Impact of Development Programmes on Scheduled Castes and Scheduled Tribes : A Critical Appraisal", *Indian Association of Social Science Institutions* Vol. 17. No 2 1998,76-92.

8. Kar, Samit, "More Determined Bid Needed in Ninth Plan", *Mainstream* Vol XXX, 45 , 18 October, 1997, 12-14.
9. Kripashankar, "Poverty in India", *Man and Development* Vol. XVIII No A December 1996, 109-112.
10. Kumar, R.S., "Panchayati Raj and Poverty Alleviation; Need for New Administrative Structure", *Prashasanika*, Vol XXII Number 2, July – Dec 1995, 5-9.
11. Mathew George, 'Ten Years On", The Hindu, Dec, 27, 2002, 10.
12. Mahesh, C., "Mobilizing Resources for Planned Development : A Case Study of Rajasthan", *Administrative Change* Vol XXXV, 10, 4 March , 2000. 823- 835.
13. Mahesh, C., "Mobilizing Resources for Planned Development : A Case Study of Rajasthan", *Administrative Change* Vol XXVI No. 2 & Vol. XXVII No. Jan./ Dec. 1999.
14. Mahesh, Prasad "Human Development Report: New Index of Poverty", *Yojana*. Sept. 20000, 11-32.
15. Mathew, Geroge, " Decentralized Institutions. Governmental and Voluntary Sector", *Economic and Political Weekly*. Vol. XXXIV , 9, 27 Feb. 1999, 529-533.
16. Mehta, Prayag; " Human Development Performance in India : State Functioning and Management Programmes", *Man and Development* Vol XVIII 2, June, 1996, 72-95.
17. Nagara,j K., "Decentralization in Kerala: A Note", Discussion Paper Series *Kerala Research Programme on Local Level Development*. Center for Development Studies: TVM Jan. 1999, 1- 11.
18. Pal, R.M., "Radical Humanism and Panchayati Raj", *Main Stream* Vol XXXVI,13,21 March 1998, 5-6.
19. Patnaik, Santhosh, " Poverty Alleviation Programmes: Fifty Years of Planning", *Social Welfare* Vol. 95 No 3 June 1998.
20. Punalekar, S.P, "People and Panchayats: Interfaces and Contradictions", *IASSI*, New Delhi: Vol. 19, January-March 2001.
21. Reddy, Rammanohar; "Poverty and Unemployment in the 1990s", *The Hindu,* Saturday, 20 Jan, 2001, 12.

22. Shrivastava, Ramesh, C., "Panchayati Raj and Rural Development in India", *Prashasnika,* Vol XXV 2 July / Dec. 1998.
23. Singh, Kanwaljit, "Micro Credit Myths: No Lending Hand for the Poor", *The Times of India*, Bangalore: Jan 30, 2003, 10.
24. Singh, Ajith Kumar. "Panchayati Raj Legislation in Selected States : A Comparative Study", *Man and Development Vol XVIII*, 3 Sept. 1996, 15-35.
25. Srivastava, I.C., "Rural Development : A New Strategy", *Prashasnika*, Vol XXV, 2, July/ December 1998, 39-55.
26. Srivastava, I.C., "Empowering Panchayats for Good Governance", *Yojana* Vol. 44 No 10 October 2000, 29-31.
27. Srivastava, Ramesh, C.. " Rural Development in India: Restructuring Poverty Alleviation Strategy", *Prashasnika.* Vol XXVI 2, July / Dec 1999.
28. Yerankar, K. Shriram, " Human Right and India", *Yojana* Vol. 44; 12, Decebber, 2000, 16-18.

Reports

1. Government of India, Report of the Team for Study of Community Projects and National Extension Service, Vol. 1, New Delhi: 1957.
2. Government of Kerala, 8th Five Year Plan, Report on JRY (Physical & Financial Achievements) Commissionerate of Rural Development, Thiruvananthapuram, 1993-97.
3. Government of India, Report of on the Team for the Study of Community Projects and National Extension Service, New Delhi: 1975.
4. Government of India, Report of the Working Group on Block Level Planning, New Delhi: 1978.
5. Government of India, Report on the Committee on Panchayati Raj Institutions (Ashok Mehta Committee), 1978.
6. Government of India, Report on Antyaodaya (1979-80) Programme Evaluation Organisation, Planning Commission, New Delhi: 1982.
7. Government of India, Planning Commission, PEO, Evaluation Report on IRDP, New Delhi, 1985.

8. Government of India, Report on Responding to the Challenge of Rural Poverty in South Asia: Role of Non Government Organisations, Bangladesh,1985.
9. Government of India, Report on the Committee to review the existing administrative arrangements for rural development and poverty alleviation programme, Department of Rural development, Ministry of Agriculture, 1985.
10. Government of India, Report on Concurrent Evaluation of IRDP. The Main Findings of the Summary, New Delhi: 1989.
11. Government of India, Report on Concurrent Evaluation of JRY. The Main Findings of the Study, New Delhi: 1992.
12. Government of India, Report of the Expert Group on Programmes for Alleviation of Poverty (M.S. Swaminathan: Chairman) Planning Commission, New Delhi: 1992.
13. Government of Kerala, Economic Review (Annual) Thiruvananthapuram: State Planning Board, 1992-2000.
14. Government of Kerala, Key indicators, Thiruvananthapuram: Rural Information Bureau, Department of Rural Development, 1996.
15. Government of Kerala, Report on the Committee on Decentralisation of Powers (S.B. Sen: Chairman) Thiruvananthapuram, 1999.
16. Government of India, Report of the National Committee on Development of Backward Areas (Sivaraman Committee) Ministry of Rural Development.
17. Government of Kerala, Administration Reports and Unpublished Official Records of the Block Panchayat Offices at Anchal, Pattambi and Taliparamba, (JRY, 8th Five Year Plan).
18. Government of Kerala, Administration Reports and Unpublished Official Records of the Grama Panchayats (Kollam) offices at Anchal, Yeroor, Edamulackal, and Alayamon and (Palakkad) Pattambi, Ongallur, Vilayur and Koppam and (Kannur) Naduvil, Chepparapadavu, Alakode and Udayagiri (JRY, 8th Five Year Plan).

Index

B

C

D

Q

R

S

T

U

V

W

Y